HEALING T

HEALING THE HIDDEN HURTS

Transforming Attachment and Trauma Theory into
Effective Practice with Families, Children and Adults

EDITED BY CAROLINE ARCHER,
CHARLOTTE DRURY AND JUDE HILLS

FOREWORD BY DAVID HOWE

Jessica Kingsley *Publishers*
London and Philadelphia

Illustrations at the beginning of chapters are kindly provided by Jude Hills.
Figures 9.1 and 9.2 reproduced with kind permission from Jonny Matthew.

First published in 2015
by Jessica Kingsley Publishers
73 Collier Street
London N1 9BE, UK
and
400 Market Street, Suite 400
Philadelphia, PA 19106, USA

www.jkp.com

Library of Congress Cataloging in Publication Data
Healing the hidden hurts : transforming attachment and trauma theory into effective practice with
families, children and adults / eited by Caroline Archer, Charlotte Drury and Jude Hills.
     pages cm
  Includes bibliographical references and index.
  ISBN 978-1-84905-548-2 (alk. paper)
  1. Attachment disorder in children--Treatment. 2. Attachment disorder--Treatment. 3. Attachment
behavior in children. 4. Attachment behavior. I. Archer, Caroline, 1948- editor.
  RJ507.A77.H43 2015
  618.92'8588--dc23
                              2014044140

British Library Cataloguing in Publication Data
A CIP catalogue record for this book is available from the British Library

ISBN 978 1 84905 548 2
eISBN 978 0 85700 972 2

Printed and bound in Great Britain

CONTENTS

FOREWORD

Since its earliest days, attachment theory has had an influence on child and family welfare practice. Admittedly, back in the 1960s and 1970s much of this influence was limited to young children's experience of loss as they moved from birth family to foster care, or between one foster home and another. Nevertheless it hinted at the growing interest being taken in young children's psychosocial and emotional development and the critical part that early care may play in that development. As the research progressed and the theory became more refined, our understanding of the critical importance of children's caregiving, careseeking and attachment experiences deepened. A key finding was the part that parents and carers played in helping children regulate their emotions, particularly at times of stress. Parenting that was sensitive and attuned, mind-minded and responsive helped children to make sense of themselves and other people as complex emotional and psychological beings. In turn, children who felt psychologically understood became good at psychological understanding. Children who had enjoyed being on the receiving end of empathic care learned to be empathic. Thus it became apparent that securely attached children who enjoyed these reciprocal relationship experiences would, in all likelihood, go on to enjoy good mental health and a decent social life.

The importance of early life relationship experiences also began to interest other scientists as well as developmental psychologists. The neuroscientists realised that the brain's ability to process stress and complex emotions depended on how well young children had been helped to recognise, understand and manage their own and other people's feelings and arousal. Similarly the concept of stress and its regulation, both physically and psychologically, began to be studied in the context of parent–child relationships.

Today we have a vast literature on children's emotional and social, psychological and neurological development. We recognise the importance of a baby's antenatal experiences. We understand why relationships have such a profound impact on development throughout childhood, from infancy to adolescence. Although this literature is possessed of wonderful subtlety and refinement, nevertheless we can tease out some basic messages. For example, children who have enjoyed good quality, emotionally attuned, psychologically collaborative care generally grow up to be socially competent, emotionally intelligent people. In contrast, children who have suffered abuse and neglect, trauma and loss find managing their own and other people's feelings and behaviour much more difficult, much more puzzling. When you are very small, vulnerable and not yet able to protect yourself, you need your caregivers to protect you, care for you and help you make sense of things, including your own self. But if the grown-ups are dangerous, scary, absent or unpredictable, then you are on your own. Feeling safe, learning to understand emotions and managing your own and other people's behaviour are very difficult if you are left to fend for yourself in an uncertain, frightening world. So you have to defend yourself psychologically against the fears of being hurt, alone, frightened and confused. Adults, especially carers, can't be trusted. Better to be in control rather than be controlled. Switch off if it all gets too much. Be wary, be vigilant. But even though you've had to find ways to try to survive, it is all very difficult, frightening and stressful. Little wonder then that being cared for by a family, taught in a classroom, taken to a nursery, sat down in therapy or driven to see your birth mother for contact are so hard.

Given the richness and rigour of current thinking about attachment, development and trauma, it is no surprise to find these ideas being picked up and appreciated by all those who have to live and work with children, especially children who have suffered abuse, loss and neglect. So one of the first things that these ideas and theories do is help parents and practitioners make sense of children and their behaviour. Being able to make sense of difficult and puzzling behaviours reduces confusion and anxiety. And when we feel less confused and less anxious, our levels of stress drop and we can begin to recover our abilities to think, empathise, connect and cooperate. The other boost that attachment and developmental research gives us is evidence that good quality, sustained, mind-engaging relationships *at any time during the lifecourse* can heal hurt minds. It may take time, often a long time, but understanding, empathy and connection can slowly make a difference.

And this is what we find in this splendid edited volume, *Healing the Hidden Hurts*, brought together by Caroline Archer, Charlotte Drury and Jude Hills.

It is rare, indeed a privilege, to read a book on attachment in that the rawness and immediacy of caring for and working with children – many of whom have suffered abuse, neglect and trauma – comes across so powerfully. The authors of each chapter speak directly of their own experience – as birth parents, adoptive parents, foster carers, teachers, therapists, social workers, children. Their honesty and candour, hurt and love burn through every page. This is attachment as lived, development as experienced, care as practised, love as given, love as received, help as offered, change as won, success as celebrated. If you want to meet and hear about the human spirit in all its undaunted brilliance read these stories, relish these accounts. *Healing the Hidden Hurts* gives us a rare glimpse of attachment in action and relationships in practice, through thick and thin. I hope that when you have read the following 14 chapters, each one as brave as it is personal, you will feel as uplifted as I did when I first had the pleasure of reading this exceptional volume.

David Howe
Emeritus Professor, School of Social Work,
University of East Anglia

INTRODUCTION

CAROLINE ARCHER,
CHARLOTTE DRURY AND JUDE HILLS

Over the years there has been a good deal of debate about what attachment is and what it means to relationships, mental health and society as a whole. Bowlby (1944, 1951, 1953) first proposed attachment as a theoretical construct from his ethological studies, work with 'juvenile thieves', evacuated children during World War II, and child guidance (psychiatric) clinics; his theories have drifted in and out of favour over the decades, beginning with Freud's psychoanalytic school (Shemmings and Shemmings 2011). However, much of Bowlby's theoretical model is currently being validated by neuro-scientific research, creating a re-awakening of interest. A current search reveals more than 7000 books with links to attachment – so why another book?

Attachment has often been seen in isolation, as an evolutionary theory (Bowlby 1969), as therapy (Cline 1992; Keck and Kupecky 2002; Levy and Orlans 1998), allocation of maternal blame (Thomas and Chess 1977), feminist debate (Franzblau 2002; Karen 1998), a health issue, both physical and mental (Lanius and Vermetten 2010), in terms of emotional regulation (Crittenden 2008), an educational standpoint (Bombèr 2007, 2011) and a social care view (Crittenden, Kozlowska and Landini 2010). It can also be viewed from an economic perspective: in a recent interview for *Community Care*, Crittenden (2010) states that attachment-based assessment tools 'can make a huge difference to outcomes and the cost of care pathways' and that 'attachment theories can solve many of the issues facing children's services'. We could go on. Sometimes it seems hard to see the whole picture as we focus on one part of it, typically driven by a professional or personal interest. 'Attachment' is primarily perceived as a theory but how does it look and feel to all of those involved with it and how does it impact their lives?

We attempt to consider different experiences of attachment from varied professional and personal points of view. Typically, Looked After Children and adopted children, troubled families and adults will come into contact with midwives, health visitors, doctors, teachers, social workers, legal services, guardians, educational and clinical psychologists, residential workers and/or therapists, in addition to parents and caregivers. Hence, as professionals, we need to see the 'big picture', not just our own bit. By bringing together case studies we hope to present that bigger picture. We include both professional and personal views since this collection is intended to facilitate moving from the detail to the overview: 'seeing the wood as well as the trees'. Each chapter stands in its own right but the chapters are sequenced to help the reader make links between them. We ask you, as you read the book or dip in and out of chapters, to remember that this could potentially be the same individual, or family, being discussed at different stages in their lives.

Since attachment theory was explored in depth by Bowlby in his ground-breaking trilogy (1969, 1973, 1980), it has formed the foundation for studies of attachment by many other researchers, beginning with Mary Ainsworth. Initially working as one of Bowlby's colleagues, Ainsworth (Ainsworth et al. 1978) is perhaps best known for developing the 'Strange Situation' to assess the type of attachment infants had with their mothers at six and 18 months. This work was developed by Main and Weston (1981) and Main and Solomon (1986, 1990), who further expanded the attachment categories. The four main attachment 'styles' or 'patterns' currently recognised are: secure, insecure–ambivalent, insecure–avoidant and disorganised (see, for example, Howe 2005). Over time, further methods of assessing attachment styles or patterns have been developed, including assessment tools for older children and adults, such as the Manchester Story Stem technique (Green et al. 2000), the Adult Attachment Interview (AAI; George, Kaplan and Main 1985), the Attachment Style Interview (ASI; Bifulco et al. 2008) and Dynamic-Maturational Model of Attachment and Adaptation (DMM; Crittenden 2006, 2014). Brisch (2004) explores the value of considering attachment styles as existing on a continuum, along which children (and adults) may move.

Disorganised attachment patterns have been a major focus of research and discussion over the past twenty years, in both social and neurobiological terms. Disorganised attachments are highly correlated with early abuse and neglect (e.g. George and Solomon 1999; van der Kolk 2005) and with disorganised developmental neurobiology (Shemmings and Shemmings 2011; Spangler and Grossman 1999). Hence our understanding of attachment has moved from a coherent but hypothetical theory of child development explaining how children develop within relationships, and the impact this has on emotional, cognitive and social development, towards a scientifically substantiated way of comprehending children's developmental attachments. This research has confirmed and developed Bowlby's proposition that children's early years with their primary caregivers are the most influential and can have a lifelong impact on individuals, families and society.

Perry (2009), Siegel (2007) and van der Kolk (2005) affirm the importance of taking account of the impact of trauma not only on the formation of attachments but also on the development of body, brain and mind. These issues are explored later in this chapter in 'The Trauma Trail' and in Chapters 1, 4, 7, 11 and 12. Young children's survival depends on their ability to stay close to significant adults and keep them attentive, in order to have their basic needs met, including a sense of security. Secure children learn to look to their caregivers to resolve both their physical and emotional distress and to protect them (Crittenden 2005). In doing so, they come to believe that their caregivers are interested in them, love them unconditionally and will keep them safe (Archer and Gordon 2013; Golding and Hughes 2012). An equally important function of these early attachment interactions is for children to experience attuned caregiving and co-regulation, so that they learn to identify and regulate their own somato-sensory (bodily) and emotional feelings appropriately (Golding and Hughes 2012). Van der Kolk (2005) states, 'Children learn to regulate their behaviour by anticipating their caregivers' responses to them. This interaction allows them to construct what Bowlby called "internal working models"' (2005, p.402).

Furthermore, within secure attachment relationships children learn to respond to 'shame socialisation' (Schore 1994), allowing caregivers to modify children's behaviour, providing they experience immediate 'repair' of their temporarily 'broken' attachment relationships (Schore

1994). Gradually, young children learn to tolerate and manage small amounts of shame through consistent co-regulation, becoming safe in the knowledge that they are still loved and safely contained. Over the decades there have been countless parenting books expounding the benefits and techniques of behaviour management, based on cognitive-behavioural theory, to establish safe boundaries. These employ techniques such as positive praise, time out, star charts and ignoring negative behaviour, often termed 'reward and punishment' methods. However, caregivers and professionals are often confounded when these cognitively based behaviour management techniques are not effective with some of the children with whom they live or work. Many children, particularly those who are within, or have passed through, the care system, have not achieved the secure attachment that allows them to internalise 'social rules' as reasonable and safe. As a result they lack adequate motivation (and practice) to allow them to respond in timely and appropriate ways to reward and punishment.

Many 'troubling' children have been exposed to early traumatic experiences, such as neglect and/or abuse, without safe caregivers to protect them and help them manage their chronic distress (Schore 2002). They have missed out on co-regulation, empathy, positive role models and social skills. Consequently, they are unable to regulate their own sensory and emotional arousal; their ability to deal with relationships is immature; their perceptions, cognitions, self-awareness and self-belief are likely to be distorted, and they are unable to tolerate or resolve shame (Perry 2009). The behaviour of traumatised children is often described as 'difficult' or 'challenging' but theirs are normal responses to an abnormal environment (Crittenden 2005). Children's 'trauma-normal' behaviour evolves as a developmental response to adversity and has its foundations in survival-based neurobiology (e.g. Perry 2009) involving the central and autonomic nervous systems connecting to the triune brain (see Chapter 1). It is therefore no wonder that they challenge social norms and expectations.

Understanding children's 'negative' behaviour as an expression of developmental trauma and distorted self-and-other perceptions and cognitions, rather than as 'naughtiness', shows us the way forward. Adults often interpret children's negative behaviour in terms of lack of motivation and ability to focus, 'attention-seeking' or 'being oppositional'. Yet without secure attachment relationships, children's ability to feel calm, or to return to that state, is impaired; they often find themselves in dysregulated sensori-emotional states (Hruby, Hasto and Minarik 2011). Traumatised children do not consciously choose to behave in 'troubling' ways: they are simply responding to imprinted patterns, neurobiological 'wiring' (van der Kolk 2014) and internal working models (Bowlby 1969, 1980) as a result of the trauma they experienced during the most formative developmental period of their lives: their first three years.

Traumatised children's issues are fundamentally regulatory not behavioural, hence behaviour management techniques, such as sticker charts or choices and consequences, are unlikely to achieve improvement. Feelings cards may also be ineffective with them, since they have not had their feelings acknowledged and 'labelled', let alone managed, by their caregivers. Behaviour management and modification techniques depend on 'top-down' modulation of children's responses by the 'thinking brain' (neocortex; see Chapter 1 and 'The Trauma Trail' below), informed by the left-hemisphere dominant hippocampus within the limbic system, via the prefrontal cortex (PFC; Panksepp and Biven 2012; Schore 1994; Siegel 2010). It is to these predominantly logical, linguistic and cognitive areas that cognitive behavioural approaches appeal. Yet these structures are known to 'come on line' later than the emotionally dominant amygdala in the right limbic hemisphere, and are seriously compromised by traumatic stress (Schore 2001b, 2014). Poor early attachment experiences are known (e.g. Levy and Orlans 2014) to impact young children's neurobiological development from the 'bottom up', hence a 'bottom-up' co-regulatory approach is required to alter children's distorted 'wiring' patterns, allowing them to take control of, and alter, their behavioural responses.

THE TRAUMA TRAIL

As research and awareness of attachment and neuroscience have increased, so too has evidence of the complex inter-dependency between trauma, attachment and development: none of these can be considered in isolation. Trauma is referred to in most of the chapters and deserves further exploration. Figure I.1 shows what happens when individuals are exposed to trauma: how the PFC, which provides vital connections to the 'thinking and reasoning' neocortex (Schore 1994, 2001b, 2002), shuts down, leaving the more 'primitive' parts of the brain (limbic and brainstem areas) in control (see Chapter 1). Trauma not only heightens sensori-emotional responses in the limbic amygdala, it also prevents the normal development of the hippocampus and PFC in young children. Responses of traumatised children, emanating predominantly from the somato-sensory and visceral levels, are therefore less mature and more prone to hyper-reactivity than those of securely attached children (van der Kolk 2014). Hence they are likely to be perceived as more troubling by caregivers and professionals.

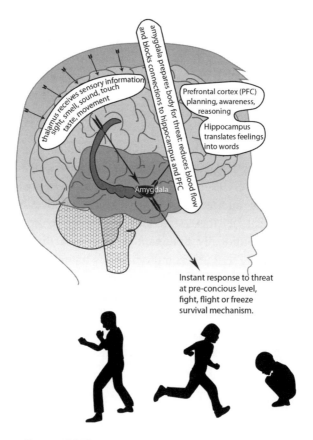

FIGURE I.1 BODY AND BRAIN RESPONSES TO TRAUMA
Source: Jude Hills

Traumatic events are known to lead to the release of stress neurohormones, such as cortisol and adrenalin (e.g. Panksepp 1998; Perry 2009; Porges 2011), leading to heightened states of arousal (hyper-arousal). However, if arousal becomes overwhelming, rapid lowering of arousal (hypo-arousal) is likely (Porges 2011). High levels of cortisol are known to affect the development of specific brain areas, such as the hippocampus (Maccari *et al.* 2014), which is highly involved in the formation of explicit, language-based, narrative memories: allowing children to learn from experience and make sense of their lives (Siegel 2014). In contrast, amygdala-based memories are emotionally charged and pre- or non-verbal. As a result, traumatised children frequently display specific learning difficulties (e.g. Sensory Integration or Executive Function disorders) and/or hyper-reactivity, increased impulsivity and reduced concentration, which looks like, and is sometimes misdiagnosed as, attention deficit hyperactivity disorder (ADHD; Silver 2013; Teicher *et al.* 2003). We may think of these heightened response patterns in terms of over-sensitised smoke alarms (Archer and Gordon 2013) that, when activated, set off tsunami-like stress reactions (Bromberg 2011) in children, leaving a trail of destruction in their wake.

Early abuse and neglect result in children failing to learn to recognise their own, and others', emotions (Bombèr 2007; Damasio 2010). However, rather than appearing impulsive, hyper-reactive or aggressive (fight-or-flight responses), some children respond, equally inappropriately, by becoming under-responsive, withdrawn and dissociative (the freeze response). Continuing our metaphor, this equates to smoke alarms triggering a 'trip switch', leading to 'systems shut-down'. This presentation is similar to children with Autistic Spectrum Conditions or Disorders (ASC or ASD), so misdiagnosis may again occur (Silver 2013); some children adopted from children's homes with minimal resources, such as Romanian orphanages, are described as 'quasi-autistic' since their behaviours are more typically associated with ASD (Rutter *et al.* 2007). According to van der Kolk (2005, 2014) and Ford *et al.* (2013) these behaviours are more appropriately understood in terms of exposure to chronic trauma, particularly interpersonal trauma, and its impact on children's neurobiological development.

In children who have experienced multiple trauma and/or have not developed secure attachments, their developmental pathways are compromised (Perry 2006; van der Kolk 2005, 2014), with long-term implications for their emotional and physical health (Healing Resources 2014; Ogden, Minton and Pain 2006). These adverse experiences compromise children's development across a broad range of domains, including stress responses, regulatory systems, perceptions, emotional literacy, behavioural control, cognition and self-concept (Cook *et al.* 2005). Their lasting effects have been shown to limit the success of therapeutic interventions (Perry 2006, 2009). When the adverse experiences are attributable to children's primary caregivers, the consequences are demonstrably more serious (Hughes 2011; Perry 2009). The term Complex Post Traumatic Stress Disorder (Complex PTSD) has been used to acknowledge the effects of exposure to multiple traumatic events in adults. However, when occurring during childhood, particularly early childhood, this symptom cluster is better termed 'developmental trauma' (Hughes 2011). Hence, Developmental Trauma Disorder (DTD; D'Andrea *et al.* 2012; Ford *et al.* 2013; van der Kolk 2005, 2014) may be the most appropriate term, as it acknowledges the pervasive impact of maltreatment and failure, or lack of opportunity, to protect by primary caregivers (see Chapters 9, 12 and 14). Moreover, it embraces many childhood diagnoses, including ADHD, ASD, and conduct, anxiety and dissociative disorders, obviating the need for co-morbid (multiple, co-existing) diagnoses and pointing the way forward towards effective treatment (D'Andrea *et al.* 2012).

Trauma, attachment and development are intrinsically linked (e.g. Cook *et al.* 2005; van der Kolk 2003; Wesselmann 2013). Perhaps the easiest way to portray this complex interdependence is shown in Figure I.2 below. Starting from any of the three points on this equilateral triangle it becomes clear that each component part influences the others and is influenced by them. Thus, secure attachments can protect children from the impact of trauma, while traumatic experiences adversely affect the development of secure attachments. Second, attachment relationships form the environment within which development occurs, hence the quality of attachment interactions directly influences children's developmental pathways; conversely children's developmental maturity and/or vulnerability influence their attachment needs, perceptions and responses. Third, traumatic events are influential in the neurobiological developmental processes that lead to well-balanced body–brain–mind systems, well-being and resilience (Siegel 2014); children who have already achieved a fair degree of developmental maturity are less vulnerable to traumatic experiences.

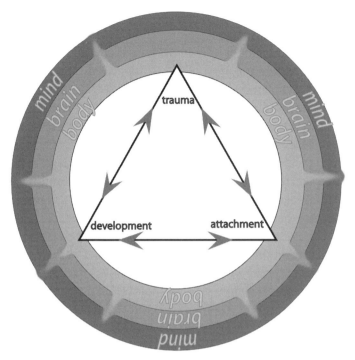

FIGURE I.2 TRAUMA TRIANGLE
Source: adapted from Archer and Burnell 2003

Children's earliest responses are physical (somatic), such as respiration, heartbeat and movement of blood around the body (e.g. Archer and Gordon 2013). Their earliest sensations are experienced from within (interoception), for example from the viscera, indicating the need for food, or from muscles, signifying the need to change position, and from without (exteroception), such as coldness of the skin, rocking movement, raised voices, loving gaze, the smell of stale urine or the taste of warm milk. Emotions are initially experienced through body sensations (Damasio 2010), only gradually becoming distinguished, labelled and regulated with the help of consistently attuned caregivers. The establishment of neural pathways to the brain are experience-dependent (Perry 2009; Schore 2002; Siegel 1999), developing from the bottom up as sensory and emotional systems become integrated and gradually linked to 'higher areas' of the neo-cortical brain – the part popularly understood as 'the brain'. The gradual, developmentally programmed formation of body–brain connections then leads to the establishment of the complex 'body–brain–mind' system (Siegel 2010), that makes us unique human beings.

Although all sensations are initially experienced in the body, they are recorded by specific areas of the brain, primarily in the amygdala and hippocampal areas of the limbic system. Memories are stored in both the body and brain (e.g. Ogden *et al.* 2006; Shapiro 2014; van der Kolk 2014), hence traumatic experiences initially recorded beneath conscious awareness continue to affect perceptions, emotional reactions, behaviours and cognitions (van der Kolk 2014). They can act as 'triggers' (Damasio 2010; see also Chapters 1, 2, 3, 4, 7, 11 and 12), when even partial reminders of the original traumatic event are encountered subsequently: neurobiologically mediated 'state dependent' memories are elicited and the original, overwhelming traumatic experiences are re-experienced in the present (van der Kolk 2014).

Therapy for children with trauma, attachment and developmental issues must begin by addressing the non-verbal and physical aspects of trauma (Ogden *et al.* 2006; Perry 2009; Schore 2014). 'Talking' therapies, although relationally based, are predominantly left-hemisphere dominant functions, based as they are on language and cognitive areas of the brain. They do not address 'bottom-up' developmental issues, such as regulation of arousal and processing of trauma that are by nature pre- and/or non-verbal. On the other hand, attachment-focused somato-sensory, co-regulatory and expressive therapies are directed primarily towards the brainstem and limbic areas of the right hemisphere, providing a sound theoretical and practical basis for the process of healing. Examples of these approaches are explored in many of our chapters.

PART 1 INTRODUCTORY NARRATIVE: HURT, HUMOUR AND PERSISTENCE

We begin with a chapter discussing the importance of how we care for, and respond to, children and young people. Victoria Drury, an experienced independent social worker, explores behavioural and self-regulatory problems in children outside of the care system. With careful exploration she locates their roots within the trauma, attachment and development triad, just as with most Looked After Children and adopted children. A broad range of early experiences can affect attachment and development (Healing Resources 2014). The trauma of abuse significantly influences children's neurophysiological, and hence psychological, development (Schore 2002; van der Kolk 2003). Research demonstrates similar destructive long-term effects through neglect (Schechter 2012). Experiences of chronic pain and illness, depression, pre- and peri-natal distress, bereavement and parental illness or separation can also have adverse effects on attachment and development (Healing Resources 2014). Examples of several of these experiences are explored in Chapters 4, 7, 11 and 12.

PART 2 EDUCATIONAL NARRATIVES: UNDERSTANDING, NURTURING AND TRANSITIONS

Chapter 2, written by an educational psychologist, begins by defining hyper-arousal, hypervigilance, dissociation and emotional dysregulation. Emma Birch explores these within an educational context, using case studies of children with poor self-regulation: their neurobiological systems are not 'programmed' to perceive the world as a safe place, hence they continue to feel distressed even within safer environments. Children with a history of disruptive, chaotic, frightening, painful and overwhelming traumatic experiences have limited top-down self-control; disorganised patterns of perceptions, responses and cognitions form their framework for navigating the world. In order to learn and achieve personally and academically they must be engaged 'from the bottom up' within safe, attuned attachment relationships (Bombèr 2007). This chapter encourages us to hold on to the belief that early negative experiences need not define children's futures: development can get back on course, self-regulation can be attained and secure attachments created when the appropriate interpersonal healing experiences are provided (Archer and Gordon 2013; Panksepp 2012).

Ann Cartwright, an experienced teacher of children with severe and complex learning disabilities (SCLD), discusses good practice for educating children with severe learning difficulties, including ASD, in Chapter 3. She makes recommendations about providing a nurturing environment, using direct sensori-motor input, recognising and responding to non-verbal elements of communication, including behavioural cues, and establishing clarity of boundaries: just as for much younger, developmentally immature, children. Cartwright illustrates how these strategies can be used effectively to encourage children to fulfil their potential while the editorial discussion proposes that this bottom-up, attachment-focused approach could benefit many schoolchildren who have experienced early life trauma.

In Chapter 4 Marie Martin explores the transition of her young adopted son into education. She gives a highly personal account, highlighting the need for a sound understanding of the impact of early separations, loss and neglect on attachment security and development. Raising awareness and educating school staff, from teaching assistants to heads, from educational psychologists to policy makers, is essential. A range of simple, but effective, developmental-attachment focused solutions is explored through the gentle musings of this nurturing adoptive mother and the subsequent editorial discussion.

PART 3 THERAPEUTIC NARRATIVES: MOVING, MENTORING, PARTNERSHIPS AND PATIENCE

Chapter 5 focuses on facilitating transitions of children from fostering to adoption as part of a therapeutic process. Although recent research into adoption indicates a disruption rate of only 3.2 per cent, the majority of families were found to be struggling, with just over a third of families reporting few or no difficulties (Selwyn, Wijedasa and Meakings 2014). Vivien Norris demonstrates how transitions can become more child-centred and effective when significant adult figures, such as foster carers, adopters and social workers, are encouraged to work together and acknowledge the complexity of children's feelings, particularly of fear, and their need to feel accepted and understood (e.g. Archer and Gordon 2013). Story-telling plays an important part in Norris's therapeutic work, allowing children to identify with 'Little Owl's' all too natural fears when faced with yet another move.

In Chapter 6, Lisa Waycott, Clare Carbis and Karen McInnes focus on the intra-familial nature of early traumatic experiences and the need to work with the whole family in experiential ways to access the pre- and non-verbal elements of early trauma. After comparing three distinct therapeutic perspectives, the authors describe how they have integrated these into their work within a therapeutic setting, creating an attachment-based approach to both assessment and therapy with fostered and adopted children. Their work draws heavily on Jernberg and Booth's Theraplay concepts (2001) and Hughes's (2009) dyadic psychotherapy approach, both of which take a developmental approach to attachment-based difficulties.

Caroline Archer describes a powerful, deceptively simple, approach to supporting adopted children in Chapter 7: using their parents as the primary agents for therapeutic change and healing within the family home (Archer and Gordon 2013). The practical principles Archer explores integrate current developmental attachment and trauma theories, with caregivers guided and 'held' by therapeutic parent mentors, drawing on the inclusive therapeutic team approach pioneered with Family Futures Consortium (Archer 2003). Her focus is on 'good kids': the children who smile, look good and can make us feel good. While the majority of children experiencing early developmental trauma 'act out' (fight-or-flight survival mechanisms), some present along a continuum of caregiving and compliance (Crittenden 2005; Lyons-Ruth, Bronfman and Parsons 1999). Crittenden (2010) highlights two notorious examples, in Victoria Climbié and Peter Connelly, where 'social workers noted that the children were happy and smiling', failing to recognise their behaviour was 'a learned defence mechanism' developed to ensure their own safety through eliciting more positive responses from inattentive, neglectful caregivers. Archer argues that 'good kids' are as needy as 'acting out' children and deserve equal, although different, therapeutic supports.

The theme of Chapter 8 is supporting attachments within the family using early intervention work. Although often perceived as less challenging than intervention work involving statutory services, this underestimates the complexity of these families' lives and the challenges they face. O'Shea and Simpson's primary focus is on creating a safe attachment space for healing, allowing them to communicate quite complex, psychological concepts to families in ways that they can 'hear', thus enabling them to make sense of, accept and develop new ideas and shared activities. Such an approach empowers family members, who have previously felt overwhelmed, disengaged and powerless: parents and children alike.

Written jointly by a clinical psychologist and social worker, Chapter 9 concerns a severely traumatised young offender who appears totally out of reach. Jonny Matthew and Tricia Skuse describe the risks they take in adopting an attachment-focused, child-led approach, challenging the usual process of containing young people and requiring them to accept the consequences of their actions directly. Although this therapeutic dialogue takes longer, and requires persistence in the face of doubts from fellow professionals and themselves, Matthew and Skuse do not give up on the boy: instead 'slowly undoing' some of the damage from his early life. The subsequent discussion weighs short-term costs against long-term benefits to individuals and society of this innovative approach.

PART 4 LEGAL NARRATIVE: ASSESSMENTS AND COURT REPORTS

In Chapter 10 Christine Gordon writes as an experienced social worker, long-standing member of the Family Futures therapeutic team and author of books and papers relating to therapeutic parent mentoring. She argues that 'best interest' assessments and decisions must move beyond mere 'feeding and watering' issues. She suggests that it is vital to acknowledge traumatised children's need for 'better-than-averagely-good' reparenting to repair the developmental attachment interruptions of their earliest years. Moreover, social workers must offer sustained support to birth parents and establish clear expectations of 'good enough' parenting, both when assessments are taking place and subsequently if children are to remain in their birth families. Finally, Gordon reminds us that timescales are very different for children and need to be more realistic in relation to their lives thus far.

PART 5 PERSONAL NARRATIVES: PAIN, PERSISTENCE AND GROWTH

Hannah Fryer is an adoptive mother who shares the story of her son's attachment journey during an extended period in prison in Chapter 11. Fryer explores the challenges that she, her husband and son faced within the depersonalised system of the prison estate and how daily contact, via Royal Mail, broke 'through prison bars' and their son's trauma-based defences to touch him at a very deep level. As Fryer makes clear, it is never too late to make good the hurts of the past: this is very much a story of the triumph of love over past experience. She contends that clear investment in early therapeutic supports for 'children who hurt' (Archer 1999) and a change in ethos of service provision for adults, both within the community and the prison estate, is an invaluable investment for all our futures. There is still clearly some way to go.

Chapter 12 is Jane MacNamara's very personal account of an often overlooked area of early trauma: clinical trauma. Despite growing up in a secure, loving environment, her son's attachment and developmental pathways were clearly impacted by his congenital heart condition and the major surgery he faced during his first two years. Although his traumatic experiences may, at first glance, appear markedly different from those of many adoptees and Looked After Children they involve precisely the same neurobiological stress responses, resulting in the same somato-sensory, perceptual, behavioural, social and cognitive response patterns. The journey she and her son take highlights the need for medical staff and families to be made aware not only of the long-term impact of trauma but also of secondary trauma.

In Chapter 13 Tamara Gordon explores her personal journey of adoption, discussing the impact that bereavement and the subsequent loss of her primary attachment figure, her adoptive mother, has had. She considers how the initial painful loss of her birth mother, the 'primal wound' (Verrier 1993), made her second loss a greater challenge, compounded soon after by the premature loss of her adoptive brother. A third strand of Gordon's narrative is the impact that her transracial placement had on her sense of belonging. This is a story of persistence, growth, self-acceptance and hope, tinged though it is with deep sadness.

PART 6 CLOSING NARRATIVE: EXPRESSION AND EXPLORATION

The final chapter, by Helen Jury, is an account of a young boy participating in art therapy, bringing with him pain, rejection, emptiness, fear and lack of self-worth. He uses the safety of the therapeutic relationship and therapeutic process to begin to confront and conquer his demons, both human and psychological, allowing him to move forward into a more positive relationship with his caregivers. As in many of the narratives, this process takes a great deal of time, patience and commitment from both child and therapist to begin to 'unravel' the long-term consequences of his early traumatic experiences.

NOTES

- We use case studies throughout the book. In all cases names and details have been changed to ensure anonymity. Some are based on an amalgamation of several different cases rather than one particular child.

- This book is the outcome of contributions commissioned and edited by members of Attachment Network Wales (see 'Useful Resources').

- The illustrations below each chapter title have been kindly provided by Jude Hills.

PART 1

INTRODUCTORY NARRATIVE

Hurt, Humour and Persistence

Chapter 1

'JOLLY WALKING'

How Social Workers Can Support Poorly Attached Children and Their Caregivers Effectively

VICTORIA DRURY

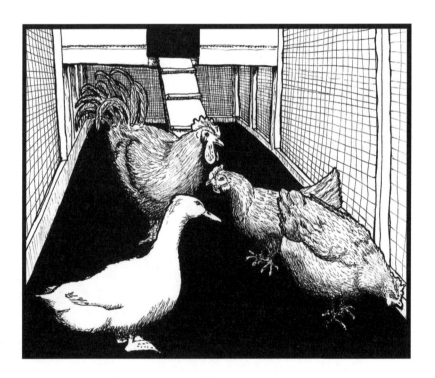

'I never expected The Waltons, *but I feel like an extra in the remake of* The Exorcist.*'* (from a very desperate parent)

Having been a children and families social worker for 14 years, I have had the privilege of walking alongside many youngsters and adoptive families, foster families and birth families who are valiantly struggling to raise traumatised and poorly attached children. Often by the time case files hit my desk the families themselves are traumatised (see Chapter 12). Many have spent years being 'good' parents, using skills and strategies that would work well with 'regular' kids, but have little effect with their children. Many have lost all sense of hope that they can 'make it' with their children: they are 'on their knees', exhausted, frustrated, angry and despairing. Many social workers themselves feel overwhelmed by the level of distress and the seeming enormity of the task in hand. The expectation of society is often that we have the answers and the solutions; we have the expectation of ourselves that we should be able to 'fix' this 'breaking family' (see also Chapter 8).

Although much of my work as a social worker is with youngsters who have experienced significant trauma from neglect and/or abuse, I sometimes find myself working with children from backgrounds where nothing initially appears amiss. They seem to be growing up in loving and supportive environments, yet their parents are distraught, with angry, disruptive, aggressive and challenging youngsters (Iwaniec and Sneddon 2001). Here I discuss some of these families. The children described are fictional characters in that they are not based on any individual child with whom I have worked; simultaneously they are very real, in that they are drawn from my years of experience working with numerous children and young people like them. I hope to introduce you to some ideas and practical techniques I have found effective when working with the 'Jacobs' and 'Zoes' on my caseload.

Poor attachment and the problems resulting from it have usually been associated with children who have been adopted or who are growing up in foster care (Bonin *et al.* 2014). Children who have experienced the trauma of neglect, abuse or poor parenting are also likely to be impacted by issues related to their patterns of attachment (Howe 2005). Attachment and trauma go hand in hand: early trauma affects healthy attachment and poorly formed attachments sensitise children (and adults) to trauma (Ogden *et al.* 2006). If youngsters experience the 'big people', on whom they depend to help them feel safe and make sense of the world, as unpredictable, unresponsive or scary, it is very hard for them to develop a relationship with them within which they feel safe and secure – a secure base (Bowlby 1988). However, as a social worker I have often found myself working with children and teenagers from seemingly 'regular' homes: where the parents worked, the children were clean and well dressed (see also Chapter 10) and where Mum and Dad were engaged and warm. In spite of this the children's behaviour bore a startling resemblance to the traumatised, abused and neglected youngsters I worked with in foster and adoptive homes. Since there is often no obvious traumatic history, these troubled and troublesome children are frequently misunderstood and families remain inadequately supported.

Many events and experiences can interrupt children's ability to form secure attachments with their primary caregiver (Prior and Glaser 2006): experiences that may not be obvious and that may not be associated with the disengaged teenager refusing to go to school, constantly getting into fights, being unable to manage peer relationships and being angry and controlling. School counsellors and teachers may be baffled as to why such children have taken another overdose, are still cutting their arms, have been excluded – again. Their parents seem to be doing everything 'right'; they have good boundaries, which are constantly pushed to the limit and walked all over. The child seems well cared for, *is* well cared for, yet continues on a path of apparent self-destruction. A little digging may reveal a history of severe postnatal depression, periods of multiple caregivers due to serious illness of a parent or sibling, or a series of painful ear infections. There may have been excessively high stress levels during pregnancy through an abusive, violent relationship, leading to toxic levels of the stress neuro-hormones adrenalin and cortisol (see Chapters 4 and 7) crossing the placental barrier and 'washing' through the unborn baby's developing body and brain. Each of these traumatic events can contribute significantly to the infant's ability to engage in the 'dance of attunement' (Golding and Hughes 2012) with their caregiver. If it looks like a duck, walks like a duck and quacks like a duck, do not assume it is a chicken because it is living in a henhouse!

THE DANCE OF ATTUNEMENT

The dance of attunement and/or attachment refers to behaviour between a caregiver and an infant where the behaviours reflect a shared emotional state without an exact imitation of behavioural expression. Stern gives the following example:

> A nine-month-old girl becomes very excited about a toy and reaches for it. As she grabs it, she lets out an exuberant 'aaah' and looks at her mother. Her mother looks back, scrunches up her shoulder, and performs a terrific shimmy with her upper body, like a go-go dancer. The shimmy lasts only about as long as her daughters 'aaah' but it is equally excited, joyful and intense. (Stern 1985, p.140)

This display of affective attunement may only last a few seconds, but there are hundreds and thousands of such experiences in the first two years of mother–child attachment formation. They serve as building blocks for the strength of the relationship. The relationship, in turn, is the basis for the full development of the child.

CASE STUDIES: ZOE AND JACOB

Let me introduce Zoe: she is 14 years old (well, actually she is 'nearly 15' as she never tires of pointing out to me). She has hair that changes colour on an almost weekly basis and, as a result, is frequently excluded from school. She is a bright kid but she is way off her targets and will struggle to complete secondary school. Her attendance is appalling and the education welfare officer is a regular visitor at the house – although my sense is that the school is not particularly disappointed when she does not show up. Zoe has taken a couple of overdoses; she will probably be 'successful' in terms of suicide at some point, as her most recent one was a 'near miss'. Her parents are distraught. They have attended a succession of parenting courses and they tell me they are attempting to put in boundaries, while high-volume expletives are directed at the tearful mum who is clearly struggling to cope. They report that Zoe's younger brother is frightened of her, and that they themselves are frightened of her: of what she may do to them but more what she may do to herself. They have tried to reason with her, to placate her, to reward episodes of cooperative behaviour. The more distressed Mum becomes the more the situation escalates. Zoe is now howling with the injustice of having such a pathetic parent and certainly does not need any help from a social worker, or anyone else for that matter. 'If everyone would just leave me alone I'll be fine, *obviously.*'

Turning to Jacob: he is 16 years old and his mum is a teacher. Jacob is about eight stone, wringing-wet, but clearly controls the entire household, standing in the doorway with Mum and Step-Dad walking around him to avoid provoking confrontations: they have learned these can quickly escalate to broken doors and windows. Jacob's parents want him to be taken into care, they are exhausted and defeated and feel they have 'tried everything' yet things just keep getting worse. When I meet Jacob and take him for coffee and cake, he is a delight of course. He chats easily and has a quick sense of humour, becoming more serious when he tells me how much he hates his step-dad who, he says, is completely unreasonable. He complains that his mum always takes his step-dad's side, never sticking up for him. The youth worker who joins us takes up the theme, pointing out that Jacob's parents just need to 'loosen up a bit' and give Jacob more freedom, 'then everything would be fine, *obviously*'.

Zoe and Jacob are both highly controlling, prone to bouts of rage, often with no apparent trigger (see Chapters 2 and 7) and show little respect for other people's belongings, space or feelings and no remorse or empathy for the evident distress of their parents or siblings. Neither accepts any responsibility for their actions either at home or school. They appear genuinely baffled as to why they were excluded for misbehaviour in class when other offenders were not; in fact their exclusion was most likely linked to verbal outbursts at their teachers when challenged over the original offences.

Talking to Zoe's parents revealed that Zoe's older brother was hospitalised for 18 months shortly after she was born. The family rallied round to look after Zoe during this time, so that Mum could spend the majority of her time with her critically ill three-year-old. Consequently, Zoe had too many people looking after her to be able to form strong, healthy attachments (Archer and Gordon 2013). All of her basic care needs were met; she was fed, played with, clean and cared for (see Chapter 10) but Mum was not there for her. She tells me that by the time Zoe was three years old she was already incredibly difficult, aggressive, destructive and prone to 'tantrums' that she never grew out of.

Jacob's mum revealed that she had separated from his father when Jacob was a few months old as the violence and emotional abuse that started during her pregnancy were too much for her to cope with. Following Jacob's birth she had postnatal depression that went undiagnosed. Although she ensured that Jacob was physically well cared for, she was unable to take delight in her beautiful son through her mist of fear and despair. When Jacob gazed into his mother's face he could not make her 'light up with wonder' and consequently had not developed the sense that he could be delightful or was wonderful.

DEVELOPING A SECURE BASE

Conversations with parents about their children's early histories are difficult. Often parents are already feeling that they have 'failed'. Beginning to explore connections between their children's emotional and behavioural development and their early experiences of being parented can trigger a further sense of blame and shame. In order to bring about change, parents need to feel optimistic about the future and confident in themselves, yet they also need to develop a realistic understanding of their children's world. To do so they need to understand how this was created (Golding and Hughes 2012), which can pose problems on many levels.

In order to develop optimally, children need their parents to act as a 'safe base' from which to safely explore the world and a 'secure haven' to which they can return for reassurance, comfort and encouragement in times of difficulty (Archer and Gordon 2013). If parents are highly anxious, exhausted and feeling helpless it is a huge thing we ask them to do: to explore a whole different set of ideas, to change their own narratives about their children and their experiences, to adopt an entirely new way of 'being' alongside their children at a point where they may feel entirely unequipped to do so. Hence we need to provide parents with a 'safe base' from which to explore this new world, and a 'secure haven' to return to for support and reassurance when the going gets tougher.

'Jolly Walking' was a description created by my son on one of our holidays that frequently included a number of youngsters of different ages. As with any group of children, especially adolescents at different stages of emotional maturity and levels of vulnerability, we encountered a range of problems of varying degrees of seriousness. On one occasion four teenagers had been playing on the beach, running and teasing and jumping on one another, as teenage boys do. Suddenly tempers and testosterone flared and fists briefly flew. Finlay, our most vulnerable and troubled boy, ran off, leaving Scott nursing bruised face and pride. I went after Finlay and spent some 30 minutes talking him down and round before he agreed to come back to the car, clearly anxious about making the transition back into the group. My own son, the same age chronologically but years older emotionally, watching from a distance, turned to the group, rolled his eyes and said, 'They'll be back in a bit, and Mum will be "Jolly Walking".' The advantage of this intervention is that anyone can do it. There is no need to have particular qualifications, no need to be a psychologist or a therapist: it is available to many, for example youth workers, teaching assistants, social workers, parents or friends. It is completely portable and extremely cheap.

It is helpful to have an idea of what is going on in the brain at times like this, in order to understand the power of what my son dubbed 'Jolly Walking'.

THE 'TRIUNE' BRAIN

The brain is structured in three distinct parts or layers. MacLean and Kral (1973) refer to this as 'triune' or 'tri-brain' theory. Each part of the brain is geared towards its own specific functions, but all three layers interact constantly with one another and with the central and autonomic nervous systems. In any threat-filled situation, specific areas of the brain react to protect us from harm. The brainstem (bottom layer) and limbic system (middle layer) respond immediately, diverting energy from the neo-cortical 'thinking' brain (top layer) and preparing the body for action. During this process, adrenalin and cortisol (see Chapters 4, 7 and 9) are released, increasing heart rate, blood pressure and glucose levels (facilitating 'fight' or 'flight') and temporarily shutting down other systems of the body. If neither 'fight' nor 'flight' is possible, the response of 'last resort' is for the whole body to shut down: the 'freeze' response (Porges 2001, 2003).

In babies and very young children who have experienced repeated, highly stressful and/or frightening situations, or whose ability to form safe, secure relationships with their caregivers has been compromised, for example through separation or chronic or acute unrelieved pain, the limbic system becomes hyper-reactive to external and internal somatic (bodily) and emotional feelings of threat. The limbic system develops markedly earlier than the 'thinking' brain (neocortex), following a 'bottom-up' developmental sequence (Schore 2001a, 2002; see also Chapters 4, 7 and 10). It takes several years for the 'thinking' brain to develop sufficiently to enable 'top-down' cognitive control; children's responses therefore tend to be 'reflexive' rather than 'reflective' (Archer and Gordon 2013). When faced with scary and potentially life-threatening situations, the 'thinking' brain does not work well: in evolutionary terms it was just not needed when encountering mountain lions or alligators!

However, the emotionally driven limbic system is not always able to distinguish the nature or 'size' of the threat. During 'normal' development with good enough caregivers, children gradually acquire these mature 'top-down' controls (Perry 2009), yet even adults may need to adopt cognitive strategies such as counting to ten when feeling angry. This allows the neocortex time to 'catch up', engage 'top-down' control, evaluate the situation and make sensible decisions. Youngsters who do not feel safe and secure spend much of their time feeling highly anxious, although they may become very good at masking this. Since their limbic systems become 'hardwired' to respond to threat, they are much more likely to over-react, sometimes with no obvious trigger (see Chapters 2 and 7). For example, Zoe quickly moves from a cajoling tone about the location of an item of clothing to screaming abuse at her mum.

Most of us will be familiar with the feeling of our mind going blank in an interview: the diverting of vital oxygen-carrying blood supplies to the limbic system, and hence to the body, leaves the neocortex 'oxygen-starved' and less able to 'read' or respond appropriately in stressful situations (Porges 2001). The answer to the interviewer's question may be in the 'thinking' brain yet temporarily unavailable; we may feel waves of panic and nausea and a racing heart as the 'fight or flight' survival mode kicks in. Most adults still maintain enough sense of what is going on, and at least some ability to regulate emotions and summon 'regrouping' strategies, such as taking a sip of water or deep breathing, to 'reconnect the neocortex' and quickly come up with suitable responses.

However, not only do poorly attached youngsters struggle to manage persistently high levels of anxiety, they also experience 'toxic' levels of shame (Howe 2005; Schore 1994). It is hard to live when continually feeling we do not fit, that the relationships we watch other people having do not match our experiences: deep down we figure, 'There must be something wrong with *me*.' This is such an uncomfortable feeling, both physically and emotionally, that it can be a relief to replace it with the more powerful and familiar emotion: anger, Schore's 'shame-rage' (1994). Although unlikely to help in the long run, it is a definite improvement on the alternative in the short term. Moreover, as children become increasingly angry, powerful and controlling, parents and professionals often feel they have only two options: to join in confrontational battles of will, or capitulate. Both of these are likely to leave children in even more anxiously aroused states: since no one is in real control, the situation deteriorates further (Archer and Gordon 2013).

CASE STUDY: JACOB

Imagine Jacob returning from school, having been given after-school detention, uncertain whether the school has spoken to his mother about this afternoon's smoking incident. He lacks an embedded sense that his primary caregiver (Mum) can 'make everything alright' or that, although she may be cross, she still loves the very bones of him. (She does, by the way; he just cannot feel this yet.) His perception is that he gets things wrong, that 'life isn't fair' and that everyone is always angry with him or letting him down. In fact, Mum does not know, as the school has decided not to ring and to manage the issue in school; staff members feel rather sorry for her and the difficult job she has with her boy. Mum has had a rare afternoon off, is feeling relaxed and looking forward to everyone coming home and the evening ahead.

Mum greets Jacob with enthusiasm: a mismatch for his current emotions that serves only to increase his distress. Jacob throws his bag down and asks confrontationally what is for dinner. Mum does not know yet, has not decided. Jacob responds angrily that she has 'been off work all afternoon, doing nothing, sitting on her arse'. Mum's fragile sense of optimism is now crushed and her anxiety about an impending 'meltdown' increases. She argues back that she has worked late every night this week and has, in fact, done much today. This swiftly escalates into a serious row, with Jacob shouting and swearing and Mum crying with hurt and frustration. Jacob's step-dad arrives home and enters the fray; he is worried about his wife, as he is aware of how vulnerable she is. He tries to de-escalate the situation by offering Jacob money for chips but Jacob now feels in 'full control', since feeling angry is 'more familiar territory' than 'people being nice'. In reality he feels 'out of control' since no one is in safe control (Archer and Gordon 2013). Neither parent is managing Jacob's 'big' emotions for him (co-regulation), he does not feel safe and his anxiety increases. And as 'it was never about the dinner', chips cannot resolve the situation. By now everyone is in a massively heightened emotional state, everyone is 'limbic'. Jacob's little brother Oliver has locked his bedroom door and put his headphones on to lose himself in a 'safer' online world. Mum asks Jacob to keep his voice down, because the shouting is upsetting Oliver. Jacob storms up the stairs, kicking out another of the stair rods on his way, shouting as he goes, 'It's always about Oliver isn't it? You don't give a shit about me.'

EMOTIONAL REGULATION

Infants do not have the ability to regulate their own emotions, relying on their primary caregivers, and subsequently other adults, to soothe them (Gerhardt 2004). Most caregivers instinctively match their infant's distress with a similar level of emotional affect. For example, a tired two-year-old, at the end of a birthday party, loses control to tears and tantrums. His attuned parent 'matches' and verbalises his emotions: '*Goodness me!* You have got yourself into *such* a state haven't you, Pumpkin? You've had *such* a busy time, haven't you? Now you just want to go home with blankie?' Using a voice conveying both animation and concern, Mum gradually 'brings down' his emotion, he allows himself to be soothed and comforted, his coat and shoes are put on and, tired-out, he snuggles into her arms feeling safe and secure. Barring post-party in-car vomiting, all will be well. Over time, children's reliance on their caregivers to co-regulate their emotions reduces, as they begin to manage this independently (self-regulation). Due to their early adverse experiences, neither Zoe nor Jacob has been able to manage this consistently, yet not being chronologically two years old, they are deeply resistant to anyone trying to help them 'calm down'. Even as adults we may not take kindly to being told to 'calm down': if we could we would! I often say to parents of youngsters, 'If I was describing your child's behaviour to you but you did not actually know how old they were, what age would you put them at?' The response is often, 'Two or three years old.'

Putting all this together, we have youngsters who do not feel safe or securely 'held', often in states of high arousal, full of shame, hair-triggered for threat responses: leaving them with poor access to their 'thinking' brains and with little ability to regulate their emotions. If my own, securely attached, son behaved like Jacob I would parent him as the 14–17-year-old he is, since he can usually access 'top-down' cognitive control and his responses are not regularly 'bottom-up hijacked' (Ogden *et al.* 2006). Securely attached youngsters who have a good grasp of consequences and an understanding that their behaviour is separate from themselves are, for the most part, able to self-regulate. However, as Howe (2005) reminds us, teenagers do experience some intense emotions, so they may need a little time to 'engage their thinking brains'. After he had taken himself off to his room and calmed down a little my son would be able to process what happened, feel some remorse at what had been said, and make some attempt to retrieve the situation, with a cup of tea and a mumbled apology for 'being a git'. He knows in his heart that he is a good kid, who sometimes gets things wrong, but he is able to change things and put things right. He has a strong sense of self-efficacy and knows he can restore our relationship, which has been temporarily ruptured. I would thank him for both the cup of tea and the apology and remind him that he still needed to make amends (e.g. apologise to everyone he had upset, or, as in Finlay's situation, perhaps help clean the sand out of the car). Less securely attached youngsters need a different response: one that matches their three- to four-year-old 'gut responses' and raw emotions (Hughes 2004).

Back to Finlay on the beach: he is not a secure boy at all. The incident itself was neither unusual nor serious, being quite typical of boys of his age, and, to be fair, Scott probably caused it, since he knows what 'buttons to push' while appearing to be the innocent or injured party. However, Finlay would have been filled with a range of emotions, mostly shame for having over-stepped the mark by doing something 'wrong'. This would have reinforced his feeling of not quite fitting in. He is the one who gets it wrong; he has hit Scott, has ruined the day. He is the one most undeserving of the treats and fun that the holiday represents. He does not know how to retrieve the situation that he finds himself in, so he runs off, shouting angrily at me to 'f*** off'. When I follow him I find him sitting against a wall, arms wrapped tightly around his knees, angry and hostile. I want to scoop him up and hug him and tell him that everything is fine but he is not going to let me get that close right now.

'Goodness me! What *are* you boys *like*? Turn my head for *two* minutes and the lot of you are rolling about on the *floor*!' My voice varies between animation and concern. My primary concern is to provide reassurance, so I need to reduce Finlay's anxiety. We can sort out the rights and wrongs of the incident itself later. There is no point doing that now: a child in high arousal will not hear or be able to process this and I will likely make things worse. Finlay looks warily at me. I sit on the floor. 'Look at the state of your trousers, kiddo... There's more sand on those than there is on the beach...shortly to be transferred into my car! Mind you, sand will make a change from chocolate wrappers and crisps packets I suppose. Maybe sand is the way to go in my car? We could feng-shui it? Do you think my car would benefit from some more harmonious placement of sand and shells among the rubbish – I think it could hugely increase its value!'

I am not reacting in the way he expected, I am being playful and a bit silly – this is what my son calls 'Jolly Walking'. The message I am sending is of reassurance and safety; nothing can ever be so bad that it cannot be sorted. Nothing can happen that I, as the adult, cannot contain or fix and I need him to understand this. This is 'Jolly Walking'. *It cannot be the end of the world if she's talking nonsense about feng-shui-ing her rubbish-filled, ancient, and battered car.* His anxiety and shame are reducing all the time; he allows himself to smile at the nonsense. 'Nothing you could do to your car would make it any better,' he says. 'What's *wrong* with *my* car? It's lovely!' I reply with mock hurt and surprise. He laughs, and we are in tune again and can begin to resolve the situation (Hughes 2004).

I sit next to him. 'You must have been really angry with Scott about something,' I state with concern; he withdraws again slightly. I nudge his knee. 'Has anyone died?' He relaxes and we talk about what happened. It is not the end of the world, but to a reactive teenager it was sufficient to trigger a strong response and it *felt* like the end of the world (see Chapters 2 and 7). A quiet conversation will be had with Scott later. 'Ready to head back? I'm *starving.*' I am aware that tensions may be high in the car on the return journey. Everyone needs to feel that the situation is in hand and the others will likely take their cue from me. I initiate a lively debate regarding the various merits of sausages over burgers, playfully threaten that I should be promoting their healthy eating by serving barbequed sprouts and recount tales of horrid childhood dinners involving chickpeas and lard-basted chickens and point out that they are all incredibly lucky I intend to cook them such 'nommy' things. Gradually the tension lessens as everyone feels physically and emotionally safe and contained (Golding and Hughes 2012).

CASE STUDIES: ZOE AND JACOB

Working with Zoe's and Jacob's parents it is important that I can help them to feel safe and secure (see also Chapters 6, 7 and 8). 'Jolly Walking' with parents looks slightly different but the principles are the same. They need me to listen hard and to really understand how difficult things are; I need to be able to articulate that I really hear them and that I will be alongside them. I need to reduce their anxiety, not by offering magic wands but by giving them hope that life can and will be different, helping them understand what is behind their children's behaviours and giving them some confidence in their abilities to parent them. They need me to give some meaning to their experiences and to reframe the behaviour of their youngsters so that they are able to view things more positively.

I talk with Jacob's parents about how his behaviour is a way of communicating his distress about something; we do not yet know what it is exactly and it may be difficult to get to the bottom of it, but this is not a horrible kid wanting to make us unhappy. It is much easier to retain some empathy for a distressed child than a defiant one. Mum is able to recognise that Jacob does not always return home from school in a difficult mood: often but not always. She has grasped that because of his early experiences, he is an anxious boy who is easily unsettled. She is able to make the connection that the boy who walks into the house in a confrontational mood is deeply unhappy about something;

he lacks the ability to sit down and tell her what that is and allow her to help him. What she described as 'simmering' she now recognises as anxiety and shame and that he himself does not understand why he is feeling so bad. Together we explore how we can start to reduce his anxiety, which is fundamental to reducing his angry and aggressive outbursts. She recognises that he needs to experience his parents as being the ones 'in control', not in a heavy-handed or confrontational way, which would likely lead to further bouts of defiance, but with a light touch, not being drawn into the child's world of anger and control. We laugh as she calls this 'wearing the flowery boss pants'.

Both Jacob and Zoe need to experience their parents as being able to contain them, even in the midst of their wildest 'tantrums': to be their secure base and safe haven when things are going wrong. Their parents begin to grasp that just as they would not punish toddlers for being distressed, nor would they try to have a sensible, reasoned discussion with them about the inappropriateness of their behaviour. Similarly, it does not work for Zoe or Jacob. Offering an environment of acceptance (not necessarily of poor behaviour, but of what that is communicating), warmth, playfulness and empathy (Archer and Gordon 2006, 2013; Hughes 2004) goes a considerable way towards providing the emotional containment youngsters need.

The new scenarios go something like this:

Jacob returns from football practice. The tell-tale slamming of the outside door indicates that all is not well and the cat shoots outside. 'Just get out of my f***ing way will you.'

'Whoa…where did that come from?' Mum replies, her face filled with concern. 'You look like you've had a rough time of it, can I help?'

'As if!' comes the retort as Jacob stomps into his room. Jacob is sitting at his desk, staring into space, when Mum puts a plate of toast and a cup of tea beside him, a small gesture of recognition that she 'gets it', has recognised his behaviour for what it is, a communication of his distress about something – not necessarily directed at her, although it usually feels that way.

'Thought it might help,' she says, quietly going to leave the room. 'That Ref is such a w**ker.' Jacob sighs and Mum sits on the bed next to him imagining what likely went on but not vocalising it. 'Did he give you a hard time again today, buddy?'

Zoe is angry this evening; it isn't fair that the Internet has been disconnected at 9pm. 'I hate you,' she informs her mother.

'I know,' Mum cheerily replies. 'I'm making some hot chocolate; would you like some? My class were blooming horrific this afternoon. I'm sure it's the weather; they always seem to go bananas when it's windy.'

'Have you ANY idea just how SO NOT interested I am?' says Zoe, following her mum into the kitchen. 'Have we got any marshmallows?'

'Sure thing, you can even have a flake…I'm going to watch *Bake Off*. Coming?'

'You're SO lame,' replies Zoe, flopping on to the sofa next to her mum. 'I know, but I make a good hot chocolate. Be grateful for small mercies, Sweetie, I might even be rubbish at that.'

EDITORIAL DISCUSSION

'Jolly Walking' is clearly jolly good fun with traumatised children – and it can be as much fun with secure children who are able to self-regulate, understand consequences and have good self-image. Moreover, it can be more effective, since it makes parents feel good about themselves as much as it does children. Who really likes feeling angry, or 'mean', or 'useless', however temporarily? It may be particularly apt when dealing with the adolescent 'terrible twos' when reason often seems to go out of the window, 'impulsivity rules OK' and parents are 'boring old *****'. This is a time when the neural networks of the brain are undergoing major changes (NIMH 2014), when teens' sleep and wakefulness 'time zones' differ from parents', carefully prepared food may be spurned and communication is predominantly through exaggerated gestures, facial expressions, squeaks and grunts. This description will sound as familiar to parents of babies as to parents of adolescents. Try saying: 'I love you too much to lend you a tenner 'cos I know how hard you find it to pay me back. I don't want you ending up feeling bad,' in a jolly, yet firm, voice. Now relax. Yes, there may be a few 'expletives undeleted' before the adolescent 'hears' what has (unexpectedly) been said, and then expressions will change and verbal battles are unlikely to ensue. Follow this with, 'But I'll pay you a tenner if you fetch the washing in and wash up after dinner,' and at least there will be two less chores to get through before enjoying an uninterrupted evening with the remote control and a glass of red!

'Jolly Walking' is also grounded in 'jolly good science': more specifically psycho-neurobiology. The invaluable examples of 'jolly parenting' in this chapter embrace an understanding of the complex interplay between attachment and neurobiological development (Howe 2006), what Siegel (2014) terms 'interpersonal neurobiology'. It has been recognised for some years that overt trauma in the form of protracted experiences of abuse within families has a profound impact on children's neurophysiological and psychological development (Schore 2002; van der Kolk 2003). Neglect, although more difficult to identify categorically, is now recognised as having equally devastating long-term effects (Schechter 2012). It is also becoming more widely recognised that a broader spectrum of early life experiences can impact attachment and development (Obradovic *et al.* 2010). These include serious clinical interventions, life-threatening conditions and chronic pain, adverse maternal experiences during pregnancy, perinatal distress, parental bereavement or loss during and in the months after birth, serious parental illness and sustained absence (examples of several of these experiences are explored in Chapters 4, 7, 10 and 12).

In neurobiological terms, the 'dance of attunement and attachment' between caregivers and infants promotes bottom-up development, from the brainstem, through the limbic areas and into the neocortex (Schore 2001a). In turn, each of the three 'layers' of the human brain come 'online'. According to van der Kolk (2003) 'biology shapes perception': good caregiving establishes good biological 'foundations' for establishing sound neurobiological structures and healthy neurobiological functioning (Schore 2002). As a consequence, children acquire self-regulation, self-awareness, self-reflection, self-control, self-confidence and self-efficacy (Archer and Gordon 2013). Conversely, maltreated children have insecure foundations and the sequential development of their neurobiological structures and functioning is compromised (Perry 2009; Schore 2002).

'Lesser' traumatic experiences, such as those listed above, also compromise developmental attachments since they can be equally stress-inducing (Schore 2002). However unavoidable or unintentional, if caregivers are unable to provide co-regulation of physical and neurobiological arousal and co-create coherent narratives for their youngsters, infants are left with unprocessed levels of distress, including overwhelming shame, sufficient to overwhelm their developing regulatory systems in the brainstem and limbic areas (van der Kolk 2005). For example, the emotionally driven limbic amygdala 'hardwires' pre- and non-verbal memories to feelings of unbearable distress and interferes with basic regulatory functions, such as heart and breathing rates (Teicher *et al.* 2002; van der Kolk 2003). Moreover, the stress hormone cortisol interferes with the development of the hippocampus (Schore 2002; Teicher *et al.* 2002): the area of the limbic brain involved in laying down verbal and narrative memories, so that children can make sense of their world.

Thankfully, the developmental attachment journey does not end here. Due to 'neuroplasticity' (NIMH 2014), that is the capacity for neural pathways to grow and change through 'interpersonal neurobiology' (Siegel 2014), it is never too late to 'repair and rewire'. 'Jolly Walking', as with other developmental-attachment approaches (Archer and Gordon 2006, 2013; Golding and Hughes 2012; Howe 2006), leads children, step by step, on the road to healing.

PART 2

EDUCATIONAL NARRATIVES

*Understanding, Nurturing
and Transitions*

Chapter 2

THE MESSAGE BEHIND
THE BEHAVIOUR

Understanding Attachment in the Classroom

EMMA BIRCH

INTRODUCTION

In the university seminar room, attachment theory can seem ludicrously simple. At its foundation lies the idea that 'the commonsensical working models a child builds of…ways of communicating…soon become established as influential cognitive structures' (Bowlby 1988, p.129). However, in practice, attachment theory is as complex and diverse as many other psychological phenomena. Identifying it depends on understanding the complexities of a child's behaviours and interpreting the message that is conveyed through these behaviours. Attempts to categorise insecure attachment styles into 'disorganised', 'avoidant' and 'ambivalent' have helped understanding to some extent, but attempting to fit all individuals into a category of behaviour leads to messy categories that 'have a tendency to proliferate and duplicate themselves' (Greig, Munn and Reynolds 2010, p.6). The messiness of some insecurely attached children's early experiences is reflected in the messiness of trying to identify behaviours and ways to respond to them. In order to try to 'pin down' some of these behaviours, a seemingly endless list of psychological terms and behavioural descriptors have been generated. These terms can be baffling to caregivers and professionals alike. However, I have found that the more experience I have of working with children with attachment difficulties, the more these terms and concepts make sense.

I would like to use this chapter to explore some of the concepts and terms that arise when talking about attachment, to use my own experience to describe what these abstract ideas look like in the classroom and to consider some helpful ways to respond to these behaviours. The behaviours and concepts I intend to cover are as follows:

- Hyper-arousal and hypervigilance

- Dissociation

- Emotional dysregulation

Each of these three concepts will be explored through a case study of a child or children I have worked with, describing their behaviours and the effect that these behaviours had on the staff working with them and on me as an educational psychologist. I will then consider the suggestions and recommendations made for school staff and explain why these recommendations were given.

I hope that in using case studies of my own work in schools, I can give readers a more practical, concrete idea of what professionals mean when they use these terms.

HYPER-AROUSAL AND HYPERVIGILANCE
Definition

Much like dissociation and emotional dysregulation, hyper-arousal and hypervigilance are linked to anxiety and stress. Some research suggests that children who have experienced early maltreatment or neglect have 'pre-raised' levels of cortisol, meaning that they are likely to react more quickly and more extremely to stress and potential dangers (Archer and Gordon 2006). Children who have experienced early trauma develop a survival strategy of being very 'aware' of everything that is going on around them and of reacting quickly to potential threat. In these children, therefore, 'fear is aroused with unusual readiness and intensity' (Bowlby 1973, p.84). If children in this state sense a potential danger, they are likely to react with a basic 'fight, flight or freeze' response. Some example behaviours for each of these categories can be seen in Table 2.1.

Table 2.1 Examples of Fight, Flight or Freeze Behaviours in the Classroom

Fight	Flight	Freeze
Controlling behaviour	**Running away**	**'Shutting down'**
Physical aggression	Running back and forth across a space	Dissociation
Fighting		Putting head on desk
Verbal aggression	Hiding	Placing of physical barriers between self and others
Destructive behaviour (breaking things/relationships with others)	Hyperactivity	
	Attempts to leave school premises	

Source: adapted from Pearce (2010, p.77)

CASE STUDY: ALEX

Alex is one of the most observant children in Miss Smith's class. He noticed when a display had changed, he noticed when she had had her hair cut and he noticed if the teaching assistant was wearing different perfume. Sometimes his comments on these things could take staff aback but it seemed nice that he could pick out details. He could be a very pleasant and chatty little boy and was sometimes really engaged in lessons. Miss Smith was concerned, however, about the inconsistency of his responses and behaviour. For example, she once promised the class that she would teach them to play 'Jacks' when she was next on playground duty. The following week, another member of staff asked her to swap a duty, so she did not go out on Wednesday as usual. The rest of the class did not notice but that afternoon Alex had a huge 'tantrum' and called Miss Smith a liar because she had not been out to play. Even when she explained that she would be on playground duty on Friday instead, Alex continued to shout and scream, hardly seeming to hear what she said. Despite eventually calming down, he was distracted and sullen for the rest of the day.

At other times, Alex seemed to 'miss' completely what was going on in the classroom. He once missed an entire activity, even though it was explained very clearly and was in his favourite subject. When his caregiver asked about his day, all Alex had been able to tell her was that the headteacher had shouted at Tommy in the corridor outside the classroom. It appeared that he had then spent the day wondering about what Tommy had done and what had happened.

In my observation of Alex, it was noticeable that he never seemed to relax or switch off. He noticed me, as a stranger in the classroom, and seemed to be constantly checking what I was doing and whom I was watching. Even during break time he was constantly checking where everyone was and what was happening. Although Alex was not in a constant state of hyper-arousal (responding to danger through fight, flight or freeze), he did appear constantly hypervigilant (on the lookout for danger).

When I spoke to school staff about this, Miss Smith was particularly upset that Alex did not trust her to keep him safe. She talked about all the work she had done with Alex and about how she felt hurt by his lack of trust. We spoke about how Alex's body and reactions were going to take a long time 'to catch up physically with the reality that

[he] is now safe and that [his] needs will be adequately met' (Bombèr 2007, p.198). We spoke about how Miss Smith's early experiences had impacted *her* own view of the world and she began to appreciate the time and hard work it would take for Alex to internalise the fact that he is no longer in danger.

Suggestions

- I find it helpful to remember times when I have been in a hyper-aroused state and to consider how it felt. For example, when I first sat my driving test, I was under a lot of pressure to pass. While I had had lots of lessons and could drive fairly well, I was so tense and over-alert that I drove quite dangerously. I reacted to anything unexpected by braking sharply; I could not process the examiner's instructions properly; and I could not reason myself out of feeling tense. Needless to say, I failed the test. Afterwards my instructor asked me what I had been thinking when I had decided to brake sharply at a crossing. I could not tell her. I had no idea what I had been thinking because, in a state of hyper-arousal, we *are not* thinking in any conscious or logical way. Remembering these events helps me to begin to understand how it feels for children who are hyper-aroused. Given their developmental immaturity, they are much less able than adults to reason and rationalise their fears: they can barely hear what others are saying to them, let alone learn from the experience.

- It is therefore unhelpful to try to reason with children or tell them to 'calm down' when they are in a state of hyper-arousal. It is more helpful to work to support children to soothe or calm themselves before discussing consequences or their behaviour.

- Be aware that children may not be able to reflect on their behaviour, even when they are calm.

- It is hard for adults to co-regulate children's stress if the adults themselves are stressed. Even if adults think they are concealing this well, they will be less effective at helping calm children if they are actually stressed, angered or upset by them. In such circumstances it would be better to call in another adult whom children know to help them become calmer.

- Staying calm does not necessarily mean staying quiet, gentle or relaxed in the face of children's emotional intensity. Children feel better understood if we 'match' the intensity of their emotion, while not matching the emotion itself (see suggestions for emotional dysregulation later in this chapter).

- Watch children for triggers or 'tells' that suggest they are experiencing high levels of stress. They may not show it overtly but may provide clues as to how they are feeling through, for example, humming, tapping, becoming rigid, increased fiddling (Bombèr 2007).

- Be aware that a high level of stress (hyper-arousal) may be masked by the child and displayed as anger, defiance, hyperactivity or another 'safer' state.

- Feeling safe may be unusual for some children. It may be necessary to 'overcompensate' and provide additional safety measures to help them feel secure. Bombèr writes: 'children with attachment difficulties need *more* information, rather than less. In their earlier experiences, uncertainty meant that hypervigilance was necessary for survival. We need to support these children by letting them know loud and clear what is happening, so that they do not have to rely on these primitive means of coping' (2007, p.123). This could include, for example, providing lots of information about changes, visual timetables or extra time for processing.

- Some children benefit from regular 'sensory breaks', for example taking five minutes to run their hands under water, smelling a calming smell, sorting out buttons or other small objects. (For further sensory break ideas, see Mosley and Grogan's (2009) *The Big Book of Calmers*.)

DISSOCIATION
Definition

Dissociation can be described as a lack of integration of sensation, emotion, action and memory (Archer and Gordon 2013) and is integrally linked to Post Traumatic Stress Disorder (PTSD). In adults PTSD is popularly associated with wars or one-off events such as accidents, natural disasters or traumatic medical procedures and involves the inability to process traumatic experiences and the 'blocking out' of memories. Childhood PTSD is now more commonly understood as a Developmental Trauma Disorder (DTD): with a symptom constellation including 'affective, somatic, cognitive, behavioural, interpersonal, and self-identity dysregulation' (Ford *et al.* 2013, p.841), with dissociation a typical feature.

As with many things, dissociation exists along a continuum. At its simplest it is a technique we all use unconsciously, from moments of daydreaming and driving 'on automatic' to 'not feeling oneself'. However, dissociation is most evident at points of stress. For example, adults involved in a car crash or 'near miss' may report feeling distanced from the events, or being unable to recall the exact details of the crash. Further along the continuum dissociation can be defined as 'extreme compartmentalisation' or 'segregated systems' (Bowlby 1980).

Dissociation in children is more complex, due to their developmental immaturity and vulnerability (Schore 2001b, 2012). It is most often associated with chronic interpersonal trauma (childhood abuse and neglect) and is typified by distressed attachments and interrupted development of 'normal' neurobiological associations, leading to traumatic neural 'wiring' (Schore 2001b). Unconsciously blocking out what is happening to them and around them is a preconscious survival mechanism affording children some protection from the traumatic threat that maltreatment and non-availability of a safe attachment figure poses to the self. Hughes writes: 'Through extreme withdrawal from the event, the child is able to diminish the affective and cognitive impact on the self' (2007, p.217). If, or when, the abuse or neglect cease, the 'trauma wiring' and traumatic memories remain; when triggered, they can prompt dissociative responses in children, even when there is no real threat.

This can be disturbing in the classroom and lead to some difficult situations for the teachers or classroom assistants. While some dissociative behaviours may be as 'mild' as getting so involved in a game that children do not notice what is going on around them, others may be more problematic in the classroom environment. For example, children may suddenly 'flick' into aggressive mode and lash out at peers, seemingly for no reason. When questioned afterwards, they may deny having anything to do with the event, despite multiple eye-witnesses. In such cases, something that looks like 'barefaced lying' may actually indicate that a child has dissociated and is unable to remember what happened.

CASE STUDY: KYLE

Kyle's teacher was at her wits' end. She did not know quite what to make of Kyle, or how to deal with him. He seemed to have real difficulties with memory – learning to do something one day and then appearing to have forgotten it the next. He was sometimes really engaged in class and seemed to be quite bright, but, at other times, he would stare into space and, on occasion, did not respond when his name was called. He daydreamed regularly and seemed to struggle to concentrate. When there was a lot going on in the classroom, he stared blankly and sometimes seemed completely unaware of what was happening around him. For example, if the class were lining up to go to PE, Kyle might join them but line up facing in the opposite direction to everyone else. At first, this seemed amusing and Kyle's teacher thought he was trying to be funny but Kyle seemed completely unaware that he had done anything unusual. When his teacher asked him about it afterwards, he looked at her blankly, almost as if he had just woken up, and did not seem to have any memory of the event. Kyle particularly enjoyed computer games and fantasy play. When engaged in these activities he appeared to block everything else out, not responding to others unless they tried really hard to get his attention.

Working with children like Kyle can be confusing and disorientating for professionals. It can be very difficult to recognise patterns of behaviour and understand what is going on for them. One moment we may wonder if Kyle's hyperactivity is linked to ADHD and the next whether he is depressed or has difficulties with memory and retaining information. It can be difficult disentangling behaviour linked to dissociative episodes from behaviour linked to other causes (all of that would be encompassed in a diagnosis of Developmental Trauma

Disorder; see Ford *et al.* 2013). While working with Kyle, I spent lots of time coming up with new hypotheses and testing them out before I started to wonder about dissociation.

Speaking to Kyle's adoptive mother about his past helped to fit some of the pieces together. It seemed that certain times, noises and feelings in the classroom were triggering distressing memories for Kyle with which he could not cope, causing him to dissociate. Once the teacher became involved in these discussions and had some basic information about the traumatic experiences Kyle had previously experienced, she could observe Kyle more sensitively, seeking to identify some of the triggers for his dissociative episodes. It seemed that sounds of shouting and crying (quite common in a primary classroom) would make Kyle 'zone out'. He would then appear disoriented and confused once he was 'back in the room'. With greater awareness of some of these triggers Kyle's teacher could try to avoid them and recognise more easily when Kyle had 'zoned out'.

Suggestions

Many of the behaviours associated with dissociation can also be linked to other issues so it is necessary to be cautious about 'diagnosing'. Where a child in class appears dissociative, concerns should be discussed with an appropriate professional, such as a psychologist, social worker or therapist – particularly if they are already involved in work with the child.

General Tips

- One of the most important things that teachers can do is to provide an environment in which children feel safe. This may involve overcompensating: making the safety of the school explicit (pointing out internal security doors) or allowing the child to have 'time out' cards that they can be helped to use when they appear uncertain or anxious.

- If resources allow, it is helpful to have a quiet, calming room that children can use if they feel overwhelmed. This provides an alternative response to threat: rather than 'zoning out' children can be helped to take some control themselves, through co-regulation with classroom staff. Initially children may need help to recognise and remove themselves from potentially distressing situations before they reach the stage of dissociating.

- Important aspects of safety are routine and boundaries. Anxiety and perceptions of threat that may result in dissociation can be reduced if children are provided with visual timetables and if plans for the day are discussed with them in advance.

- Prior knowledge of what will happen helps children manage anxiety. 'Surprises', such as unexpected visitors or sudden changes to the timetable, can trigger stress reactions and dissociation. Acknowledgement of this to children and support to handle these changes can mitigate distressing reactions.

- Introducing routine, mechanical tasks, such as sorting, organising, categorising, building and clearing up, into the daily classroom routine can be invaluable in creating a calmer environment and minimising dissociative episodes.

- Collaboration with other staff members can ensure a consistent, positive approach allows the identification and management of dissociative episodes in ways that do not result in children feeling judged or rejected.

TRIGGERS

Triggers are events that remind children of past traumatic experiences. Triggers may seem insignificant to observers but to the previously traumatised child they are associated with intense feelings, such as abandonment, terror or pain. They are most commonly experienced as sensory, motor or somatic sensations that partially replicate the original traumatic feeling state and are mediated by the pre- or non-verbal, procedural memory system and unconscious 'reflex' reactions. They are not, therefore, available for conscious recall or mature reflection.

- Spend time observing, or ask someone else to observe, the child in question. Consider the moments before the child 'zones out' or has sudden mood changes. Discuss whether there are particular noises, images, smells, requests or activities that act as triggers.

- Common triggers to watch out for are physical contact (such as another child bumping into the child), certain noises (yelling, crying, sirens), bullying (as victim or witness), certain names or labels ('You're lazy', 'Don't be stupid') and particular, or over-stimulating, environments (newly painted classroom, busy, echoing hallway, brightly lit assembly hall, dirty or smelly washrooms).

- Obtaining basic information about children's traumatic experiences will help with identification of triggers. If a child was verbally abused by a caregiver, a raised or authoritative voice or a 'hard look' may cause 'freezing' or 'zoning out'. Similarly, early experiences of being kept in a dark room may mean that switching off classroom lights to watch a film clip could trigger sudden mood swings.

Responding When a Child Dissociates

- If you think a child is currently experiencing dissociation, try to remain calm yourself and breathe deeply. If children sense anxiety in your voice, they will feel heightened anxiety. If possible, it may help to take the child to a calm, quiet space.

- When they are recovering from an episode, it may be helpful to remind children where they are, who you are and that they are safe.

- Younger children may have a particular toy or object that helps them feel secure. This could be made available to them when staff become aware that they are beginning to become 'wound up' or are 'zoning out'. With older children, objects may need to be more subtle but are still helpful.

More information and tips are available from the website for the International Society for the Study of Trauma and Dissociation (ISSD) at www.isst-d.org/default.asp?contentID=101.

EMOTIONAL DYSREGULATION
Definition

Emotional regulation refers to the things we do to influence our sensory and emotional feelings and express them in acceptable ways. Mothers regulate babies' emotions by soothing, feeding, singing or making them physically comfortable. Hughes writes that:

> the parent's calm and soothing presence enables the infant's physiology to match that of the parent. The infant cannot self-soothe, but rather is soothed by the parent's calming presence that sensitively responds to the more agitated, irregular presence of the infant. (Hughes 2007, p.17)

Effective parental co-regulation of children's feelings facilitates their capacity for self-regulation.

Self-regulation allows thoughts or behaviours to 'modulate mood, self-calm, delay gratification, and tolerate transitions' (DeGangi 2000, p.18). An example of self-regulation may be when someone recklessly pulls out in front of you when driving. Emotionally, there may be the urge to drive into the back of their car, or pull up alongside and yell out of the window. Rationally this is not a good idea; considering the consequences allows regulation of anger and impulsive responses: perhaps by muttering inaudibly about terrible drivers (behaviour), or reflecting on one's own poor decisions on the road (thought). Using conscious reflection to think things through and modulating behaviour to influence our sensory and emotional feelings provides self-regulation. However, if children have not had their feelings regulated consistently by a caregiver, they cannot learn to regulate their own emotions or action tendencies.

CASE STUDY: KAREN

Karen, aged five years, sometimes seemed like the little girl in the nursery rhyme: 'When she was good, she was very, very good and when she was bad she was horrid!' She could be quite sweet and easy to work with sometimes, especially on a one-to-one basis; sometimes it felt like she really was trying hard and wanted to please. However, when encouraged to do something she did not like, she would 'kick off' within seconds. She loved playing outside and playing with water and sand. The problems began when her group had to stop playing and go inside. As soon as she heard the instruction to line up, Karen would start screaming and hitting anyone who was around her. She needed to be forcibly led inside, still kicking and screaming and throwing anything within reach. Sometimes these outbursts would last for nearly an hour and seem totally out of proportion.

At first her teacher thought that Karen was just used to 'having things her own way' but as the behaviour continued, he wondered if there was something else going on. Once a teaching assistant offered to take Karen back outside again if she would calm down. This had no effect on Karen, who continued to shout, scream and throw things for a further ten minutes. Occasionally, Karen would also become upset, crying and sobbing in the classroom. When asked what the problem was, she could not tell staff or other children. She continued to cry uncontrollably and did not want to be touched or spoken to, although eventually she would calm down. When spoken to about the event afterwards, she would refuse to discuss it and often just walked away if staff continued to question her.

Karen's behaviour was not only disruptive in the classroom but also quite scary for those working with her. Sometimes Karen hurt herself while having a 'melt-down' and she has threatened to hurt others. Watching a small child become so violent and inconsolable was really upsetting for Karen's teacher and he has tried all sorts of things to get her to stop but none seem to work consistently. Her distress and uncontrolled rage has led staff to try all sorts of drastic measures in an attempt to make it stop.

Suggestions

- A first step in supporting children to self-regulate may be helping them to recognise their own emotions. Just as a mother will talk to a crying toddler, articulating their cry into, 'Oh dear, you fell over and hurt your knee. Yes, it hurts doesn't it? I know...', so an adult may need to try to articulate or comment on the emotions displayed by an insecurely attached child.

- It is important to comment on the full range of emotions (positive and negative) and to articulate 'clues' to that emotion. For example, an adult may say, 'I noticed that you started to frown and kick the wall when the whistle went. I wonder if you may be feeling angry that break time has finished,' or, 'You seem happy that it's time for messy play.' This can help children begin to notice their own feelings and responses. Sometimes a visual metaphor for feelings may be helpful, for example, 'I notice you're starting to tap your pencil and wonder if you are going into the red zone on our "worry thermometer".'

- It is important to stay calm when children are experiencing and showing their feelings (e.g. anger, upset) very intensely. However, staying calm does not mean remaining quiet and relaxed while a child is screaming at you. Hughes suggests that the child will feel more understood if you match 'the vitality of the affect…[rather than] being detached from it' (2007, p.52). See Table 2.2 for an example.

Table 2.2 Examples of 'Matched' and Non-Matched Responses to Intense Feelings

Child says	Adult says	Child feels
'I *hate* you. I wish I'd never been born. I hate this school. It's rubbish.'	In a very calm, soothing voice: 'Now, you don't mean that. You need to calm down and not say such nasty things.'	I *knew* they wouldn't understand me. No one takes me seriously. I must be a freak. Even my feelings are wrong…I'll get more angry to show her that I really mean it.
'I *hate* you. I wish I'd never been born. I hate this school. It's rubbish.'	In an animated (but not angry) voice: 'Wow! You are *really* angry at me. Was it because I took the pen or because of something else?'	Well…at least Miss understands where I'm coming from. She's even interested in what the problem is. If she can understand me, maybe she can help sort it out.

- Children need to learn that their feelings can be tolerated, managed and overcome. They need to know that it is OK to feel anger (for example), that adults can cope with them being angry and are not going to respond by leaving or getting angry themselves. Staff may need to support children in finding ways to calm down, doing the logical thinking for them when they are unable to.

- Children may need help to practise relaxing *before* they begin 'melting-down'. When early signals that they are becoming anxious appear, these should be 'noticed' out loud (as above) and appropriate soothing and calming activities suggested, for example, 'I notice you're kicking the desk and looking annoyed. Shall we go and get a drink of water from the hall? Or would you rather we did some deep breathing?'

- Working with children who struggle to regulate their emotions can be emotionally draining. Staff need to develop strong support networks; other professionals, such as educational psychologists, social workers and counsellors, can be useful to process what is going on.

EDITORIAL DISCUSSION

One of the most vital things to remember about attachment behaviours in the classroom is that they are always communicating something (Archer and Gordon 2006, 2013). If we saw a friend throw down his pencil and suddenly get up from what he was doing, we would not assume he was 'just being naughty' or 'trying to wind me up'. We may wonder out loud if he had forgotten something important or suddenly felt unwell. Similarly, when children act in particular ways, there are always reasons behind what they do and ways of reflecting on these empathically with them. It can be hard work to 'get to the bottom of' what the behaviour is 'telling us' but once we know something of children's trauma and attachment histories it becomes easier to work out the messages implicit in their behaviour. This can then inform effective, attuned interactions with children, providing them with the safety, co-regulation and shared understanding they so desperately need to fulfil their potential, both at school and in the broader community.

Clearly there will be times when children's insecure attachment behaviours can be very draining, upsetting or irritating. Adults working with traumatised children need to have good support networks and coping mechanisms in place. These may include having a colleague or trusted adult with whom to discuss feelings, 'switching off' by taking part in another activity (e.g. walking, reading, singing in the shower) or spending time with family, friends or the dog. Adequate rest, good nutrition, exercise and mindfulness are also essential. It is vital to be aware of the possibility of developing secondary trauma, or secondary traumatic stress, through caring for children who have experienced attachment trauma (National Child Traumatic Stress Network (NCTSN) 2014). NCTSN propose a 'triad of psychoeducation, skills training, and supervision' to enhance 'resilience to secondary stress' (2014, p.4).

SECONDARY TRAUMA

Secondary trauma can occur as a consequence of chronic or severe single event exposure to other people's traumatic experiences (e.g. as a witness or service provider). Staff in military field hospitals, emergency response workers, psychotherapists and mental health service professionals have been shown to be vulnerable to secondary trauma, popularly known as 'burn out' or 'compassion fatigue'. Less recognised, yet equally important, are the long-term effects of caring for traumatised children, as primary caregivers (Archer and Gordon 2013; Levy and Orlans 2014) or as caregiving staff. Symptoms are likely to include reduced capacity for self-regulation and reflection, altered perceptions of self and others, hypo- or hypervigilance, 'hair-trigger' responses, irritability, aggression or passivity.

While working with children with attachment difficulties can sometimes be very rewarding, it can also be incredibly hard work. There are seldom 'quick fixes' and caregivers, parents, teachers and other professionals need vast amounts of patience and resilience to provide support to the children in their care. Hughes states: 'Professionals working with these children need to face their responsibility with humility, dedication, care and creativity if they are to make the difference' (2006, p.vii). This can be a big call and it is important to be mindful, on a daily basis, that early negative experiences need not determine the rest of children's lives. While 'baby brains' are highly vulnerable to traumatic insults, neuroplasticity, the capacity for neurobiological change and healing (Siegel 2007), continues through the lifetime. If life circumstances and intersubjective experiences with caregivers change for the better, becoming consistent and sensitively attuned (Hughes 2009), so too can children and adults change. Staff members need to hold on to the belief that early traumatic hurts can be repaired and developmental attachment 'gaps' filled when the right healing experiences are given based on a sound understanding of the effects of early traumatic experiences on children's somatic (physical) states, perceptions, cognitions and behaviours (Archer and Gordon 2013; Panksepp and Biven 2012).

Chapter 3

NURTURING THE EDUCATIONAL ENVIRONMENT
Creating Safe Space for Children to Learn

ANN CARTWRIGHT

Our second son was born with profound and multiple learning difficulties (PMLD). I gained my Post Graduate Certificate of Education as a mature student and worked as a supply teacher in mainstream schools before being offered supply work in the special school, Ysgol

Crug Glas (YCG), my son attended. I was surprised how much I enjoyed it.

Sixteen years later I still teach in that school. Currently the school is attended by 50 pupils aged from three to 19 years. All our pupils have PMLD or severe and complex learning difficulties (SCLD). All have associated communication, behavioural and sensory difficulties; a significant number have very specific healthcare requirements. A growing number of our pupils are on the autistic spectrum and have challenging behaviours. We consider each pupil to be a unique individual, with the potential to develop and learn. One of our stated aims as a school is to find the means to maximise this potential.

In total we have eight teachers (plus an Art/Design Technology teacher) who are supported by Teaching Assistants (TAs); most of our classes have a ratio close to one-to-one. Some pupils require one-to-one support because of challenging behaviours, others due to chronic medical needs: realistically few of our pupils are able to participate without one-to-one support. Our school is recognised as a centre of excellence not only by ESTYN (the education and training inspectorate for Wales), who awarded us 'excellent' in every area at our last inspection, but also by other educational establishments. Since 2006 our head has organised and run an accredited Graduate Diploma in Professional Development (SCLD/PMLD).

Alongside our remit to provide and meet the requirements of the National Curriculum, our ethos is to:

> provide a caring, supportive and safe environment that promotes the social, physical and moral development of each child by the provision of a curriculum and details that promote self-worth, confidence and independence. No child can learn effectively and reach their potential unless they feel secure.

A major school aim is to:

> work as partners with parents and with other professionals to provide the highest quality of education.

Our school vision emphasises the importance of showing pupils that they are valued, that their achievements are recognised and celebrated, that they will be treated with dignity, and that their communication has value. Using techniques derived from 'infant–caregiver' interactional models, Nind and Hewett (1994) propose making the pupil and communication central to good teaching practice. As very few of our pupils have speech, we utilise communication aids like the Picture Exchange Communication System (PECS) and iPads to enable pupils to communicate their needs and wishes. Augmentative communication like Makaton, symbols, gestures and cues are also used by staff and pupils to assist communication and understanding.

Pupils' good behaviour is recognised and positively reinforced rather than staff focusing on and punishing pupils' bad behaviour. McDonell (2010) found 'the behaviour of staff has significant impact on the management of challenging behaviours' and that staff may 'inadvertently trigger challenging behaviours' (see also Chapters 2 and 7). At YCG our behaviour policy requires that staff use a 'low arousal' approach. We seek to defuse potentially difficult situations by calm, non-confrontational language and posture: remaining reflective, and mindful while focusing on appropriate behaviour.

Our behaviour policy states that we should provide:

> a nurturing environment in which our children and young people can thrive. Here they can, for example, feel accepted and safe: allowing them to learn to identify and communicate their needs in the expectation that these will be met appropriately and consistently.

Hence our children can achieve optimal physical and emotional comfort, participate socially and reach their full potential (Hughes 2012). To achieve this goal the school behaviour policy proposes:

- creating an environment where good behaviour is more useful than bad

- noticing good behaviour as powerfully as bad behaviour

- allowing for feelings arising in pupils

- discussing feelings and debriefing after inappropriate behaviour

- modelling good and appropriate behaviour

- managing challenging behaviour effectively

- establishing safety and security

- establishing well-being

- helping pupils learn self-control

- providing exterior control, using discipline that is confident, clear and demonstrates empathy for pupils' feelings.

Most of our pupils arrive aged three years and are well-placed with us for the entirety of their school career. A small proportion move to a Specialist Teaching Facility (STF): a small class within a mainstream school with high pupil-to-staff ratio. Other pupils arrive at the end of Key Stage 1 or 2 when it has become clear that their current provision no longer suits their complex needs.

CASE STUDY: ALED

Aled came to the school from the STF he had attended since he was three years old. Relationships between home and school had become very strained and his mother felt embarrassed when greeted at the classroom door every day with a list of Aled's behaviours. The teacher told us that Aled caused approximately £100 worth of damage each month to the school. He was clearly a good, committed teacher who liked Aled but felt he and his STF staff did not have the resources to deal with his special needs: in particular his challenging behaviours. Aled is an attractive 12-year-old boy with bright eyes and tremendous agility and energy. He has SCLD and a diagnosis of autistic spectrum disorder (ASD).

Aled had reached the end of Key Stage 2 and needed to select a secondary school placement. He would never have been seen as a candidate for our school at three years old but over the years the gap between school demands (intellectual and social) and Aled's ability to meet those demands had widened. As a result, he did not feel safely contained and his level of anxiety increased, resulting in increasingly frequent outbursts of anger and aggression to people and property. Hence, although Aled's previous school was, in theory, more suited to his educational needs, it did not meet his social and emotional needs and, therefore, in practice, was not meeting his educational needs (Geddes 2006).

Benefits to Aled of Moving to Ysgol Crug Glas

The school has been able to focus on Aled's socio-emotional needs, providing him with the one-to-one support and understanding that allow him to engage with his learning environment and increasingly experience success.

We are fortunate to have a staff ratio sufficient to provide Aled with one-to-one support; all our teachers have the support of suitably skilled TAs. His previous class teacher reported that Aled's challenging behaviour was often triggered when the adult who had been supporting him turned their attention to another child or adult. Bombèr (2007) states that children need designated support staff they can perceive as 'theirs' and fortunately we are equipped to provide this.

We have been able to provide Aled with:

- a supportive and friendly atmosphere (for pupils, parents and staff alike), within a small school, providing a secure base and safe containment

- high pupil-to-staff ratio where teachers and TAs understand triggers that may cause anxiety that leads to violent outbursts, and so can pre-empt by distraction or by taking Aled to another activity

- individual visual time-lines giving predictability, and therefore reassurance

- iPad with a 'Proloquo app' (using symbols/pictures and sound), enabling Aled to request activities and talk about things that are on his mind, such as when is he going out with his respite carer whom he loves

- calming, safe physical input

- personal space at lunchtime where Aled can do jigsaws, play games on the iPad or curl up in the beanbag, reducing his anxiety and promoting feelings of well-being (Bombèr 2007)

- weekly one-to-one sessions with Phil, our music therapist; Phil follows and echoes Aled's playing generally but sometimes Aled indicates that he wants Phil to play while he curls up and listens – and that is OK, too

- regular access to the school's hydrotherapy pool, which provides both relaxation and boisterous play with familiar class staff and a limited number of fellow pupils

- designated small safe area (Bowlby's 'secure base'; Bowlby 1988) in the classroom where Aled can go to calm down during and/or after an outburst; Aled is free to kick/hit the wall here as he needs to: there is nothing for him to throw or break, and Aled is willing to be led to this safe area

- 'circle of attachment' with designated staff as secondary attachment figures (Bombèr 2007) forging strong links with Aled's parents. The home/school book is sent back and forth daily – Aled's mother gives us a brief description of his moods and activities the previous evening and that morning, and school comments on his day – we are honest but not damning, and we have a great rapport with home: his family are so happy to see their son less anxious and therefore less challenging

- summer playscheme at the school staffed by experienced staff, many of whom work at YCG and therefore greet Aled around school on a daily basis.

All our staff are aware that many children with ASD are calmed, reassured and grounded by firm patting on the back and shoulders (Cartwright and Morgan 2008); Aled's mother confirmed this to be true for him. Moreover, Aled's sleep patterns have been much improved since having a weighted blanket on his bed and his mother reports that he often wanders around the house with a duvet around his shoulders, no matter what the weather. However, in Aled's mainstream STF, touching pupils in this way, to provide comforting deep pressure touch, was taboo. Since some of our pupils are Looked After Children (including respite provision) we know that there are similar rules around 'safe care' in their foster homes. Our school timetable includes daily activities, such as dance, massage and access to soft play areas, again providing vital sensori-motor feedback and improving proprioception and spatial awareness (Reebye and Stalker 2008).

In accordance with the school's behaviour policy we use reinforcement of positive behaviours, by offering activities to motivate Aled, offering him his choice of 'earned reward', such as going on the bikes or swing, or doing jigsaws, rather than punishing his inappropriate behaviours. We never remove a privilege after inappropriate behaviour because we feel Aled lacks the understanding to link the two. Also, once a favourite activity has been removed, what motivation remains for a person (adult or child) to comply? Aled responds well to his 'First…Then' board: *First* he must complete a task – as shown by picture of activity. *Then* he can have what he wishes – as shown by the picture of the activity he chooses. This visual prompt helps him in times of non-compliance. We are consistent, so he feels confident. He knows he can trust us from previous experience.

We believe every day is a new beginning, and staff genuinely enjoy working with Aled. They look forward to their turn on the rota supporting him (one week per month) because Aled is eminently teachable and fun to be with. Frankly everyone is amazed by his progress. He is able to access activities around school and in the wider community because he is more predictable, as well as less anxious. Within one month of his placement Aled's mother reported that he was calmer and happier at home. He began to sign 'school' and 'taxi': indicating his enthusiasm for his new school.

Triggers and Avoiding Challenging Behaviours

Aled still has challenging outbursts during which staff follow Aled's Reactive Plan. Reactive Plans describe cues and triggers that are known to affect the pupil's behaviour, activities known to distract the pupil, and strategies for dealing with inappropriate behaviours. Staff working regularly with the pupil are familiar with the Reactive Plan as part of the school's behaviour policy and a copy is available for supply staff. The Reactive Plan was written by the class teacher in conjunction with the TAs in Aled's class, approved by the management team and then shared with Aled's parents. Once agreed with parents, Reactive Plans are shared with all school staff. 'Schools that adopt and successfully implement a whole-school approach to behaviour have the most positive impact' (ESTYN 2006).

Staff do not need to make 'on the spot' decisions in response to Aled's behaviour when they, and he, are feeling anxious and stressed; they feel they share responsibility as part of a team. Their sensitive responses allow Aled to 'feel felt' and safely contained, allowing him to gain insights into, and more control over, the feelings that trigger his outbursts. There are no verbal recriminations concerning any inappropriate behaviour, neither immediately following an incident nor later. Behaviours are, of course, discussed by the class team later to identify possible triggers: 'Was it something in the environment?', 'Had something happened earlier?', 'Is Aled feeling unwell?', 'Is something going on in Aled's home life, perhaps cancellation of Respite?'

Observation and experience help staff understand what may trigger frustration and/or anxiety (McDonnell 2010), resulting in inappropriate behaviour in pupils. These are the most common triggers we see:

- Child feeling unwell, tired, hungry, thirsty, constipated.

- Issues at home or in transit to school.

- Medical issues, for example hormonal changes, general mental health.

- Lack of understanding or an inability to communicate.

- Transition from one activity to another, or change of staff.

- Unexpected loud noises.

- Unexpected changes to routine.

YCG's behaviour policy states:

Whatever their particular needs, we believe that pupils should be involved as actively and independently as they can be in all activities and should experience a broad, balanced curriculum that will enable them to reach their individual potential.

The school has an inclusive and supportive ethos where all pupils are treated with respect and dignity. All pupils have equal access to all aspects of the school's provision. The school considers pupils' needs, abilities and backgrounds carefully.

The school provides a positive, caring and welcoming environment with a wide enough range of suitable resources to meet the needs of learners.

AIMS OF SCHOOL'S BEHAVIOUR POLICY

- To create a positive, caring and happy atmosphere where pupils and staff feel safe and secure.

- To recognise and reward achievements and appropriate behaviour.

- To enable pupils to reach their full potential educationally, socially and emotionally by reducing behaviours that inhibit learning or cause risks to the individual or to other pupils.

- To provide support for pupils and staff by accurately assessing risks and triggers, so preventing and minimising situations that trigger challenging behaviour.

- To ensure an agreed, whole-school approach to positive behaviour management.

EDITORIAL DISCUSSION

This account of best practice relates to a child with SCLD and ASD. However, the principles relate equally to children with emotional or behavioural special educational needs. By identifying and prioritising children's socio-emotional needs for security, nurture, structure and consistency, the basis for attachment and hence development globally (Levy and Orlans 2014), we optimise their learning potential and maximise their life chances. This case study demonstrates the necessity to identify the most appropriate learning milieu for each child. Geddes (2006) states that, since learning requires a step into the unknown and acceptance of change and uncertainty, children must feel comfortable in their physical environment and assured of the capacity of classroom staff to provide safety and containment.

Bombèr (2007) speaks of differentiating academic tasks and targets from those facilitating the emotional and social well-being of children; in particular she proposes broadening this focus to include children who have experienced trauma and loss. Many such children have weak sensori-motor integration (Streek-Fischer and van der Kolk 2000) and would benefit, like Aled, from focused sensory input within the daily curriculum. 'Everyday' caregiving interactions (often eschewed in schools due to risk aversion), such as massage, pleasant smells and sounds can create a sense of calm (in recipient, caregiver and others in the nurturing environment) due to the secretion of the neurotransmitter oxytocin (Shemmings and Shemmings 2011). 'Reading' and responding to children's non-verbal, including behavioural, communications (Archer and Gordon 2006, 2013; Geddes 2006) and respecting their feelings while being explicit about expectations and boundaries (Bombèr 2007) also play a major part in enabling all children to engage successfully in the classroom.

There are clear resource implications in extending a socio-emotional needs-based service across the board. However, in the long term, by enabling children to fulfil their potential and gain the self-confidence, life skills and independence that will allow them to take their rightful place in society, the gains far outweigh the initial costs.

Furthermore, all students would benefit from the calmer, more comfortable learning environment that adopting such measures across the learning lifespan would facilitate.

Chapter 4

'NONONONONO, MUMMY, I WANT TO STAY WITH YOOOOOU!'

The Challenges of Starting School

MARIE MARTIN

My two-and-a-half-year-old, Ben, lies in the middle of the road howling, his small body wracked with sobs. His arms and legs are thrashing so violently I struggle to get a grip on him. 'NOOOO, Mummy, NOOOOO I don't want to nursery.'

It is a quiet road but I am terrified that a car will come along – that anyone will come along and witness this scene. As I succeed in hauling him up and into my arms he goes limp and I stagger as he slips down again. I wrestle him to the curb, trying to keep the desperation and, let's face it, outrage out of my voice. 'Come on, honey, you love Susie, remember?' I grumble through gritted teeth. 'And the singing? And sweeping the paths in the park?'

'NoNoNoNoNo, Mummy, I want to stay with YOOOOOU!' he howls.

Ben attends nursery two mornings a week with a day in between. At this point he has been going for about ten weeks. It is like this every time, although by collapsing in the street instead of on the steps he has upped the ante considerably. I wrestle him to the door where he is met by kindly arms and smiling faces. They bundle him in and the door shuts firmly. 'I love you, my honey!' I find myself saying to the door. They do not approve of parents coming in. I think they are wrong, but this is by far the most thoughtful, gentle, playful and child-centred of the nurseries we visited, so we've decided to trust their wisdom. I retreat to the car and weep. I call my partner and shout at her, 'I hate doing this. It is horrible. It can't be right.' She makes sympathetic noises. She is used to this. We have talked it through a million times and keep drawing the same conclusion: I need this nursery time to stay sane.

Previously I was going nuts managing my busy, active, ferociously determined, scarily bright, staggeringly gorgeous, immensely challenging toddler single-handed five days a week. I can't do simple chores: if I take my attention away from Ben even for a few seconds he clings to me and tries to sabotage whatever I have been doing. When told 'No' he flies at me, pulls my hair, punches and kicks. He looks for things to throw and smash. If he has my full attention he is delightful, imaginative, funny and very chatty – we stopped counting his words many months ago, as he speaks in complex sentences and delights in replacing short words ('light') with long, fancy ones ('chandelier').

To say I adore him with every fibre of my being is an understatement. And yet, when he pulls all the books off the shelves *again*, for no reason I can fathom, and flings them at me, laughing as if demented, I have begun to shout at him, nastily. When he looked me in the eye and threw a pretty cup so it smashed on the floor one day, I smacked him. I would never have believed I had it in me to do such a thing. Sure, my mother had been a 'mega-shouter'; a 'well-deserved-smack-on-the-bottom' was the parenting norm back then. But I knew better, and I had still done it. I was appalled at myself and began to become depressed: meaning I was even less able to handle Ben, so his behaviour became more extreme. A terrible cycle was becoming established. I needed help. Nursery was the obvious answer. Those weekly six hours 'off' were a fantastic breathing space for me, an opportunity to get a few things done in a reasonably straightforward way. And yet…

Ben never seemed glad to see me when I arrived to collect him: no hug, no eye contact – very different from the other little ones who seemed joyful, relaxed and full of happy chatter. Staff said Ben's crying stopped as soon as he was through the door and he was happy to participate in all activities. Ben said he spent his time in nursery 'wandering about, crying'. The staff looked perplexed, assuring me it was not so. I did, however, think it odd that they never commented on his prodigious communication skills and sociability – everybody else did. Still, friends, family and nursery staff all assured us that his behaviour was common and normal. Yes, he was taking a particularly long time to stop resisting, but all would be well. But Ben's background was not common or normal. We had adopted Ben, having started out as his foster carers, taking him home from the hospital three days after his birth.

Jane and I were in our late 40s and had been together for nearly 25 years when Ben came into our lives. Adoption had not been an option for lesbian and gay people when we were contemplating having children with the rest of our peer group. Many of our friends had had children via in-vitro fertilisation (IVF), but we did not really feel comfortable with that. We had a rich, busy life, loved being 'Aunties' to our friends' kids, and enjoyed being respite carers for two children with serious physical and mental disabilities. We had talked about fostering for a long time; Jane in particular thought it would be interesting to look after newborns. We thought we would give it a try; our relationship felt rock solid; we were certainly mature, physically fit, emotionally intelligent, and loved to hang around with babies. Among our friends were teachers, play workers and psychotherapists, all of whom took childrearing very seriously. We, too, had read all the books, and felt we could give a baby a rich, stable, loving start in life.

BEGINNING AT THE BEGINNING

Ben was born on Friday, and though we were standing by, to be ready at a moment's notice, we were not called until Monday to pick him up from the hospital. When we arrived, we first glimpsed him tucked firmly under the ward sister's arm as she sat at the desk talking on the phone. The ward was frantically busy, and a fault in the alarm system meant a siren went off every time the door opened. I remember asking if I could take a photo of the nurse most involved with Ben, having been well trained to think in terms of Life Story Books. This would not be the last time I received looks of blank incomprehension from officialdom. Apparently, from his birth three days previously (his birth mother having left the hospital as soon as she was physically able to do so), baby Ben had been haphazardly picked up, fed, changed and cuddled as and when anyone with a minute to spare was able to do it. Most poignantly for me, the space on the medical record of the birth next to 'Skin-to-Skin Contact' had a line through it. After a long round of form-filling, briefings from the social worker and a swift demonstration of feeding and 'nappying' from a midwife, a beautiful new human being, perfectly unique, unutterably precious, was bundled into our car-seat-basket. Awed and elated, we took our great adventure home.

BEN'S BACKGROUND

Perhaps understandably, we thought we were bringing our little one home as a more or less clean slate. We felt his first experiences after birth were far from ideal but were sure that all the love and care we were ready to flood him with would soon mitigate his rough beginning. But the child in our basket was deeply traumatised, and not only from the unfortunate circumstances of his birth. His mother had herself had a brutal childhood, and had already lost a child to adoption when Ben was born. The pregnancy had been intensely stressful for many reasons: her developing foetus had floated in a high cortisol 'broth', affecting his neurobiological development (Shemmings and Shemmings 2011; see also Chapters 7 and 12) and subsequently the way he would react to stress, perhaps for the rest of his life. Furthermore, his birth mother had a phobia of hospitals and had faced the birth with terror, increasing this 'toxic wash'.

Having been through a difficult time *in utero*, and having survived frightening and stressful birth experiences, her newborn infant was whisked away from all familiar sounds, smells and tastes. There was no one to greet him for the joyful miracle he was. He landed on earth to the noise, chaos and general hubbub of the busy and (largely, for him), impersonal maternity ward. His experience was of complete abandonment in a terrifying and unpredictable place, the antithesis of what we now know new babies need in order to carry on healthy neurobiological and socio-emotional development. It was three days before Ben felt a truly loving touch, and by then he was so deeply buried inside himself he would scarcely have noticed it and did not react.

To sum up the damage of Ben's very early experience:

- Pre-birth:
    - toxic wash of stress hormones *in utero*, deriving from the mother's previous loss of a child to the care system, her break-up and make-up, possibly including violence, with the baby's father, and the requirement of a dreaded hospital birth ahead if she was to have any hope of keeping this baby.

- Birth and immediately after:
    - stressful delivery
    - abandonment by birth mother with no skin-to-skin contact or time to bond
    - sensory overload without co-regulation (bright lights, noise, clinical smells, unpredictable environment)
    - alarm system broken: ringing constantly
    - multiple caregivers: no specific person looking after him
    - lack of routine
    - limited rocking movement.

Understanding the importance of what had happened to Ben was still way down the line for us: for the moment we were puzzled by Ben's lack of response. He cried when hungry, when fed, and when having slept. I had been present at two home-births and knew how curious and open to the world tiny babies could be, and how important and delightful eye-contact with them was. Ben just did not seem to be 'home'. Finally, when Ben was five days old, it occurred to me to try baby massage. I gently but firmly stroked his little arms and legs (see also Chapter 12), when suddenly, with a shudder, Ben's eyes flew open and there he was! What I felt at that moment was a lightning zing of total connection and pure joy. I bent low over him, cooing and smiling and radiating a love I had never felt before. His eyes held my face. Was that? It was! A gurgling reply! The ensuing conversation, totally miraculous, yet as ordinary as sliced bread, went on until he fell sweetly asleep.

It is my contention that at that moment, Ben began to heal from his rough passage, and we began to belong to each other. Once Ben 'woke up' he became amazingly alert, drinking in everything around him with vast enthusiasm. He held his head up at just over two weeks old. We did not realise yet that this precocious behaviour was a reaction to his terrifying journey into our lives, a hypervigilance (see Chapter 2) caused by his bodily assumption that he was essentially 'on his own'. However, to us, his progress was excellent, and we were very happy. Sadly, a long and sometimes treacherous journey through the care system awaited us, and the scars that remain will be challenging for a long time to come.

One major difficulty we immediately faced as foster carers was the list of official restrictions around caring for Ben, which interfered with natural opportunities to develop attachment in newborns, including:

- We could not be naked with Ben, nor could he sleep in our bed.

  We pushed the cot as close to our bed as we could, and I slept with my arm through the bars so he had human contact as he slept.

- No swaddling allowed due to fears of baby overheating.

  This we guiltily defied, because he seemed to need it so badly.

- The contact arrangements with Ben's birth parents, who were applying for custody: one hour of contact daily began at six days old. We had to take this tiny new-born out in bitter winter weather, handing him to birth parents who took him away to a room without us. Ben slept for the duration.

At least we were able to take him ourselves, hand him over with pleasant conversation and kisses goodbye, and receive him back again with love and reassurance. Sadly many infants arrive at, and go home from, contact visits in taxis.

EARLY YEARS

Gradually, Ben begins to thrive; life at home feels calm, rich, loving and joyful. We pay for treatments from a cranial osteopath and cranial sacral therapist, for his difficulties with sleep and digestion. These are the first people to speak to us about the shock and trauma of his beginnings, the brutally broken bond to his birth mother and about the ongoing physiological and psychological results of these events. We are shocked that our dear Ben had actually experienced these events as painful, and that the results of that pain and fear could potentially be developmentally damaging.

Meanwhile, social workers and health visitors comment on Ben's excellent eye contact, his surpassing of developmental targets and the quality of our relationship with him. 'Never seen a baby do so well in care.' We are bonding tight, tight, tight.

However, when Ben is five months old, the court orders that he and his mother should stay at a Mother and Baby Unit for up to three months, where her ability to parent him would be assessed. It takes six weeks, almost a quarter of his life to that time, massively important to neurobiological development and attachment, for the assessors to decide that Ben's birth mother has failed in her attempt to provide adequate care for him. It is decided that Ben should be placed for adoption.

We collect Ben from the Unit, now aged six-and-a-half months. He seems 'a shadow of his former self', dull and withdrawn. He does not respond to us with recognition, but when he sees our house he recognises it and laughs with joy! Ben wakes at night, screaming and screaming.

We begin to rebuild our relationship, and, once again, Ben 'wakes up' and begins to thrive. We decide to apply to adopt him. The new social worker and adoption agency refuse to assess us, despite crediting us with having been superb foster carers. We go to court.

Nine months of extreme stress follow, including being required to move house to a new city. During the last few months of the court process, Ben's social worker (number 12!) said if he had been with us when we had applied to adopt, he would have supported us wholeheartedly. Fortunately, at the end of the day, Ben's guardian ad litem, well-schooled in attachment, convinces the judge of the definite harm that would be caused to Ben if he were removed from us. We become a legal family and move back to our true home. Ben is 21 months old. During our 'exile' Ben has acquired an attachment, or transitional, object: 'Duck' (see also Chapter 5). At aged two years he told a family friend, 'I love my duckie because he is mine. He helps me not be scared.'

Ben begins nursery group aged two-and-a-half, for two mornings each week. He shows extreme resistance to going, and is responsive but withdrawn during sessions. By now we have found Adoption UK and are learning much more about attachment: we are realising that he has almost certainly been harmed by experiences in early life, but everyone around us says that his reactions are normal for his age.

NURSERY, AGE THREE-AND-A-HALF

Ben enters our local primary school nursery: five half-days each week – with similar resistance to going in, as in nursery group. I try going in with him, staff welcoming, although they 'advise against it'. He has to be 'peeled off me' inside rather than outside. I suggest staying for a morning. They reluctantly allow this, but set me to work with a group of other children. Unable to have me to himself, Ben's behaviour becomes wildly disruptive (see also Chapter 3). Although Ben begins to say he loves his school, going in is pure hell. We get tough. He takes a deep breath and runs in to cheers from the staff.

Duck is lost. Ben copes, but life is grim.

Ben 'goes to pot' after several good months. He is miserable again, cannot bear to let go of me at the school gate. We are mystified: finding out much later that a staff member he has bonded with has gone off on long-term sick leave. Several weeks later, Ben is happy to go in again (staff member has returned).

Ben finds a duck he likes and accepts him as his new 'special friend'.

RECEPTION, AGE FOUR

Ben attends five full days each week: same room, same teaching staff, same nightmare going in. His previous beloved teacher is not available to him in the same way. Bedtimes become horrendous as well as mornings. Ben runs amok, biting, kicking, choosing heavy items to throw at us, while laughing like a lunatic. We've learned that the laughter is a terror response (that is why our shouting is counter-productive) – he fears going to sleep, and school in the morning. He tells me that he is pretty sure I will not be coming to collect him from school. We are all in bits.

Jane meets with Ben's teacher (I feel I'll appear too emotional at this point – the 'interfering parachute mother of the manipulative child' – or will not be able to control my rage if the meeting is unsuccessful). Jane explains that Ben needs an assigned staff member whom he knows is his 'special person', to greet him at the gate and be available as a sort of 'touch stone' during the day. They say OK, and sort it for the next day! Astounding result overnight; it costs nothing; staff are not monopolised. Happy Boy! Happy Family!

Ben's behaviour's suddenly terrible again. We discover his 'special person' has been re-deployed because staff thought he was 'sorted'. He is a wreck.

One day I am five minutes late picking him up. He flies to me, clinging and sobbing. His teacher is astonished; she says he was a bit quiet while waiting but 'fine'.

Yet another teaching assistant reaches out to Ben at the gate each morning, chats in a friendly way for as long as it takes, makes eye contact, takes his hand, tells him she has an important job for him to do, walks in with him. This works. If she's there, all is well; if not, he cannot bear to let go of my hand. He struggles right up to the last day of school.

We need help. We access Therapeutic Parent Mentoring support (see Chapter 7) and Theraplay (see Chapter 6). We learn about the big gaps in Ben's developmental attachments. He assumes deep down that he can only rely on himself; he cannot trust us to be there for him or keep him safe. We work on nurture and structure: loving touch, safety and boundaries. We practise these with acceptance, playfulness and consistency. We become better skilled at matching our interventions to the developmental level that Ben presents moment-by-moment: be it frightened baby, anxious toddler, or stroppy five-year-old. Ben feels safer, copes better with the less structured school holidays and manages well with a long flight to Australia to see relatives! Our confidence as parents also soars: a wonderful virtuous circle.

YEAR 1, AGE FIVE

Every morning is difficult, but Ben's new teacher is on board. She meets him at the gate and does what we suggest. He hides behind me, clinging for up to five minutes, before he can be persuaded to make eye-contact with her. But he does, and manages to get in. When she is not on the gate, we go to the door where she is. His behaviour within school is considered 'very good' (none of the ongoing power struggles we have at home), and he is described as 'very curious, bright, happy and delightful'. He still sticks close to his teacher and particular playground staff rather than playing much with other children. We understand the effort it takes him to hold his emotions together during school time, making the often explosive behaviour after school almost inevitable.

YEAR 2, AGE SIX (PRESENT)

Hooray! Ben has the same lovely teacher, in the same classroom. He still clings to me for a moment most mornings, but even when she is not at the gate he is able to go in happily. He is finally developing relationships with other children, and no longer talks of being lonely at school.

However, at 'pick-up' recently Ben is preoccupied with another child and does not come straight out, although he spots me waiting. I turn and walk a few steps to pass on a message to another mother. When I turn back (less than a minute later) Ben is clinging to the fence, tears running down his face. I hold out my arms and he runs to me; we land on the ground and I pull him into my lap and rock him while he sobs. He had been sure I was leaving him. Still!

INTO THE FUTURE

We have a brilliant school with loving, responsive teachers. Ben is known, loves and is loved by all: we are confident staff will work with us if problems arise. We continue to learn, grow and become better at parenting him and looking after ourselves. I rarely shout now, not just because it is counter-productive, but because I have dragged myself out of my old patterns of response and learned new habits that work better for myself and our child. I am so grateful for the help and support that has enabled me to moderate my own behaviour.

Ben still saves his 'acting out' for us at home, and is mainly cheerfully well-behaved and enthusiastic in school. He is making good relationships with peers, playing well with individuals and in a group. Duck is still with him: staying in his school bag – but Ben is allowed to 'visit' him during stressful times. We are hopeful that Ben will continue to develop confidence and trust in this warm, supportive environment. Even though staff do not exactly 'get it', they are prepared to follow our lead and this seems to be enough. We are hopeful of a smooth transition to juniors (new teacher, new room, new regime), as the school is gently and positively introducing the children to their new teachers and classrooms. We are, however, prepared for tricky times.

Our 'roller-coaster' story with Ben is a series of beginnings. Each time we gain a measure of understanding of what makes him 'tick', or have an insight into our own behaviour as parents that helps or hinders his healing process, we have an opportunity to start afresh. In this step-by-step journey of discovery, we are building an ever warmer, more trusting relationship with our child, and marvel as our own maturity grows in step with his. Our task now is to share our developing understanding with the professionals who will contribute much to the shaping of his future and life chances: his teachers.

The suffering our son survived in his first year resulted in a deep-seated sense of abandonment, for which he (and indeed we ourselves) feels (wrongly) responsible and ashamed. We can only begin to imagine the abyss of terror that an abandoned new-born experiences. Ben survived this, was 'rescued', held, nurtured and loved, only to have everything he knew disappear in an instant, with the slam of a car door. For years Ben refused to enter a car without one of us there; he sobbed if asked to get into a taxi – echoes of being driven off for his birth mother to 'have a go' at parenting. After these six weeks of haphazard care and neglect, such relationship as he may have established with her was abruptly terminated. Once again he was driven away with strangers: us. Thank heavens our house, neutral and beloved, could be safely remembered (the first stage of Object Permanence; see also Chapter 7) without terror of further loss and rejection. We, after all, were the ones who suddenly, inexplicably 'sent him away' (as he perceived events). For a long time he played a game with us where he said he was a little worm, or a little slug, whose mummy and daddy had chopped him up into bits and put him in the rubbish, and the bin-men had taken him to the dump. We would say, 'Oh how horrible for you! Sweet little one, we will look after you, and love you forever and ever.'

It is hardly surprising that the separation anxiety, common in young children, has persisted for much longer in our son. To leave us is to stand again on the brink of that terrible abyss, to feel a deep 'knowing' that he may never see us again. Without a loving presence to anchor him, to remind him that he is not utterly alone, to give him faith that all will be well, he existed in a fog, 'wandering around crying' unable to connect with other children, unable, certainly, to relax enough to learn anything (see also Chapter 3). Even now, on occasions when I pop into school (to help with 'road safety', for example) his desperate need to cling to me looks merely silly in a strapping seven-year-old lad who is otherwise doing fine. Teachers do not understand, unless we are able to tell them, that much of his 'good' behaviour in school is still driven by anxiety: he is terrified of being triggered by their disapproval and of losing control.

The fact that our son's school is a nurturing one, the teachers loving, happy to listen and adopt new strategies with parents, has made a great difference to his development. He is learning, because there is kindness and predictability everywhere he turns, to find his own 'anchors', among the lunchroom and playground staff, as well as in the classroom. The confidence this has given him has enabled him to build relationships with other children. These days, his stories of playtime are all about who he played which games with. The lonely wandering times seem, for now, to be a thing of the past. We are profoundly grateful that our choice of school turned out to be the right one, and that Ben's, and our family's, ongoing healing journey can continue seamlessly through his day.

We have been greatly helped in recognising, understanding and dealing with the difficulties we faced as an adoptive family by information we acquired from Adoption UK, from our Therapeutic Parent Mentor and through Theraplay (Booth and Jernberg 2010). The developmental attachment-based strategies we were offered (Archer and Gordon 2006, 2013) enable us to be creative in exploring the best ways to help Ben make sense of, and feel safe in, the world we share. We know that we face new challenges as Ben navigates his way through life but we now feel confident he, and we, will succeed.

EDITORIAL DISCUSSION

Ben's earliest stressful experiences, *in utero* and during his first days in hospital, and the resultant release of cortisol left him with a legacy of high physiological arousal (Schore 1994; Shemmings and Shemmings 2011) and hypervigilance (see also Chapters 1, 2, 7 and 9). Furthermore, a lack of consistent soothing, cuddling and soft voices and exposure to distressing lights, smells and sounds precluded the secretion of oxytocin, a 'feel good' neurotransmitter, which would provide a counterbalance to the over-secretion of cortisol, a 'feel bad' neuro-hormone (Shemmings and Shemmings 2011). When taken home he appeared 'shut down', a fundamental survival mechanism (Porges 2001). Fortunately, baby massage 'woke him up' and allowed him to benefit from the calming effects of deep touch (Field 2004). Skin-to-skin contact (Richardson 1997) and safe swaddling (Heller 2002), precluded by safe care rules for Looked After Children, would have improved his capacity to regulate distressing arousal, including heart rate, body temperature and sleep patterns (Richardson 1997; Shemmings and Shemmings 2011). The hospital environment, with its auditory, olfactory and tactile sensory overload, limited adequate vestibular stimulation and lack of one-to-one care, created overwhelming sensory experiences, increasing the likelihood of sensory integration difficulties (Heller 2002).

Ben's weekly contact visits, as a young infant, echoed the distressing experiences of unpredictability and changes of caregiver on the ward. Sleeping throughout contact indicated neurobiological and social shut-down typical of the dissociative 'freeze' response described by Porges (2001). Attempts at rehabilitation with his birth mother compounded the devastating effects on the development of a 'secure base' (Bowlby 1988), trust and Object Permanence (OP; van Gulden 2010a) of his early disrupted care. The slamming of car doors continues to trigger preconscious memories of loss and abandonment (van der Kolk 2003) associated with travelling to the contact centre. (For a discussion of many of the factors described in the previous paragraphs, see Chapter 7.)

On his return from failed rehabilitation, Ben was unable to recognise, or feel comforted by, his foster carers, although the delight he showed as he entered their house suggests he had established the earliest stage of OP development (van Gulden 2010a). Gradually, Ben was able to experience the love, security, protection and consistency that his mothers strove to provide. However, his hypervigilance, high activity levels, 'attention-seeking', sleep issues, defiance and destructive behaviour indicated that his physiological and emotional arousal remained unmodulated and that he often felt overwhelmed during social activities, change and brief separations. The odds were stacked against him when starting nursery, experiencing staff changes and transitions between classes.

Ben's use of 'Duck' as an attachment, or transitional, object (see also Chapter 5) helped him, to some extent, manage his huge separation anxieties. It was, however, the school's willingness to listen and provide secondary attachment figures and designated safe spaces (Bombèr 2007) for Ben that gradually enabled him to engage in the social and educational environment. Ben's ability to behave well in the school setting was typical of many traumatised, adopted children (Archer and Gordon 2013). Further difficulties may occur for Ben when faced with further challenges, such as transitions into junior and senior school, but the understanding of trauma and developmental attachments his parents have gained should stand him in good stead.

PART 3

THERAPEUTIC NARRATIVES

Moving, Mentoring,
Partnerships and Patience

Chapter 5

'NOT AGAIN, LITTLE OWL'

Transitions from Foster Care to Adoption

VIVIEN NORRIS

Then one day (after a very long time) Rabbit came along. 'Help,' thought Little Owl. 'It's Rabbit, I know what this means.' And she was right, because guess what Rabbit said?

Rabbit said, 'A little owl needs someone to look after her forever. We're going to find you someone new.'

'NOT AGAIN!' cried Little Owl. 'PLEASE, NOT AGAIN!'

And this time Little Owl felt very sad. "But I wasn't being jumpy or shouty and Badger is my best friend,' she said, 'And I don't care about forever,' she said. 'Please, Rabbit, just go away. Please, Badger, make Rabbit go away.'

This excerpt is from a therapeutic story written for a four-year-old child about to face moving for the sixth time. This young child finally feels safe where she is. She is tired and scared of moves, and she does not understand. Why would she want to move? The idea of forever has no meaning. 'Not again, please not again,' she thinks but does not say. And the adult plan moves forward regardless, with excitement and anticipation. A special book arrives and everyone gears up for this long-awaited outcome – adoption. Unintentionally, the gap between the child's experience and that of the adult widens. In some small sequence of everyday details the child realises she is alone in this confusion. And she knows exactly what to do.

She has been here before. She survives. She works hard to look fine, to interpret which course of action is likely to be safest, perhaps to throw herself on the new parent and push the old one out, or flirt and endear herself, to keep negative parts of herself out of sight, and she does this unconsciously and expertly. The adults are delighted, 'Everything is going well, what a relief.' In spite of everyone's good intentions to support this child through the move, in the end she is alone, contorting herself to fit. The stage is set, farewells are said and she starts her new life parallel to, rather than with, her new family. Expectations and hopes will be impossible to sustain and it is only a matter of time before the façade starts to crumble. She wonders how long it will take before her new family realise that they have made a mistake.

Adoption is one of the sought after outcomes for providing vulnerable children with the love, stability and support they need within a family. However, issues arising from early life experiences, often of abuse and neglect, 'are not resolved simply by being adopted' (House of Lords Select Committee on Adoption Legislation 2013, p.5). Alongside the profound impacts of early trauma and lack of responsive care, all children who are adopted or fostered have experienced the upheaval of moving family at least once and many have had multiple family moves. While adoption may be the longed-for outcome for new parents and support services, for the child the process can be confusing and traumatic.

The process of moving from a foster family to an adoptive family is an area where there has been surprisingly little research and it is unclear on what basis common practice has developed. Standard practice is for transitions to occur over a two-week period, or less for younger children, and for there to be a recommended gap of several months before the foster carer(s) visit(s) the new family 'to allow the child to settle'. Personal experiences of how this transition process is managed differ vastly. Where one adoptive family may report that their children did not realise they were leaving their foster home until they were in the car and never saw the foster carer again, another adoptive family may report a wonderful experience, having embraced the foster family as part of their extended family, at times ignoring advice and organising informal visits soon after a move. Each transition will be different with a range of factors impacting on decisions made.

Families and those in the professional support networks know from experience that difficult transition processes can have long-term negative impacts on the new families. And while there is growing recognition about the critical importance of providing support across placement transitions and of finding ways to address issues of early trauma in order to ensure stable, enduring placements, many people are uncertain about how to do this in practice. 'In many ways I don't think we've ever really recovered from our bad beginning. When she came to us it was so traumatic and badly managed. In her mind we did that to her,' reflects a struggling adoptive parent five years in.

The focus of this chapter is on what moving family means for children: how we may help children and their families make sense what is happening, of the specific challenges that arise due to the impact of developmental trauma, and how the adults involved may be able to stay alongside children to help mediate the profoundly difficult process of changing family. Although the age of the child and context has a significant impact, similar issues can arise for transitions from foster care to adoption as from short-term foster care to long-term foster care. Drawing on recent advances in our understanding of the development of attachment in children who have had fractured relationships, this chapter presents an approach that uses developmental trauma as a guiding framework and draws upon Theraplay (Booth and Jernberg 2010), Dyadic Developmental Psychotherapy (Hughes 2006) and narrative approaches (Moore 2012) to create coherence in the way we support families. This model emphasises the centrality of the child's main caregivers as the child's main attachment figures in all aspects of the work and is represented in Figure 5.1.

DEVELOPMENTAL TRAUMA

Developmental trauma refers to the pervasive impacts on children of the experience of abuse and neglect early in life at the hands of their parents or caregivers. These impacts can greatly compromise the child's development across a broad range of domains, including the development of attachment relationships, regulatory systems, behavioural control, cognition, self-concept and response to stress (Cook *et al.* 2005). The majority of children entering the Looked After system will have experienced developmental trauma; it is therefore essential that those caring for them have a coherent understanding of its impact and of the most effective ways to help them. During family transitions there are core difficulties that are likely to come to the fore. The child's fragile sense of trust in adults and sensitivity to being triggered into a survival state, or to regress to earlier ways of relating, are likely to mean that they move away from, rather than towards, their main attachment figure (the foster carer) at times of significant stress. Children are also likely to hide their fear and 'mis-cue', that is, give signals that they are fine and self-sufficient when they are feeling frightened. Children's capacity to think and make sense of what is happening to them is likely to be highly compromised and exacerbated by fear (Porges 2001, 2003). They may not be able to process and retain information or respond to logic and their sense of time is likely to be distorted. Foster carers will often report that things have been explained clearly to a child but 'they act as if they haven't heard it'. One young adolescent described this as 'having holes in my memory'; when stressed, information just 'falls out'. Alongside a child's age-related limited concept of time, children who are highly anxious may be able only to think in minutes or seconds and any discussion of the future beyond that may be meaningless.

DEVELOPING A COHERENT NARRATIVE

Transition points naturally bring the past, present and future into focus as children prepare to leave one place in order to move on. Because their lives have been fragmented and without the level of responsive care needed to help them make sense of their experiences (Golding 2014), many children struggle to have any sense of coherence about their day-to-day life, let alone their life history.

When children are at the point of moving to an adoptive family there is often confusion among professionals about producing a 'life book' (a child-friendly history of children's lives that is given to them and their new families) or engaging in the process of trying to make sense of what is happening in relation to their family history, a 'life story' process (see also Chapter 6). During the period of a transition to adoption, children are often facing multiple losses and changes. There may be final meetings with birth family and siblings shortly before the idea of a new family is introduced and along with this the impending loss of almost all elements of everyday life. Some of these changes are unavoidable but much more can often be done to provide emotional and practical 'scaffolding' for the child.

Short-term 'life story work' is sometimes carried out at this stage with the aim of helping children realise what is happening. In my experience children frequently become overwhelmed or re-traumatised if workers arrive with photos of birth family members; we need to think much more carefully about what kinds of processing children are able to manage during this highly stressful period. The process of developing a narrative of one's life happens gradually and at different developmental stages and is much more likely to be helpful as part of a gradual and ongoing therapeutic relationship with a safe adult (such as with the adoptive parent or an experienced therapist with the adoptive parent alongside) at a time when the child is in a safer position.

When thinking about coherence in the context of a family transition, I am referring to the basic links between one thing and another ('They are taking you to the park and then they will bring you home – you will see us again at tea time'), to finding ways of connecting with the child's emotional experience and 'here and now' concerns ('If they knew I bit people would they still want me?'), and to providing as much continuity as possible across contexts. Experienced caregivers of traumatised children keep life predictable and patterned for their children, with frequent concrete reminders if anything is to change. Within this safe predictability and with high levels of attuned care, children are gradually able to relax and have a sense of 'felt safety' that allows them to start to make some sense of their experiences.

Children who have experienced developmental trauma often struggle to communicate their inner life or to find the words to be able to engage in the sort of to-and-fro dialogue that helps develop new meanings. Advances in neuroscience are helping us understand how the brain is designed for relating. When caregivers are able to establish safety and acceptance and engage in an attuned dialogue – much like the storytelling that occurs between parents and infants – then children become less defensive and more able to allow adults to have a positive influence on them (Schore 2001a; Siegel 2007; Trevarthen 2001). The sorts of dialogues that are helpful are of this 'melodic', rather than directive, kind: looking under the surface, guessing, telling a story that chimes with children's inner experience: 'Oh so much is going on, you're excited, and worried, and happy and wobbly, oh my goodness, what a lot!'

Using a PACE (Playfulness, Acceptance, Curiosity and Empathy) approach in the way we engage with children can be very helpful (Golding and Hughes 2012). With genuine, emotionally connected engagement with children, difficult topics can be commented on, or explored for a moment and then moved away from, in a way that is manageable for them. This is likely to be an organic process using guesses and wondering aloud to try to find moments of connection with children's experience. It can feel like 'jumping in and out of puddles': moments where children feel that the adult has 'got it' and moments when they 'have a rest'.

Creating coherence also comes about via personalised rituals, small sequences particular to the child and caregivers that may be soothing, delightful and specific. Many of these develop naturally within intimate relationships. Theraplay (Booth and Jernberg 2010) uses a wide range of simple activities that promote to-and-fro connections between a caregiver and child, deepen attachment, help support physiological and emotional regulation, give insight into a child's and caregiver's particular needs and preferences, generate a shared sense of joy and fun, and incorporate the core dimensions relevant to the development of healthy parent–child relationships using Structure, Engagement, Nurture and Challenge (Booth and Jernberg 2010). Theraplay-based ideas can be particularly helpful in establishing shared, connecting experiences between caregiver and child without having to talk about the past and can be introduced at any stage of family life. Many of these activities can also hold deep symbolic value: for instance, a game of peek-a-boo ('You may not be able to see me but I'm still here') or running under a blanket from one person to another (a way of safely rehearsing leaving and re-uniting).

Another vital component is obtaining as detailed as possible a history about the child, both information about history and events and specific experience-based knowledge, from those who have cared for the child. These would include: what they are like beyond basic routines, what soothes and excites, how to recognise when they are upset, the small things that are important to them (a particular shortcut, the way they like their food organised, a special signal or ritual). It is hard to overstate how dramatic the changes are that each child has to manage. Apart from the loss of familiar relationships, the whole sensory context will be different: the feel, smell and sounds of the house, routines, food, colours (Archer 1999). Children who have experienced trauma typically demonstrate a high level of vigilance and attention to minute detail. Hence it is often through careful provision of continuity of the sensory environment and attention to non-verbal means of communication (for instance, via touch, rituals, music and transitional objects) that caregivers are able most effectively to provide some coherence for children as they move. 'It's really hard for new parents to resist the temptation to try and start afresh. It takes a strong person to try and hold all the pieces together' (foster carer).

Children use Transitional Objects to help them 'take their caregiver with them' during separations. Where babies may trail their 'blankies' around (however dirty or ragged); young children may use treasured toys or 'things that smell of Mum'; older children might choose key-rings with personal photos or idiosyncratic items, such as 'special purple socks'.

HELPING CHILDREN TO USE THEIR MAIN ATTACHMENT FIGURE FOR SUPPORT

The overall aim during the transition process is to facilitate the transfer of the child's attachment from the current attachment figure (the foster carer) to the new one (the adopter). It is now widely accepted that new relationships form more easily if a child has already had experience of a good attachment to a safe caregiver. Every effort should be made to strengthen these relationships even where they may be recognised by the adults as 'short-term'. If this is our aim, it makes sense to focus on these central attachment relationships throughout the transition process. (It is worth noting at this point that 'short-term' is a misnomer and can mean a couple of years, which for young children may be more than half their life. Similarly, young children will not understand fully, if at all, the implications of being temporarily in a family).

Once the child has been removed from a chaotic or traumatic birth family context and a court process is under way, the intended message to the child is 'you're safe here'; the adults work hard to understand the detail of the child's underlying needs and interpret their behaviours accurately. Children need to feel able to seek comfort and move towards the main attachment figure – here the foster carer – for soothing. As children become more able to do this it is seen as a sign of progress. However, once the idea of a new family, a 'forever family' is introduced, the focus seems to change abruptly. So often 'new Mummy and Daddy' are 'talked up' and children encouraged too quickly into intimate exchanges. Moreover, what may be interpreted as positive signs of the child attaching to the new parents is more likely to be survival behaviour. The new parents are strangers. The child does not know what they are like, whether they are to be trusted, whether they will stick around. Children have felt lied to and let down profoundly by adults in the past, so why should these promises be different? Often this reality contrasts dramatically with the new adoptive parents' perceptions: that may be filled with excitement (and anxiety) and an (idealised) attachment to the child that started well before this initial introduction.

Effective, practical interventions should be based on an understanding that the current attachment figure(s) (the foster carer(s)) are children's main source of comfort and safety. When foster carers and adopters are able to work together, with the new adults actively deferring to the knowledge and safety of the more established relationship, the world may start to feel less frightening to children. For instance, the adopter may say: 'I'm not quite sure. We're just getting to know each other; let's check with (foster carer) as she's been looking after you for such a long time.' When children actively try to exclude their main attachment figure, and children do this frequently (for instance, pushing their foster carer out of the room, or finding ways of being alone with the adopter), it is helpful for the adopter to rein this in: 'Hey, I think we need to all stick together. We need her to help us know all the special ways you need to be looked after.' In practice this approach requires high levels of trust between foster carers and adopters and, if not done as a team, can easily lead to difficulties: with the foster carers being seen as clingy or intrusive, or the adopters as lacking confidence. If the focus remains on children and what may be most helpful to them, it is easier to negotiate a responsive, more comfortable path. For children, seeing these crucial adults working together on their behalf is incredibly reassuring. What commonly happens then is that children's survival behaviours start to fall away and we see them using their main attachment figures for support again at this most stressful time. Although some more ambivalent behaviour may emerge, this is a good sign as children are now expressing, with safe adults alongside, their deeply mixed feelings and muddle (Howe 2006).

The issue of ongoing contact with foster families is complex. However, if we consider things from children's perspectives, then a clean break and lack of continuity in their relationships make no sense. A foster carer expresses her change in view:

> I used to think it was good to just cut off and have no further contact. Now I think it makes no sense: I was the first person (the child) trusted. What would (he) think had happened to that relationship if I just evaporated?

Certainly, a visit from a foster carer may well unsettle a child. However, if managed well by all parties the message given to the child is, 'I haven't forgotten you and I can see you're going to be OK here,' and the adoptive parents can demonstrate to the child that tricky things are manageable. My experience is that though things may begin intensely and with some anxiety, over time all parties become more relaxed and the gains for children in having some infrequent contact with the people who cared for them when they were small is very powerful.

KEEPING CHILDREN'S EXPERIENCE CENTRAL

Why is it so hard to keep children's experience central during the process of transition, in spite of adults' motivation to do just that? My view is that we are often working within a 'trauma organised system'

(Bentovim 2011). Often the pain and distress inherent in the process is too hard for the adults involved to bear and so systems have developed that are emotionally manageable. A seminal paper by Menzies (1961) described hospital practices and asked a similar question (see Chapter 12). When patients need consistency and tenderness, how is it that a 'caring' system develops that appears to work in the opposite direction, with staff rotating from patient to patient and becoming less able to respond sensitively and personally? Her compelling conclusion was that this system served to alleviate staff anxiety by protecting them from getting too close to vulnerable patients, and that, over time, this function obscured the primary task of providing responsive care to patients.

With respect to family transitions, there are many pragmatic reasons to keep moves relatively short and to a set plan. These include length of adoption leave, time off work, large distances travelled, the needs of other children, and levels of exhaustion for both foster and adoptive families. However, another component typical of the attitude towards transitions is to keep things upbeat, to focus on the excitement and possibilities, as captured in many children's adoption books, with a reluctance to look beneath the surface and get closer to the child's world. From my experience of facilitating a range of transitions there is often pressure to 'lighten' and speed up transitions in order to protect the adults from feeling overwhelmed at what the child faces. In the words of a senior colleague: 'If it takes too long the shine comes off.'

Why do we need things to 'shine'? Changing family encapsulates multiple complex and competing experiences, including a great deal of loss. Children entering new families who are only encouraged to show particular parts of themselves are in a much more vulnerable position for the future. My view is that, by maintaining close attention to non-verbal cues and the underlying fear inherent in the process, transitions provide unique opportunities for processing trauma. Children who have experienced developmental trauma and multiple changes in caregiver usually have poor emotion regulation and are easily triggered into survival states. When caregivers are enabled to make sense of children's behaviour and cues and to support them to make use of their main attachment figures for comfort during this stressful period, then children need not carry their feelings alone. This establishes an attachment context for relationships to deepen.

Potential issues

The child:

- has a fragile sense of safety and a reliance on adults

- is easily triggered into survival state (fight, flight, freeze) and into earlier ways of relating when stressed (self-sufficiency, presenting as if fine, dysregulating)

- mis-cues, hides fear, tries to fit in and please adults

- has a compromised sense of time and ability to process information (also age-related development)

- is likely to fill times of uncertainty with fantasy and anxiety

- has a fragmented sense of history and a sense that no one holds all of the pieces – finding it easier to block off difficult issues than to integrate

- feels confusion and grief at ending contact with birth family members.

With a sibling group, the attachment to the new parent(s) needs to be prioritised, since siblings' existing inter-relationships can challenge or undermine the formation of reliance on/attachment to the new caregiver(s).

All of the above increase with length of exposure to trauma and the number of moves.

→

Implications for therapeutic work

- Promote development of attachment and reliance on adults even in short-term placements.

- Closely observe what excites, what dysregulates and what calms.

- Focus on the child's 'felt sense' of safety; assume that fear underlies many behaviours.

- Introduce attachment-forming interventions early.

- Introduce the idea of new parents only once they are ready to meet child.

- Repeat information simply with visual cues.

- Provide non-verbal sensory continuity across contexts.

- Treat the child's history as a detailed and personalised 'dictionary' (Archer and Gordon 2013) to help understand behaviour; take an interest in specific details of events and people to see how the child shows stress and seeks comfort.

- Use the joint sessions to provide connecting experiences as well as for exploring difficult themes with the main attachment figure alongside. Start while in the foster placement, and continue across introductions and after the family move.

- Remember that adult time for discussion is essential – increase the capacity of adults to bear inevitable distress and mediate process on behalf of the child.

- Mark the passage of time via non-verbal rituals.

- Organise timings to follow the needs of the child rather than being rigid and adult-led.

→

Goals

Child to form a strong attachment to their permanent family. The new family should:

- be able to understand, withstand and grow through challenges – to 'keep going'

- draw upon understanding of the impact of child's early experiences to make sense of behaviour and remain empathic, accepting, curious and playful (from Golding and Hughes's (2012) PACE)

- expect and make sense of rejections and personal attacks within the development trauma context

- share moments of connection, belonging.

The adult should:

- be able to interpret the child's cues accurately, and be aware of mis-cueing, and the adult should respond to the unmet need that lies under the behaviour

- quickly initiate repair of the relationship after ruptures in attunement

- be increasingly able to support the child's capacity to regulate via co-regulation.

The child should:

- turn to the adult for comfort when distressed

- take the risk of sharing fear and confusion.

FIGURE 5.1 DEVELOPMENTAL TRAUMA AS A FRAMEWORK (ALL ADULTS INVOLVED WORKING TOGETHER)

WHAT IS 'TRANSITION WORK'?

There are many different views as to what constitutes 'transition work', how it should be done, whether it should be done and whether outside professionals are needed. Most transitions from foster to adoptive families are supported internally by the agencies making the placements and many are managed well by foster carers and adopters with minimal intervention from professionals. However, for some 'hard to place' children, particularly older and very traumatised children, there may be the need for outside support. From my own clinical experience, a process of sessions using Theraplay (Booth and Jernberg 2010) as an overarching structure within which more difficult themes can be explored has been very effective. During the introductory period, providing some joint work where foster carer, adopter and child play 'getting-to-know-you' games together (for instance, checking how warm people's hands are and how soft their hair is) has proved powerful. Where sufficient training and support is provided, these kinds of interventions can successfully be provided by a range of workers. A new adoptive parent commented: 'He was really ready when he moved and he came to me for comfort. This was very new for him and I think the work made a big difference. It wasn't so much about talking about the past, more like working out what a mum is.'

Whatever route is taken, it is essential to keep children's experience central and to use whatever key relationships are available to help mediate the experience on their behalf, rather than children having to manage alone. This requires the adults to work collaboratively and share a guiding framework reflectively. For the prospective adoptive parents, the process of matching and introductions is laden with intensity.

An adoptive parent reflected: 'When I think back to our transition process we were all in a state of shock. We were under-prepared and under-educated about attachment and trauma…they [adopters] need someone to hold their hands almost throughout the process.'

The need for high-quality support and training to be available to adopters (and foster carers) during the early stages of formation of their new family should clearly be part of routine provision and can often significantly impact on prevention of future difficulties (Hudson 2006).

DISCUSSION

When a family opens their heart to a new member, it is tempting to try to provide a 'fresh start', but we know that children bring their early histories with them into the new relationships and, if unaddressed, difficulties often arise at a later point. In the words of Sally Donovan (author and adoptive parent of two traumatised children): 'The problem with trying to "lock up" the past is that no lock is strong enough to keep the past from spilling out all over the present and the future' (personal communication). If the adults involved can be supported to recognise and bear the inevitable fear and complex feelings evoked by changing family, children can experience being emotionally held by their attachment figures and begin to develop the 'neuroception of safety' (Porges 1998). This leads to firmer foundations in the new relationship, where the children feel seen and understood (Hughes and Baylin 2012). The adopters, too, will feel 'felt' and understood and confident that they will be able to help their child heal from the developmental trauma they experienced so early in their lives (Archer and Gordon 2013; Levy and Orlans 2014).

> But Rabbit didn't go away. 'What's happening?' cried Little Owl. She felt very small and all alone again. Badger took Little Owl into her arms and held her tight. 'This is a hard thing to do,' she said, 'but I will be here and we will work it out together.'
>
> Rabbit and Badger tried to explain that this would be the last time she had to move and that Little Owl would be safe in her new home forever. And Badger told Little Owl all about Squirrel. Badger said it would be different this time. Badger promised to stay with Little Owl and hold her tight. She said that she would teach Squirrel all the special ways that Little Owl needed to be looked after. About how to tuck her in her bed. About what to do when she was sad. About her favourite dress and cuddly toys. About all the things that had happened to Little Owl.
>
> Little Owl was scared but she also wanted to know all about who this Squirrel was. She had lots of questions. 'Will Squirrel be fun or mean? Will she be fast enough? Will she have strong arms? If I fly too high or bite her will she go away?'
>
> Squirrel came to visit every day to try to get to know Little Owl and Little Owl tried to get to know Squirrel. And Little Owl began to think that maybe Squirrel would be soft, too. But she

knew to wait and see. And Badger stuck close by Little Owl until she was nearly ready, like she promised she would.

Then the moving day came and along came Rabbit. 'NOT AGAIN!' cried Little Owl in a quiet voice.

'I know,' said Badger, 'this is a hard thing to do.' 'I know,' said Squirrel, 'this is a hard thing to do.' Then Squirrel said, 'Things can feel in a big muddle but we will work them out together.' The Squirrel took Little Owl in her big strong arms and carried her to her new home.

Chapter 6

DEVELOPMENTAL TRAUMA AND ATTACHMENT

An Integrative Therapeutic Approach

LISA WAYCOTT, CLARE CARBIS AND KAREN MCINNES

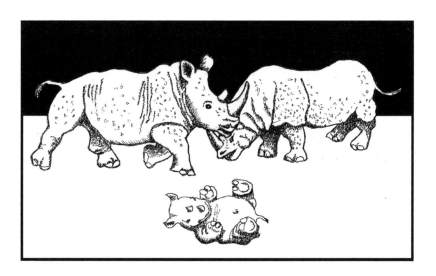

INTRODUCTION

This chapter explores how therapists working with adopted children and Looked After Children use different theoretical models and techniques to help them make sense of their early life experiences and build new attachment relationships. An overview and critical discussion of three therapeutic models will be provided:

- Non-Directive/Child-Centred Play Therapy (Axline 1947; Landreth 2012)

- Theraplay (Booth and Jernberg 2010)

- Therapeutic Life Story Work

This will inform parents/caregivers and professionals of the strengths and limitations of the different therapeutic models for working with this specific client group. Combining these approaches the therapists have developed a Trauma–Attachment Integrative Model, which will also be explored. Case studies and therapeutic techniques will be used to illustrate how these different therapeutic interventions are applied to clinical practice.

Childcare professionals often express uncertainty regarding the different therapeutic approaches available when working with this specific client group. This chapter aims to inform practitioners of differing therapeutic models for working with Looked After Children and adopted children.

NON-DIRECTIVE/CHILD-CENTRED PLAY THERAPY

Non-directive play therapy originates from the work of Virginia Axline (1947). Axline adapted principles from the work of Carl Rogers (1951) and applied this to using play as a therapeutic intervention for children. The most cited work by Axline is *Dibs: In Search of Self* (1964). Axline's work is based on her eight key principles that underline the theoretical origination of non-directive play therapy. Building on the work of Axline, Landreth (2012) developed child-centred play therapy.

The British Association of Play Therapists (BAPT) defines play therapy as a way of helping children to express their feelings and deal with their emotional problems, using play as the main communication tool (BAPT 2014). In non-directive play therapy the therapist's role is to recognise the:

> feelings that the child is expressing in speech and play and to reflect these back so that the child can get some insight into its own behaviour. There is no attempt to direct play or hurry the child. The only limits are those necessary to keep the therapy anchored to the real world and to make children aware of their responsibilities to the therapy. (McMahon 1992, p.29)

This approach is helpful for adoptees and Looked After Children as it allows them a safe environment in which to process their past traumatic experience at a developmentally appropriate level.

Morse and Wiley (1997) state that, for children to recover from trauma, they require safety and security so that they are able to deal with unprocessed emotions associated with the event and are able to secure social networks with well-formed attachments. In non-directive play therapy sessions the therapist creates an environment (playroom) that allows the child to feel safe and secure while forming an attachment to the therapist, enabling them to form secure attachments outside the therapy room. Non-directive play therapy is typically undertaken with children and young people aged between three and 12 years (McMahon 1992; West 1992); however, it can be effective with older children, if they are functioning at a younger developmental stage, and with adults (Landreth 2012).

Case Study: Tom

The following case study demonstrates Tom's experience of non-directive play therapy. Tom, a six-year-old boy, lived with his mother, father and sister. His mother left the family home after a number of years of physical and verbal violence from Tom's father that Tom witnessed. He was accommodated as his father was unable to manage his difficult behaviours at home. Tom appeared to use his play therapy sessions to process his experiences through the use of projective play with the toy animals. He spent time organising toy animals into two lines facing each other, 'the mums' and 'the dads' (e.g. two rhinos were facing each other and then two tigers facing each other). Tom selected one male and one female animal and made them fight, and then introduced a small animal that he placed to one side and stated, 'He's watching the animals fight.' The therapist was able to reflect the feelings of fear and sadness that the small animal may have felt. Tom went on to play out the little animal hiding behind objects in the play room due to his fear. He appeared to be using the animals initially to explore some of his experiences, and, second, to project some of his feelings and behaviours through the use of the small animal.

The research and literature suggests that there are a number of limitations when using this approach with children with attachment difficulties, including the child's caregiver not being present in the play therapy sessions and the child being in control of directing the play (Barnes 2007; Bratton *et al.* 2005), that may result in a child choosing not to explore their past experiences due to fear of evoking difficult emotions (West 1992). West further suggests that children who have experienced trauma may require a more focused intervention in addition to their non-directive play therapy.

Non-directive play therapy is often seen as a long-term intervention, which has financial implications for parents and commissioning agencies. Bratton *et al.* (2005) suggest that the optimum number of non-directive play therapy sessions is 35–40 sessions. However, currently there is a shortage of qualified play therapists in many parts of the United Kingdom (West 1992) and, from the author's knowledge, the majority of play therapists in Wales are self-employed. 'Play therapist' is not a protected title in the UK and therefore 'play therapy' remains unregulated. There are two professional bodies that regulate their members: the British Association of Play Therapists (BAPT) and Play Therapy United Kingdom (PTUK). (For further information about training please refer to the professional bodies' websites.)

THERAPLAY

Theraplay®[1] originated in 1967 and is defined as 'an engaging, playful, relationship-focused treatment method that is interactive, physical and fun' (Booth and Jernberg 2010, p.21). Based on attachment theory, the model aims to create healthy secure attachments. Theraplay sessions, attended by children and their parent(s) or caregiver(s), allow children to experience for the first time, or after a lapse, the benefits of attuned, responsive care that leads to them developing a sense of trust and a positive inner working model of themselves. Theraplay is based on four dimensions that are essential in developing healthy attachments: structure, nurture, engagement and challenge.

The key principle of Theraplay is to put the child's caregiver(s) firmly in charge of addressing and meeting the child's needs through playful activities (Barnes 2007). An initial assessment of the child–parent relationship is undertaken via the Marschak Interaction Method (MIM; Marschak 1960).

---

1   Theraplay is a registered service mark of The Theraplay institute, 1840 Oak Avenue Suite, Evanston, IL, 60201.

THE MARSCHAK INTERACTION METHOD

The Marschak Interaction Method (MIM) Assessment is used to observe the child's interactions with his or her parent(s) or caregiver(s). It allows therapists to identify patterns in children's attachment relationship: both positive factors and those areas of the attachment relationship that need to be enhanced through therapeutic intervention. The MIM consists of a set number of developmentally appropriate tasks categorised according to the Theraplay dimensions of Structure, Engagement, Nurture and Challenge, as well as playfulness. The MIM tasks are located in Jernberg and Booth (2001). Professionals facilitating a MIM assessment are required to undertake training accredited by the Theraplay Institute.

Children and their caregiver(s) are videoed or observed by the therapists completing a set of playful tasks, which represent healthy attachments according to the four dimensions. Through the MIM, the therapists are able to observe patterns in the interactions between children and their caregivers that inform the development of individualised treatment plans for them.

Theraplay is used throughout the UK and worldwide with Looked After and adopted children and is a useful short-term therapeutic intervention, as it seeks to enhance and develop secure attachments between children and their caregivers (Booth and Jernberg 2010). Theraplay sessions involve the therapist(s) initially modelling activities with the child, before caregivers are invited to undertake these activities with their child(ren). Once confident with the tasks, caregivers are invited to undertake these activities at home with their child(ren). As a result, these playful experiences, of structure and nurture, for example, can be transferred to the home environment and both caregivers and children have the tools to continue after direct treatment is complete (Booth and Lindaman 2000). Although Theraplay requires few resources or toys, the intervention does require parents or caregivers who are willing and able to engage in the therapeutic process. However, it does not focus on helping the child deal directly with difficult life experiences and it is recognised that adopted children may require an alternative or additional therapeutic intervention in order to process and make sense of these experiences (Booth and Lindaman 2000).

Weir *et al.* (2013) explored the effectiveness of Theraplay as the clinical treatment for adoptive families, and outlined a new approach entitled Whole Family Theraplay (WFT) that integrates Theraplay with family systems therapy. Their findings indicated that WFT treatment may lead to statistically significant benefits to children's overall behavioural functioning, family communication and adults' interpersonal relationships. Theraplay training requires candidates to be qualified, registered professionals in a field that prepares them to work with children and families (e.g. social worker, play therapist or teacher). Theraplay training is completed in stages from Level 1 to certification as a 'Certified Theraplay Therapist' (Jernberg and Booth 2001).

THERAPEUTIC LIFE STORY WORK

Life story work (see also Chapter 5) has its origins in social work practice and dates back to at least the 1960s (Rees 2009). Over the past forty years various approaches to life story work have developed in order to meet the complex needs of children who are looked after and adopted (Hendry 1988; Rees 2009; Rose and Philpot 2005; Ryan and Walker 1985). The Adoption and Children Act 2002 states that children must be given comprehensive information about themselves on placement with their adoptive families and that some form of life story work should be carried out prior to adoption. In practice, there are many children placed for adoption who do not have a life story book; some have a memory book or box or photo album but do not have an accompanying narrative.

The concept of 'life story work' is distinct from 'life story books'. Historically, life story work has focused on creating a life story book that starts in the past and ends in the present. Rees's (2009) model starts with the present and then explores the child's past before returning to the present. In more recent years a number of digital approaches to life story work have been developed for working with Looked After Children and adopted children (Ahmond and Betts 2003; Hammond and Cooper 2013).

Therapeutic life story work is a therapeutic process that allows children to understand their life experiences and process their internal feelings associated with their past, leading to resolution for the child or young person (Fahlberg 1994). Therapeutic life story work focuses on the process rather than the final product (life story book) and is based on developmental and attachment theory and practice. Children and young people typically attend 12–14 sessions with their parent(s) or caregiver(s), and sessions are facilitated as part of a therapeutic process by suitably qualified practitioners. During the sessions factual information about their narratives is shared in an age-appropriate manner, using a reflective process that allows children and young people to communicate their own perspectives and feelings related to their past experiences. At the end of the process the children and young people are given life story books containing the information shared during the sessions and their own reflections on the process.

The following provides an example of a child's experience of therapeutic life story work.

CASE STUDY: PETER

Peter was nine years old when he was referred for therapeutic life story work. At the point of referral he displayed aggressive behaviours both in his placement and at school. He had experienced more than 20 moves since he had begun being looked after, resulting in him having a deep mistrust of adults. Peter was made subject to a full Care Order, due to experiencing early developmental trauma and neglect. He had witnessed domestic violence between his mother and her past partners. Peter and his foster carer attended 20 sessions of therapeutic life story work. The therapist used a three-stage approach to working with him. The initial stage involved the therapist carrying out in-depth research into Peter's history and compiling a developmentally appropriate life narrative to use in the therapeutic life story work sessions. The second stage involved developing a therapeutic alliance with Peter and his foster carer through the use of focused play techniques to engage Peter. These techniques (e.g. family play genogram, 'getting-to-know-you' game, feelings masks) focused on enabling Peter to communicate his thoughts and feelings about himself and his past experiences. The third stage used a life line to map out his history; in Peter's case he used a river. During the sessions developmentally appropriate information was shared with Peter and he was invited to add his own thoughts and feelings to his 'river of life'.

On completion of the sessions a celebration was held and Peter chose to invite his social worker and the foster carer's supporting social worker. He was keen to share with his social worker his river of life and completed life story book. The professionals present in the closing session were invited to add comments to the final part of the river of life.

With younger children, a play-based approach to therapeutic life story work is required. The therapist engages children (in the presence of their caregiver(s)) using focused play techniques to help them understand their past experiences. Our approach involves the therapist acting out the child's narrative using a car mat or train track and play materials. Younger children use the play materials as a form of projection to express their own feelings and experiences from their past.

A criticism of therapeutic life story work is that it is often not carried out in the context of a relationship with the child, but seen as a routine procedure for children who are looked after or adopted. The timing, pace and depth of the work need to be carefully considered as this is often overlooked by busy professionals. It is recommended that all workers should undergo their own life story work before undertaking the process with children and young people (Ixer 1988).

Unlike other children and young people, many adoptees and Looked After Children experience difficulties in obtaining accurate information about their past. They often have gaps in their understanding of who they are, their past experiences and the reasons why they no longer live with their families of origin. Frequently, they do not have access to baby or family photos or birth certificates. For example, Katie was nine years old when her therapist shared her birth certificate with her; this was the first time she was aware she had a middle name!

It is common for practitioners helping children and young people prepare their life story books to 'gloss over' the reasons why they are in care, which can result in them developing distorted thoughts about themselves, their past and the reasons why they no longer live with their families of origin (Fahlberg 1994). There is currently no required professional qualification or supervision requirement for practitioners undertaking life story work or therapeutic life story work.

CONTEMPORARY PRACTICE: TOWARDS AN INTEGRATIVE APPROACH

Integrative approaches of working with children and their caregivers have been developed in response to clinical experience and research. Research and literature within the field of child therapy conclude that one model of therapy or counselling does not fit all children (Barnes 2007; Gil 1991; Schaefer 2001). 'Play Therapy is carving its own niche, drawing from the psychoanalytic, behavioural, gestalt and transpersonal schools, but resting mainly on the Rogerian person-centred approach' (West 1992, p.197).

The Stepping Stones (Child Therapy Consultants) Integrated Model

This is our integrative model that will be outlined using a case study from our clinical practice to illustrate. Our theoretical orientation as therapists is primarily humanistic (Axline 1947; Rogers 1951; West 1992). Our approach to therapy is creative and integrative. It is based on the principles of Theraplay (Booth and Jernberg 2010) and the work of other attachment-based therapists, including Hughes (2009) and his work on developmental re-parenting. It is also influenced by the neurobiological research of Perry (2006).

The Stepping Stones Integrated Model for working with Looked After Children and adopted children with developmental trauma and attachment difficulties is a five-stage model. The stages are outlined below:

- Stage 1: Family Assessment

- Stage 2: Report and Professionals Feedback Meeting

- Stage 3: Intervention: Designed to meet the individual needs of the family

- Stage 4: Therapy Review meetings

- Stage 5: Preparation for endings and final family session

The following case study is used to outline Stepping Stones Integrated Model and includes research findings in relation to this piece of clinical practice with a Looked After Child.

CASE STUDY: ALICE
Background Information

Alice was ten years old when she was referred for therapy. She had lived with her foster carers, Amanda and John, for two years. Prior to this Alice had seven different placements, including a potential adoptive placement that broke down due to the aggressive and attention-seeking behaviours commonly observed in children with similar histories. Alice had been removed from her birth mother due to neglect and her birth mother's mental health difficulties. She was referred for therapy by her social worker due to high levels of oppositional, and attention-seeking and aggressive behaviours towards her foster carers. These behaviours were possibly linked to high anxiety resulting from fear of separation from caregivers.

Assessment

Prior to the Family Assessment, Amanda and John were sent a series of questionnaire assessments to complete:

- *The Play History Questionnaire* (Taylor, Menarchek-Fetkovich and Day 2000). This provides information regarding the child's play preferences.

- *Day in the Life Form* (Family Futures 2014). This provides a snapshot of a child's behaviours during the course of a typical day.

- *Strengths and Difficulties Questionnaire (SDQ)* (Goodman 1997). Based on caregivers' reports this questionnaire identifies the extent of children and young people's emotional and behavioural problems. It is scored to produce an 'overall stress score' and also indicates whether a child or young person is likely to have a significant problem in one or more of the following areas: hyperactivity, emotional symptoms, conduct and peer problems. In addition, the SDQ also provides a score in relation to pro-social behaviours (positive social behaviours).

Alice had a total difficulties score of 22/40 on the Strengths and Difficulties Questionnaire (SDQ), placing her in the high needs category. She scored very highly for behavioural difficulties (7/10), peer difficulties (5/10) and impact on daily life (7/10). She also scored highly for emotional distress and low for kind or helpful behaviours. The Family Assessment is structured as follows:

- Welcome and introductions – including rules consisting of boundary setting, confidentiality and behaviour in the therapy room.

- Family Group Picture (adapted from Smith 1985) – a non-verbal, projective, interactive task designed to obtain information regarding family interactions swiftly. All family members are asked to create a 'family picture' and therapists observe how the family engages with the task and family interactions. Discussion between therapists and family follow completion of the picture.

- Family Obstacle Course – the family are asked to create an obstacle course together and then complete the course individually/with assistance from the other family members. The purpose of this task is to assess the family's dynamics while working together: for example, is appropriate structure provided by the caregivers, or does a family member attempt to dominate the task?

- Refreshment break – during both this break and the lunch break the family are provided with food which they use to make their refreshments and lunch. This provides an opportunity for the the therapists to observe family dynamics in relation to food and nutrition that can be problematic for Looked After Children and adopted children.

- Marschak Interaction Method (MIM) (Marschak 1960; see page 106).

- Lunch break.

- Child(ren) and caregiver(s) sessions – an individual session is held with one therapist and the child(ren), with a parallel session between a second therapist and the caregiver(s). The individual session with the child(ren) provides an opportunity for them to ask questions and for the therapist to observe their ability to engage in non-directive play therapy. (When there are two children a sibling session is undertaken.) The individual session with the caregivers provides an opportunity to ask questions and for the therapist to review assessments completed before the session.

- Review of the day (whole-family feedback).
- Ending game (using Theraplay based games).

During the course of the Family Assessment, family interactions and dynamics are observed alongside the attachment styles of the child(ren) and caregivers. In addition, the caregivers' capacity to provide structure and nurture to the child(ren) is observed alongside their ability to be playful with their child(ren). The children's ability to accept structure and nurture is observed and their developmental stage is assessed through observation. The family's ability to engage in the therapeutic process is assessed along with their level of interaction and engagement with the therapists. The information is recorded during the assessment using the Adult–Child Interactions Assessment Checklist (Waycott, McInnes and Carbis 2012).

Report and Professionals Feedback Meeting

Following the Family Assessment, caregivers and professionals already involved with the child and family (such as social workers) attend a meeting with the therapist(s) where feedback from the Family Assessment is given and therapeutic recommendations are made and explored. A report is provided, detailing the observations and recommendations.

Intervention

The intervention is designed to meet the individual needs of the child(ren) and family within their current living environment, based on the observations from the Family Assessment. The therapeutic plan of intervention has several essential elements, which are explored and managed simultaneously. In Alice's case the following interventions were recommended:

- *Six caregiver consultation sessions.* The focus of the sessions is psycho-educational and helps caregivers develop theoretical knowledge of attachment and trauma behaviours and strategies to manage these behaviours within the home and school environments. In addition to the psycho-educational components the sessions also offer caregivers the opportunity to reflect on their own childhood experiences and attachment styles and how this impacts on their parenting of their child(ren). Self-care techniques and managing the potential effects of caring for traumatised children (such as exhaustion, anger, depression, ill-health or secondary trauma) are also discussed. For more information about secondary trauma see Chapter 2.

  These sessions are usually conducted in parallel to the family trauma and attachment sessions.

- *Fourteen family sessions.* Children attend these sessions with their caregiver(s). Sessions focus on enhancing children's attachment (use of Theraplay-based techniques), meeting their unmet developmental needs and creating a structured and nurturing environment in order for children to process their feelings and past experiences through the use of therapeutic life story work.

- *Therapeutic review meetings.* Typically these are held every six months.

PARENT AND CAREGIVER PERCEPTIONS OF THE MODEL: RESEARCH FINDINGS

Perceptions of the assessment process and sessions were obtained through a semi-structured interview with Alice's caregivers. Initially, family members were unsure what to expect from the assessment process. Once this was clearly explained, they found the focus of both assessment and intervention being on the whole family reassuring: 'It's helpful; you're seen as a family and you're assessed as a family. She's not seen on her own; it's a family issue, not her issue.' They found the initial questionnaires thought-provoking and Amanda stated that it made her think about their daily life, consider the inconsistencies in Alice's behaviour and why that may be.

The whole-family assessment session was quite difficult at times but they all felt they had learnt about themselves and their relationship as a family unit. The Family Group Picture was considered difficult by both Amanda and John as it was not an activity they would usually engage in. They also found it difficult not to try to analyse it as they were going along but as they relaxed into the activity they found it enjoyable and worthwhile: 'It was interesting to see where she saw herself and our family.' Amanda and John were curious about the activities within the MIM but could understand that the activities were designed to look at different aspects of their interactions. Amanda particularly liked the nurturing activity as it was an opportunity to be close to Alice and enabled her to reflect on how difficult this can be for Alice at times, and why that may be.

Amanda and John could see clearly how the assessment process fed into the intervention and were able to make links between aspects of the intervention and the different assessment activities. They felt the therapeutic life story work was a complementary part of the intervention and that they really came to understand Alice's history and the impact on her life and behaviour now: 'These things have happened in her life and you know the reasons she has the attachment issue and she's having issues with me now because of what happened eight or nine years ago.' They also found the parenting consultation sessions helpful in understanding family dynamics and how to work as a family: 'It's made us stop and think about how we're parenting her; it's made us rethink some of the things and strategies to deal with her.'

SUMMARY

Drawing on relevant literature and empirical research, this chapter has provided a critical overview of non-directive and child-centred play therapy (Axline 1947; Landreth 2012), Theraplay (Booth and Jernberg 2010) and therapeutic life story work and how these models may be used when working with adopted children and Looked After Children. A range of case studies of the authors' work with children has been described to exemplify the different therapeutic models discussed. The three models have been combined into an integrated trauma-attachment model – The Stepping Stones (Child Therapy Consultants) Integrated Model. Development and research of this integrated trauma-attachment model is an ongoing process. Current experience indicates that it is an effective therapeutic model when working with adopted children and Looked After Children.

EDITORIAL DISCUSSION

Therapeutic work with children has developed side by side with a greater understanding of attachment, behavioural systems and neuroscience, including brain development. While many therapeutic interventions remain grounded in theoretical models and techniques, modifications have been introduced to the more traditional therapeutic approaches, plus new interventions designed to address specific needs of children and their families. The circumstances of Looked After Children are often complex, and pivotal to their healing is the development of healthier attachments with caregivers. This chapter describes an integrated trauma-attachment model that uses assessment to discern the most appropriate approach for each individual child and their caregivers. The model supports the caregivers, using separate parenting sessions to introduce effective strategies. 'Support and therapeutic efforts therefore have to help parents not only understand and emotionally "stay with" these children but also develop a range of responses that can distinguish between children's behaviour in terms of their socio-emotional age' (Howe 2006, p.133).

Due to the intra-familial nature of adopted children and Looked After Children's early traumatic experiences it is vital to nurture healthier attachments within their current families (Archer and Gordon 2013; Golding and Hughes 2012). An integrative approach that includes non-directive play therapy, exploring children's histories with children and their families, parent mentoring (see also Chapter 7), and shared, playful experiences for caregivers and children creates a sound basis for healing for families, within families. For example, the focus in Theraplay on nurture and structure recreates vital stages of attachment: providing comfort, protection and co-regulation to facilitate the development of a secure base and a safe environment within which children can begin to explore the world and acquire self-regulation and self-awareness. The use of assessment tools, such as the Marschak Interaction Method (1960) can establish a baseline, enabling therapists to establish 'where children and families are' and identify the developmental-attachment needs of the children with whom they are working.

Furthermore, due to the predominantly pre- and non-verbal nature of their traumatic experiences, expressive therapies can be particularly effective in changing children's developmental-attachment patterns within the current caregiving context. In evolutionary terms, learning has primarily occurred during play (Panksepp 1998, 2010). Structured playful interactions with caregivers (and siblings) provide healing experiences (Hughes 2009) through activating the neurobiology of attachment (Levy and Orlans 2014): establishing new, healthier neurobiological patterns and hence more secure patterns of attachment (Levy and Orlans 2014; Orlans and Levy 2006). To do so, caregivers need safe space, information and support (Hughes 2009) to adopt and practise effective, developmentally based reparenting strategies (Archer and Gordon 2006, 2013): all of which separate parenting sessions can provide (see also Chapters 7 and 8).

Finally, the integrative nature of the Stepping Stones model reflects the essentially integrative nature of developmental attachments. Traumatic experiences fundamentally interfere with healthy psycho-neurobiological integration: the earlier the traumatic events occurred, the greater their impact (Schore 2001b, 2012) and the more important it becomes to establish the point at which 'bottom-up' developmentally sensitive attachment interactions should be addressed. Caregivers, however secure their own attachments and couples relationships, are unlikely to have the in-depth understanding of their children's developmental, therapeutic reparenting needs (see Chapter 7) that is essential to effecting healthy changes (Howe 2006). For example, a cognitive-behavioural approach to managing and 'correcting' behaviour may effectively alter the behaviour of children who have age-appropriate shame-socialisation (Schore 1994) and robust attachments. However, for traumatised children, having experienced toxic levels of shame in their earliest years, this approach is more likely to be experienced as punitive (Archer and Gordon 2006, 2013) and humiliating (Siegel 2010): triggering dissociative fight, flight or freeze reactions (Lanius, Bluhm and Frewen 2013). It is therefore likely to compromise their current, and future, attachment relationships rather than strengthen them.

Chapter 7

SMILE THOUGH YOUR
HEART IS ACHING

*Therapeutic Parent Mentoring for
'Good Kids' and Their Families*

CAROLINE ARCHER

I am an adoptive parent and have worked as a therapeutic parent mentor for many years, within attachment-based therapeutic teams and independently for local authority and independent adoption and fostering agencies. Most referrals relate to 'acting-out' children whose caregivers struggled to develop healthy attachment relationships with them. Frequently caregivers report verbal and physical aggression towards themselves or vulnerable family members, struggles with rejection, compliance, destructive behaviour towards relationships or possessions, 'attention-seeking', 'lying' and 'stealing', alongside school and peer group difficulties. Work here focuses on finding effective strategies to help caregivers understand and manage their children's chaotic and incomprehensible behaviour.

This chapter, however, will focus on the often 'invisible child', the 'acting-in', 'good kid' whose smiles and eagerness to please conceal the terror and hurt of rejection and neglect. The mentoring and therapeutic aims are essentially the same: using a developmental-attachment based approach to enable caregivers to nurture their children towards sensory and socio-emotional literacy, well-being and resilience. However, the therapeutic reparenting process must take into account fundamental differences (Archer and Gordon 2006, 2013; Crittenden 2005). 'Acting-out' children need support to recognise and control their own emotions and behaviours and become sensitive to those of others. 'Acting-in' children require encouragement to 'be themselves': to acknowledge and express their own needs and feelings rather than attempting to identify and meet those of their caregivers.

The therapeutic mentoring programme comprises 90-minute home visits with one or both caregivers. Meeting family members at home reinforces their security and confidence, allowing me to engage with them and observe children's interactions and behaviours 'in their natural environment'. I aim to develop a 'secure base' (Bowlby 1988) for caregivers, enabling them to explore their frequently ambivalent feelings towards their child, their own experiences of being parented and their current attachment and parenting styles. This enables us to identify their strengths and opportunities for changes that could benefit them and their families and to begin to work as a 'therapeutic attachment team'.

I explore the principles of therapeutic (developmental) reparenting (Archer and Gordon 2006, 2013) at length with caregivers and together we 'practise' making sense of children's current behaviour in terms of their past history, learning to understand the 'language of trauma' (Archer and Gordon 2006, 2013) and consequently developing a tailor-made, attachment-based parenting approach to 'reparenting the child who hurts' (Archer and Gordon 2006, 2013). Pivotal to establishing credibility, mutual trust and confidence is the experience of 'having been there, wished I hadn't done that'. This allows me to empathise with distressed caregivers, and offer support and strategies based on in-depth understanding of the lasting impact of early intrapersonal trauma on attachment and development.

During introductory family meetings and subsequent sessions with caregiver(s) I pay close attention to the 'identified child', remaining alert for references to siblings: their attachment histories, how adults feel about them and their relationships within the family. Alarm bells sound when I hear how siblings differ from the 'difficult' child: how little trouble they are, how rewarding and loveable they seem. It requires subtlety to help caregivers recognise this could indicate that their 'smiling, good, willing or quiet child' may be as 'hurt' as their 'acting-out' sibling. Inconspicuous 'acting-in' children deserve as much attention, understanding and help to achieve physical, emotional, social and intellectual health as their 'in-your-face' counterparts. Their neurobiological organisation, beliefs, perceptions and behaviours are often as distorted as 'acting-out' children's (Crittenden 2005; van der Kolk 2005). While serious difficulties may not become apparent until adolescence, when hormones surge, neural networks undergo radical reorganisation (NIMH 2014) and the developmental challenges of separation are 'revisited', it is vital that interactive repair occurs as early as possible, when 'neuroplasticity' is optimal (Schore 2001b, 2012).

THE MILBURNS' STORY

I was asked by the Milburn family's adoption support manager to provide therapeutic parent mentoring sessions to Alison and Nick regarding their elder child Deano. His behaviour was becoming more troubling, both at home and in school, and his adoptive parents were increasingly disheartened. From his social worker I received a brief account of Deano's early history and his adoptive placement at 15 months, alongside an account of the difficulties his adoptive parents were experiencing. I then spent time with the adopters as a couple, listening to their story and their growing struggles. After a brief 'honeymoon period', the troubling behaviour seen in Deano's previous placement had returned, alongside increasing aggression towards Alison and children at nursery school. Deano frequently rejected Alison's caregiving and was becoming increasingly uncooperative.

When Dreana, Deano's half-sibling, was born a year after him, their mother Marnie was co-habiting with Dreana's father. Marnie had concealed her pregnancy until her third trimester. Since her appearance and health had improved and her flat seemed adequately furnished and reasonably clean, Marnie was offered family support to help her care for Dreana. She contracted to remain drug and alcohol free. However, within weeks Marnie's partner disappeared and evidence of drug and alcohol abuse re-emerged. At six months old Dreana was placed with foster carers while an adoptive family was identified. An adoption assessment had already begun for Nick and Alison; the family was introduced to Dreana when she was 11 months old.

Dreana's placement exacerbated Deano's troubling behaviours, precipitating extended 'melt-downs', the taking and hiding of food, destruction of the parents' valued possessions, running off and refusing to get ready for school. Now, with Deano aged four-and-a-half and Dreana 12 months younger, Alison and Nick expressed growing concerns for Dreana's safety and were unhappy about leaving the children together unsupervised, even for short periods. Although they were both feeling increasingly inadequate as parents, they were supportive of each other, committed to their children and ready to try 'anything' to make their family 'work'.

I met both children in the family home, observing their play and interactions while 'chatting to Mum and Dad'. Deano approached me immediately, attempting to climb on my lap, talking excitedly, leaping on furniture, throwing toys, shouting loudly, demanding sweets. He took little notice of his parents' responses and gave Dreana sly digs when their attention was elsewhere. In contrast, Dreana remained close to Mum, smiling and sucking her teddy. When Alison suggested Dreana play with DUPLO® bricks she did so, humming tunelessly to herself, occasionally turning towards Alison for reassurance. Later, still humming, she wrapped teddy in a blanket and sat rocking gently.

Although Dreana kept her distance from Deano she showed little response to his hurtful behaviour. Both parents appeared protective of her and were visibly upset at Deano's actions.

During subsequent, weekly home visits I mostly saw Alison while Nick was at work, Deano in school and Dreana at morning nursery. However, immediately following visits I wrote letters addressed to both parents exploring and expanding on issues that had arisen. This removed some of the burden of practising therapeutic parenting herself from Alison's shoulders and simultaneously helping Nick make sense of, and implement, my suggestions. I re-emphasised to both that they were the 'primary therapeutic team', the most important part of the children's healing process, that I believed they were good enough parents (Winnicott 1958) and that eventually they would, too.

My immediate aim when meeting with Alison was to create a secure base in which she felt psychologically held (Siegel 1999) and able to explore painful feelings. I gave her permission to speak honestly about the effects that Deano's behaviours had on her feelings and responses towards him and on her self-image. We talked about the stresses his behaviour placed on the family both at home and at school, the responses of extended family and friends, and Alison's growing sense of isolation, since Deano was often excluded from play and party invitations. Alison also experienced 'distancing' from other caregivers at school pick-up times and during informal 'cups-of-coffee-and-chats'. Alison was sad that, as a consequence, Dreana had fewer opportunities to socialise with her peers.

Alison and Nick had become increasingly confused about how to respond to Deano from the mixed advice they received from friends, family, social media and 'parenting manuals'. Prompted by their search for understanding they now wondered whether Deano had 'ADHD or Asperger's'. They felt they were 'failing' as parents since the star-charts, 'ignoring negatives' and 'thinking step' advice they had received was proving ineffective. Despite the confidence their social worker had in both parents, Alison wondered whether she was 'the right mother' for Deano, as he continued to resist her attempts to care for him and she began distancing herself from him. She acknowledged that alongside Nick's support, it was the loving relationship between herself and Dreana that helped her keep going. Whenever Alison mentioned Dreana her face lit up and she seemed visibly to relax.

The Way It Was

I encouraged Alison to tell me more about Dreana's development, her behaviour and both parents' feelings about her. She could tell me little about the pregnancy or birth, other than that Dreana was below average birth weight and remained in hospital for several days. I requested Dreana's case notes and arranged for Nick to join us to discuss them. Records indicated that Marnie had not acknowledged her pregnancy for several months, attending ante-natal classes only late into the pregnancy. Labour was long and Marnie received strong pain relief; Dreana was delivered using forceps when monitoring indicated foetal distress. Marnie did not remain in hospital with her baby, although she visited for brief periods daily.

Nick and Alison were visibly moved when we discussed the effects of these experiences on Dreana's early neurobiological, and hence socio-emotional, development. Marnie had been exceedingly anxious that 'they' would remove her baby if they learned she was pregnant: inevitably her high levels of anxiety flooded her developing baby with stress hormones, such as cortisol, disturbing Dreana's long-term neurobiological development (Schore 1994, 2011). Marnie's use of restrictive, concealing clothing and late engagement with ante-natal care would also impact Dreana's well-being. It was likely, given Marnie's history, that Dreana was exposed to the adverse effects on her development of drugs, alcohol and tobacco. Additionally, peri-natal distress, exposure to analgesia and forceps delivery would all have negative consequences on her development (Gitau *et al.* 2001).

Records written by family support staff indicated growing concerns about Marnie's caregiving. Workers visiting twice weekly noted that the television was always on at full volume. When Marnie bottle-fed Dreana she held her away from her body, sitting cross-legged and using her smartphone to text or access social media sites. Although she mostly kept the baby adequately 'fed and watered', support staff became increasingly aware that Dreana spent much of her day in her baby-seat or cot. When encouraged to engage with Dreana, Marnie would say the baby was tired, was 'poorly and needed to rest', or 'liked her own company' and disliked being picked up. Things came to a head when workers found Marnie passed out, cradling an empty vodka bottle, while Dreana lay cold, wet and hungry on the floor.

Dreana was removed from Marnie's care according to the terms of the parenting contract.

Alison described Dreana on arrival in their home as a quiet, small-for-age baby who slept for long periods and cried infrequently; she needed encouragement to feed. Her play was 'not as forward as expected' but she responded with pleasure to nursery rhymes and cuddles. Dreana did not crawl; her first steps were taken at 16 months but she did not walk independently with confidence for some time. Her speech and fine motor development were 'a bit slow'. Alison described Dreana as: 'a lovely little girl, so good and so loving. She's always telling me she loves me. She puts up with Deano, shares her toys and seldom complains. She's been a bit slow developmentally but then she was premature and the health visitor says she'll soon catch up.'

During each visit Alison and I took time to reflect on both children's early histories: at what happened to them and how this affected their attachment, development and behaviour, their perceptions of the world and sense of self. We explored these in parallel so that we could see the similarities and differences between the children's experiences and how this could explain their different behaviour patterns (Crittenden 2005). The information was put in writing and given to Nick and Alison to strengthen their shared understanding of past events and their meaning now: the details would always be there for them to refer back to if they felt confused or out of their depth. I gave them my email address, allowing them to ask further questions or raise other issues as they arose; having my mobile phone number meant that they could text and arrange mutually convenient times to talk. These steps served to help Alison and Nick feel 'held in mind'. Rather than fostering dependence, this ongoing connection encouraged them to work through problems for themselves, increasing their confidence and strengthening the secure base they sought to provide for both children.

Deano had clearly experienced serious emotional and physical neglect, alongside physical abuse. The period Dreana spent with her mother seemed superficially less challenging, particularly in relation to her physical care. However, access to birth and care records allowed us to identify subtle traumatic stressors in her early life. For Dreana, connections with her mother, beginning in the womb, were compromised by Marnie's heightened emotional state and sub-optimal self-care. Peri-natal birth trauma interfered with essential neo-natal attachment experiences and continued to affect Marnie's parent–infant interactions with Dreana.

Marnie's self-preoccupation and lack of insights meant that she was unable to sustain good enough caregiving or provide the stimulation and co-regulation that Dreana needed. Dreana internalised that she could not rely on her mother and that her needs would not be met. In order to survive the intense neurophysiological and emotional arousal she experienced she learned to shut down her feelings, make few demands and inhibit her movements. Thus, while both children shared inner working models (IWMs; Bowlby 1988) of the world as unpredictable, unsafe and hurtful, Deano responded with impulsive, demanding behaviour, whereas Dreana's lack of positive sensori-motor and socio-emotional experience led to somatic and emotional constriction and behavioural compliance.

The Way Forward

It is possible to provide only an outline of the regulatory, somato-sensory and socio-emotional reparative interactions that Dreana's parents undertook over the subsequent year. I am using a composite case study of a young child, which will be familiar to many childcare professionals, to spotlight issues allowing early identification of potential difficulties, facilitating early intervention and optimising outcomes. With some lateral thinking it becomes possible to devise acceptable, age-appropriate alternatives for pre-teens to the attachment and developmentally based strategies discussed. For extended exploration of these, and many other therapeutic reparenting strategies see Archer and Gordon (2006, 2013).

I discussed Alison and Nick's anxieties about Dreana's physical progress, to establish our 'base-line': the 'bottom-up' developmental level from which we would work to heal Dreana's developmental-attachment issues. It was evident that Dreana's brainstem and vestibular functions had been compromised, affecting her physical relationship with the world, the 'wiring up' of basic regulatory functions, such as heart and respiration rates, facial muscle functions (Porges 2001, 2003) and physiological arousal (Ogden *et al.* 2006; van der Kolk 2005). Since these difficulties developed in the context of dysfunctional primary attachment relationships, healing also needed to occur within primary attachment relationships, that is with Alison and Nick, using developmental reparenting principles.

Alongside the accounts of reduced movement opportunities in the womb and early months, Dreana's parents spoke of her delayed motor development and general discomfort with movement. Discussion revealed that Dreana tired easily, had difficulty running and jumping, disliked rough-and-tumble games, see-saws, roundabouts and slides, and suffered motion-sickness. This picture is typical of children with compromised vestibular system functioning (Goddard 1996), which is critical to balance and positional security and consequently attachment security (Archer and Gordon 2013; Kranowitz 1998). Poor brainstem–vestibular integration also affects the development of auditory and visual processing and speech and language development (Porges 2001, 2003; van der Kolk 2005). This was evident in Dreana's discomfort with unpredictable noise, her tendency to create her own background noise (like humming), difficulties with following instructions and unclear speech.

Together we devised a 'sensori-motor diet' for Dreana, to be introduced by her parents using PARCEL principles (Archer and Gordon 2006, 2013): Playfulness, Acceptance, Responsiveness, Curiosity, Empathy and Love (based on PACE; Hughes 1998). Children learn through joyful childlike *Play*; serendipitously they cannot experience separation anxiety or fear simultaneously (Panksepp 1998). *Responsiveness* included monitoring Dreana's body language to detect signs of discomfort to avoid overwhelming her vestibular system (Goddard 1996). *Accepting* 'this is hard for you' allowed Dreana to 'feel felt' (Siegel 2007); being *Curious* enabled Alison to wonder whether 'not being able to move around a lot when you were with Marnie makes it scary now'. *Empathy* allowed Dreana to hear how sad her parents felt that 'we weren't there to look after you when you needed us'. *Love* formed an integral part of all these interactions: of being and playing together, exploring 'what you like and don't like' and practising feeling and being loved.

Tri-phasic Developmental Approach

Therapeutic strategies were introduced in three intrinsically related phases embracing neurodevelopmental and attachment sequences:

1. Sensori-motor issues: gravitational security

2. Developmental attachment, secure base and Object Permanence (OP)

3. Exploration stage of attachment

1. Sensori-motor Issues: Gravitational Security

The initial focus on gravitational security echoes therapeutic parenting principles: that development is 'bottom up' and supports the proposal that 'Safety Trumps Fear' (Porges 2003), allowing social interactions and co-regulation to occur. Strategies included rocking, shared action rhymes, bear-hugs, bouncing, rolling, swinging and rough-and-tumble play (all subject to tolerance), with appropriate rhythmical accompaniment. Bottle-feeding was encouraged, since stimulating oral muscles strengthens facial muscles integrally linked to the brainstem (Porges 2003), facilitating social engagement and hence promoting attachment.

Cradling in the 'nursing position' provided Dreana with feedback to her vestibular system; an accompaniment of mutual gazing, 'motherese' and nursery rhymes provided co-regulation, auditory stimulation, closeness and comfort, also invaluable in establishing social engagement and attachment interactions (Porges 2003), a secure base and OP. Many older children are comfortable with bottle-feeding or, following the same developmental attachment principles, more 'grown-up' alternatives, such as sports bottles and 'curly-wurly' straws; caregivers can sit alongside, arms around them, chatting, reading aloud or singing.

2. Developmental Attachment, Secure Base and Object Permanence (OP)

Endearing though Dreana's 'funny little ways' were, given Dreana's early history, they would be based on internalised beliefs that caregivers would not or could not meet her needs, that she was intrinsically 'bad' and did not deserve good care. Fearing rejection, Dreana developed an attachment pattern predicated on being sensitive to, and meeting, others' needs in order to 'control' proximity and interactions (Crittenden 2005) – inverting the normal parent–child caregiving hierarchy.

Her 'funny little ways' included:

- being able to locate Alison's possessions while unable to find her own

- asking 'What do you think?' when given choices

- repeatedly whispering 'I love you Mum'

- saying 'Mummy needs cuddles or stories?'

- being desperate to help with household chores

- sharing her toys and sweets.

It can be difficult for parents and caregivers to see beyond the socially engaging behaviours of 'good children'. 'Being good' is what we are raised to be; having 'good children' gives us pleasure and makes us feel good. Smiling, an integral component of the social engagement system (SES; Porges 2001), creates positive feelings within and stimulates observers' mirror neuron systems: creating similar body feelings that inform their emotional well-being (Carr *et al.* 2003; Schore 2003). More obviously upsetting to her parents, Dreana became distressed and hid if they seemed upset or distant. She sometimes 'went into her own world' (dissociated), appearing startled when addressed. During occasional 'melt-downs' she became inconsolable, kicking and pushing her parents away.

PHYSIOLOGICAL AROUSAL

Infants learn to manage their neurophysiologically based sensori-motor and emotional arousal through consistent external regulation by 'attuned' caregivers (Schore 1994, 2001a, 2003). Early traumatic separation, loss, neglect, abuse, chronic illness and clinical interventions interfere with this interpersonal neuro-developmental process, leaving children in persistent states of hyper (over) or hypo (under) arousal and unable to follow normal developmental sequences culminating in 'top-down' self-regulation (Schore 2001b). This lack of integration is often evident in dissociative 'shut-down' or 'melt-down'. In the longer term it compromises children's capacities to learn (Bombèr 2007) and increases susceptibility to poor social functioning and physical and mental health issues in adulthood (van der Kolk 2005, 2014).

Rewiring and integrating Dreana's trauma-driven neurophysiology required knowledge of developmental sequences, the ability to make sense of children's behaviour, sensitivity to respond to her 'real needs' and controlled child-like playfulness. We explored how Marnie's failure to recognise or respond to Dreana's needs left her with serious experiential and developmental 'wiring gaps'. Without sufficient experiences of co-regulation of sensory and emotional arousal, Dreana managed her distress by distorting or limiting her SES responses and 'shutting down'. Dissociation (see also Chapters 2 and 9) underpins the attachment patterns of 'good kids': avoidance of sensory and emotional feelings and of being seen or making demands, alongside heightened sensitivity to the needs and feelings of others. This behavioural pattern is consistent with Crittenden's (2005) insecure attachment 'A' classification. Inevitably, there will be occasional 'melt-down' incidents: episodes of uncontrolled hyper-arousal, including aggression to self or others, followed by intense feelings of toxic shame.

Dreana's 'funny ways', and shut-down, were therefore worrying in developmental-attachment terms: contrary to common perceptions that such endearing, or non-challenging, behaviours are pro-social behaviours, to be welcomed and encouraged. True pro-social actions require active, positive choices, unlike 'pleasing' interactions based on fear of rejection and dissociation. Dreana's 'melt-downs', although occasional, were highly distressing for her parents; they found them confusing and out-of-character. For Dreana these outbursts reinforced her shame and deepest preconscious fears that she was 'bad': her parents' reactions confirming that she was unacceptable and unlovable. It was vital that Alison and Nick understood this dynamic and were supported to respond calmly, showing acceptance and empathy for her distress. They would stay with Dreana, holding her or remaining close, speaking quietly to her, learning to 'decode' her behaviour and verbalising her unspoken feelings. They needed to show Dreana they could 'read', validate and 'hold' her emotions for her: providing the essential co-regulation that leads to self-regulation, just as caregivers would with their infants. They might say:

- 'I'll stay here with you until you feel calmer.'

- 'I wonder if you feel you're bad and we'll send you away. Sorry! You're stuck with us!'

- 'I know it hurts and it's scary. We can do this together.'

- 'I love you. I love you even when you say you hate me.'

- 'I can keep us both safe. It's hard for you but I know one day you'll know that, too.'

Alison and Nick also explored ways to 'discharge' the stress hormones, like adrenalin, that drove Dreana's 'melt-downs': bouncing, running, singing, dancing or shouting loudly together. They also learned to model expressing and managing 'bad' feelings in safe and playful ways.

Much of Alison and Nick's 'work' focused on enabling Dreana to 'feel her feelings' and improve her sensory and emotional literacy. Integral to this was learning to 'decode' Dreana's 'encrypted' behavioural communications, accepting, verbalising and responding to them, seizing every opportunity to anticipate her attachment needs and meet them pro-actively. For example, they instigated 'hugging time' before separations (however brief), following signs of upset, with changes of activity, or in unfamiliar situations. They would provide gentle cuddles while acknowledging and validating Dreana's reactions:

- 'You've gone very quiet. I wonder if you're worried we're angry.'

- 'Maybe you're scared I don't love you when you keep telling me you love me or "Mummy needs cuddles".'

- 'Maybe you're worried I won't come back when I'm not around? Remember, you're always in my heart and in my mind.'

Alison and Nick were asked to initiate 'rapid-response' approach responses, promoting healthy attachment interactions through facial expression, body-language, prosody and simple statements. This would turn interactions with Dreana 'the right way up', from 'bottom up': beginning with the brainstem, informing and influencing limbic areas and encouraging the maturation of the neocortical reflective, self-regulating brain (Perry 2009).

Neglected children perceive their world as unpredictable: they need extended, consistent availability of caregivers to alter these cognitions. We discussed reducing Dreana's sessions at nursery to

xiety and strengthen her sense of Object
Constancy (OP and OC); a local toddler
ore beneficial short-term alternative. (For
OP and OC see Chapter 12.)
edtime, were eased through acknowledging
ing predictable, relaxed sequences through
nd transitional objects (see also Chapters
photos and items of Alison's that Dreana
ning'. Her parents would tell Dreana that
minutes to see you' and 'be thinking of you
ey 'did not disappear' when not physically
g acquisition of OP included peek-a-boo,
', covering parts of each other (excluding
later by hide-and-seek and 'Sardines'.

L
b
4
'c
th
alv
wit
hun
faces,

3. Exp| |achment

Core d   ting principles, including co-experiences,
both p   nal, are vital for both 'acting-out' and
'acting-   ver, the strategies used must be 'tailor-
made'. '   ase in children like Dreana specifically
involves g   their behavioural repertoire: to reduce
inhibitions   positive socio-emotional experiences, self-
awareness, s   and spontaneity. Therapeutic caregivers
should contin   ring', while encouraging and modelling
merriment, mes   istake-making.

Dreana's pare   lled 'being impulsive', 'discovering new
things', 'controlled   king' and 'you-don't-know-until-you've-
tried-it' activities w   maining mindful of her trauma-based
perceptions, cognitions   behaviours. Shared playfulness and
amused curiosity are invaluable components of this personal and
social learning. Creating ways of stimulating good kids' under-
developed PLAY circuits attenuates their PANIC and FEAR circuits
(Panksepp 1998), promoting a positive 'feeling and learning' cycle.
Simultaneously, making children 'head-strong' increases their vitality
and thirst for life.

Laughing at themselves and with children offers caregivers
non-threatening ways of interacting that challenge distorted power-
dynamics and reduce habitual fear responses. By making themselves

look ridiculous, giggling and enjoying themselves, adults liberate 'acting-in' children, giving them permission to have fun without fear. Child-like mischief plays a large part in these 'reparative experiences': allowing children to expand their behavioural repertoire, develop self-confidence, self-awareness and autonomy.

Books, cartoons, dolls, puppets and role-play introduce the concept of acceptable naughtiness in funny, non-challenging ways. The counter-intuitive strategy of daring 'good children' to be 'wicked', or praising them for being mischievous, counters their beliefs that they are 'bad' and must strive to be 'perfect' at all times to avoid hurt and rejection. Since perfection is unachievable, they are frequently overwhelmed by shame, leading to 'shut-down' or uncontrollable 'melt-downs': caregivers, and other adults, such as grandparents and nursery school staff, need help to understand this dynamic to be accepting and play their part enthusiastically.

Opportunities for 'messy play' allow children to experience messiness safely. Neglected children like Dreana are often left dirty, then experience disgust and rejection from caregivers or peers for being unacceptable. These experiences affect their developing sensory systems, leading to dissociation of bodily feelings (Ogden *et al.* 2006) and habitual sensory-seeking or sensory-avoidant behaviours. Activities such as finger painting, digging in mud, splashing in puddles, sucking sauce-covered spaghetti and making bread, with suitable protective coverings, can be indulged in, laughed over and then 'cleaned-up-and-tidied-away' with gusto.

To maltreated children, making mistakes triggers fears of abandonment and annihilation. Challenging such deeply held beliefs requires that caregivers model accepting and dealing with their own mistakes: allowing children to explore this concept and its implications while feeling sufficiently 'held' psychologically. Where verbal reassurances that 'it's OK' or 'there's no need to feel scared' are frequently ineffective in changing maltreated children's IWMs and characteristic behaviour patterns, seeing and experiencing mistakes alongside immediate interactive repair leads to positive changes (Archer and Gordon 2006, 2013).

Finally, caregivers need infinite patience with their children, accepting and empathising with their once adaptive perceptions, beliefs and behaviours throughout these three developmental phases. There are often 'slip ups' and regressions during the process that may recur during subsequent developmental periods, such as age-related changes through school and puberty. During such transitions families need access to therapeutic mentors to receive 'top-ups' in understanding these new challenges and their impact on their children, alongside age-appropriate strategies.

On Their Way

Over a period of months Alison and Nick embraced therapeutic reparenting principles, gaining insights into Dreana's behaviour and encouraging her to believe they could and would accept her, keep her safe and love her. With each other's support they grew in confidence in their capacity to manage the challenges they faced with both children and to devise appropriate reparenting strategies themselves. They felt reassured that they would have access to 'top-up' support, notably through significant developmental events, such as Dreana's transition into full-time school, from infant to junior departments, into senior school, and during the challenges of adolescence, including individuation-separation. Reducing Deano's impulsive and 'attention-seeking' behaviour using PARCEL principles created safe physical and emotional 'space' for Dreana to blossom. She is increasingly able to articulate her needs and feelings, manage separations and engage in spontaneous play at home and with peers.

DISCUSSION

Therapeutic reparenting embraces attachment as an experience-dependent, developmental process (Schore 1994). Through synchronic interactions within primary attachment relationships infants learn about the world and about themselves. They 'mind-share' (Siegel 2010) information-processing systems, allowing them to 'download vital data' and organise their central and autonomic nervous systems from 'bottom up' (Archer and Gordon 2006, 2013; Siegel 2007). This developmental sequence begins in the brainstem, governing arousal and involved with sensori-motor processing (Ogden et al. 2006), followed by sensory, emotional, attachment and learning functions within the limbic system and eventually the neo-cortical reflective brain (Siegel 2007).

Early traumatic adversity, such as neglect, abuse or chronic illness, seriously compromises neurobiological organisation (Schore 1994, 2001b, 2012), leading to insecure or disorganised attachment patterns (Crittenden 2005; Spangler and Grossmann 1999). There are strong correlations between early neurobiological disorganisation and serious mental health issues in adulthood (Levy and Orlans 2014; van der Kolk 2003, 2005). Therapeutic reparenting therefore requires access to children's early history, to establish levels of developmental attachment-trauma, and interpretation of the impact of such experiences. This enables caregivers to help children alter their 'neurobiological wiring' and attachment patterns, enhancing long-term well-being and resilience (Siegel 2007).

The tri-phasic approach to therapeutic reparenting emphasises the neurobiological and socio-emotional developmental sequences occurring within primary attachment relationships. Early emotional and physical neglect lead to poor modulation of somato-sensory and affective arousal. The effects of poor attachment experiences compromise the development of a secure base, positive IWMs, the capacity for exploration and mature top-down modulation (Schore 2001b): consistent with van der Kolk's (2005) proposed diagnosis of Developmental Trauma Disorder (DTD; see also Introduction) for children experiencing early, chronic intra-familial trauma.

Traumatised children fitting Crittenden's 'A' attachment classification (2005) run the risk of being overlooked in terms of their developmental attachment needs: 'looking good' and making adults feel good, they adopt 'pro-social' adaptive behavioural strategies to achieve proximity, protection and attention. Their behaviour is highly organised around survival (Crittenden 2005), leaving them dissociated from their basic needs, which affects their somatic, psychological and relational developmental integration and functioning over their lifetime. Since their 'default' behaviours are organised towards rapid 'shut-down' responses to actual and perceived threat, difficulties frequently arise when they are placed in foster or adoptive families (Perry 2009), since trauma-organised perceptions, behaviours and cognitions tend to be inflexible (Schore 2001b). It is essential to tailor developmental attachment interventions to their fundamental need to feel safe enough to know and be all of themselves, for themselves.

Chapter 8

GETTING THE RIGHT FIT

The Team as a Secure Base for Supporting Families

HELEN O'SHEA AND ELAINE SIMPSON

This is the story of a family and the Family Intervention Team (FIT) project working to support that family's changes. I will first introduce you to Mollie and her family, to our team and the Family Support Practitioner (FSP), Lara, who worked with them, illustrating some of our thinking and ways of working to make life a little happier for a child and her mum and step-dad.

MOLLIE AND HER FAMILY

Mollie is eight years old and lives at home with her mum, Alana, her stepfather Richard, and 18-month-old brother, Corey. She is a pretty little girl with long, dark hair that she wears in plaits. She can look thoughtful and wary but when she smiles it is warm and friendly. Mollie lives with her parents in a rented terraced house in a small 'valleys town' in South Wales.

THE FAMILY INTERVENTION TEAM (FIT)

The authors of this chapter are a clinical psychologist and a service manager working for Action for Children, a national children's charity. The project we describe is an early intervention project for children with social, emotional and behavioural difficulties. The project has been subject to numerous evaluations evidencing its effectiveness in reducing problem behaviours and generating social value. The project team is made up of the FSP, a clinical psychologist, a part-time manager and business and administrative support. We are based in a major 'valleys town' and support children and families across the borough. The project is a referral-only service taking referrals from a wide range of professionals. The families that use us are often experiencing multiple challenges such as separation or divorce, abuse, bullying, domestic violence or bereavement. Children may be showing their emotional distress through physical aggression, challenging and non-compliant behaviour, having difficulty making or keeping peer relationships, or school refusal. They often have low self-esteem, fears and phobias or a need for rigid routines.

HOW WE WORK

The service is based on a systemic approach (Carr 2009; Stratton 2010) using attachment theory (Bowlby 1969) that helps us think about family patterns of relationship and how we provide a 'secure base' for our families.

A SYSTEMIC APPROACH

A systemic approach is based on the idea that people cannot be viewed as isolated individuals, but as connected and interdependent within numerous groups and networks. Any intervention therefore must take account of the child and family's relationships, interactions and the interactional patterns and dynamics that are present.

A secure base is fundamental to any successful caregiving environment and therefore at the heart of our therapeutic interventions. The FSP seeks to provide a place of trust and emotional safety to which caregivers can return without fear of reprisal, enabling them to practise new and potentially challenging ways of thinking and acting with their children.

We use a reflective approach throughout our work (Finlay and Gough 2003; Hargreaves and Page 2013; Schon 1983); initial referrals are discussed by the team where we consider carefully whether we are the best service for a family. We accept families where children have newly emerging social, emotional or behavioural problems and have not had extensive involvement from other services. We do not see children who, at the point of referral, are involved with statutory Social Services or who are already receiving support from another service such as Child and Adolescent Mental Health Services (CAMHS). Parents must be in agreement with the referral and want to work with us. If we do not accept a referral we will recommend other appropriate support. If we accept the referral we provide an individualised book recommendation from the Bibliotherapy list and an invitation to our Wellbeing Groups, if this seems appropriate. The Bibliotherapy scheme provides a list of useful books about common childhood difficulties. Since it requires a high degree of literacy and organisational skills it is helpful for only a proportion of parents. Our weekly Wellbeing

Groups are run by systemic psychotherapists, allowing for a high level of containment of group dynamics and individual distress. They are open to the community for all parents looking to improve emotional well-being.

We offer families a 12-week intervention. One of our strengths is that we are not constrained by any single model but draw from a wide range of therapeutic tools according to the needs of the family. We arrange an initial meeting and assessment in the family home, where we invite the family to share their story about their concerns and what has led to the referral. From this we construct an initial formulation that we share with the family.

FORMULATION

A formulation is a theoretically based explanation or conceptualisation of the information obtained from assessment.

The assessment is not intended to 'diagnose' the 'problem', but rather to explore with the families their stories and how they make sense of the events that have happened to them, their hopes for change and fears about past, current or future life. It is co-constructed with families based on how they, rather than professionals, perceive and make sense of these. From this our intervention is developed. As every family's story is unique, so every intervention is unique to that family. The initial formulation will be tentatively offered to them as a way of checking out that we have heard and understood the important parts of their story and also as a way of explaining how the service works. The formulation enables the clinical psychologist and FSP to plan a 12-week intervention that is carried out by the FSP. At six weeks a mid-way review is held with families. This focuses on the work that has been done so far, what has been achieved and how best to use the remaining time. At the end of the intervention an end-review is carried out with the family and FSP, reviewing what has been achieved, how to maintain this and whether any further referrals need to be made to other services.

The assessment and formulation is shared at a weekly clinical team meeting where FSPs and therapists can pool ideas, ranging from the theoretical to suggestions for games or activities that may encourage children to think and talk about a particular issue that is worrying them, or think in a different way about something that has happened. Cases are also brought to a team meeting half-way through the intervention following the mid-way review and again at the end after the end-review. This reflective approach is underpinned by monthly clinical supervision and the team also ask one another for support with ideas at any point of the intervention (Hawkins and Shohet 2012).

MOLLIE'S STORY

Mollie was referred to the project by her school health nurse. Mollie had been eating very little at mealtimes and this was really worrying Alana who had asked the school if they could monitor how much she was eating at lunchtime. Although school staff had no concerns, they could see how worried Alana was and asked the school health nurse, Sally-Anne, if she could meet with Alana and give her some advice. Sally-Anne tried to reassure Alana that Mollie was within the normal weight range for her age and height but Alana remained anxious. Sally-Anne began to ask more questions about the reasons for her worries and learned that Alana was very concerned about Mollie's behaviour at home. As Sally-Anne was aware of our work, she asked Alana if she would be happy for her to refer the family to our service.

We are a very busy project and it is not uncommon for families to have to wait many months before they can receive a service, so it was not until several months had passed that Lara, the FSP, contacted Alana to see if the family were still interested in working with us. From our first point of contact the focus is on developing the relationship between the FSP and parent that forms a foundation for the work. Especially in the early stages it is important that parents feel in control of the process, so things like the location of the meeting and who is present are important. Lara arranged an appointment and Alana requested that it take place in the family home while Mollie was at school. A week later, Lara and I arrived for the first appointment.

We walked into a living room so dark that I stumbled walking in. Curtains and furniture obscured the views of the mountain-side outside. Alana and Richard sat together while Alana told her story. Alana said that Mollie's main problem was her 'attitude'; she answered back, was cheeky, shouted at her mother and was rude and dismissive to Richard. She ate little during the day but about 8:00pm would start snacking and then refused to go to bed. Bedtime was a time of anger, with Mollie shouting, kicking doors, throwing things and threatening to hit her mother or stepfather. Mollie was frequently awake at midnight and so was tired and grumpy in the mornings. She was often unwilling to go to school, becoming angry and tearful. School attendance had been a problem, although the involvement and support of the education welfare officer had helped and Mollie was now doing well. Alana was very proud of this and said she was determined that her daughter should do well and achieve more in life than she felt that she had herself.

Alana started to tell us about Mollie's early years, sharing that for most of the first four years of her life Mollie had lived with her grandmother. Although Alana had seen Mollie when she could, there had been no regular routine for contact. When Mollie was four years old it was agreed that Mollie should move to live with Alana, where she has been ever since. Alana felt frustrated by Mollie's current behaviour because, although she felt Mollie had been settled at home with her for a long time, instead of improving, Mollie's behaviour was deteriorating. Alana had left Mollie's biological father, Jason, as he had been violent, some of which had been witnessed by Mollie. Alana said that she herself had been diagnosed with Bipolar Disorder and Borderline Personality Disorder and that she had a named community psychiatric nurse, whom she had not seen for more than a year. She also shared that she was not taking her medication regularly and often felt very low. The constant arguments with Mollie were making her feel very depressed and that she could not cope.

Lara and I listened and I asked open questions to help Alana tell her story. Then I shared with Alana and Richard my understanding of their story from what they had told us so far. I said that I thought that Mollie was a little girl who had experienced separation in her first four years as her mum had been going through a really hard time. It seemed that the two had not had a chance to form a secure attachment and this may be affecting times of separation, such as going to school and bedtime (Ainsworth and Bell 1970). It could also mean that Richard was seen as a rival for her mum's affections, rather than a source of support within the family. I thought that this may also link back to what Alana had told us about her own childhood. Alana had said that she did not get on with her mum, had left home aged 14 years and had Mollie at 15 years. Although her mother helped with Mollie, Alana felt resentful that she needed this support.

Infants learn how to manage their emotions through their relationship with their primary caregiver (emotional co-regulation) (Howe 2011; Trevarthen 2001). I suggested that the early adversity (maternal separation) Mollie had experienced may have made this more difficult for her. I said this was my understanding of the story so far: Alana said 'yes', nodded and I continued. I suggested that it could be helpful to begin working on increasing security and predictability within the home, helping Alana and Richard understand what Mollie's behaviours may mean and how to manage them by focusing on emotional co-regulation, rather than perceiving Mollie as 'naughty'. We explained that we used a relational (Systemic Attachment) way of thinking that meant we would be exploring Mollie's views: helping her explore her relationship with her mother and finding ways to support her with her worries and concerns and to understand her feelings. Alana agreed that this seemed a helpful way forward.

This verbal summary is tentatively and respectfully offered as a way of checking that we have understood what the family has told us. It gives the family a chance to correct anything we may have got wrong and can be a way of introducing some psychological understanding of the situation, such as linking Mollie's and Alana's current difficulties with their early years of separation and attachment distress.

School Observation and Discussion with Class Teacher

Lara observed Mollie in school so she could see her in an alternative environment to the home. Children are not told that they are being observed, to minimise disruption within the classroom and also to get a sense of how they would normally behave in that setting. Lara talked to Mollie's class teacher who described Mollie as a delightful and hard-working pupil who got on well with teachers and, although quiet, was popular with other children. The teacher was evidently very fond of Mollie and anxious to help.

First Home Visit with Mollie

Lara's first session with Mollie took place at home. This was in order both to increase security for Mollie and reinforce the message to the whole family that this is family work rather than individual work with the child – which risks reinforcing the idea that the 'problem' lies within the child. Our approach is that the problems and solutions lie in the relationship between the child and parent(s) rather than locating the problem and/or solution in one or other of the individuals (George, Iveson and Ratner 2006). In the first appointment Lara suggested that they could play a game or do some artwork: providing a limited choice offers the child some degree of control within secure boundaries (Erikson 1963).

Fortunately, Mollie loved art, so that Lara was able to use an activity Mollie enjoyed and felt skilled in through which she could explore complex ideas. Lara asked Mollie to draw a picture of her family. She drew herself and her mother with a big heart between them with red lines linking them both to the heart. She explained that the picture showed that she loved her mother and her mother 'has a lot of love for me'. Lara noticed that Mollie's voice and expression at this point were very sad. She reflected to Mollie that she seemed sad when she talked about this. Verbalising this incongruence allowed Mollie to explain that things were difficult at home between her and her mother. Lara asked how things might look if they were different but Mollie could not answer. At this stage Mollie did not have any vision of what a happier life could look like and was therefore unable to think of what could change. Mollie wanted to give her picture to her mother and gave permission for Lara to tell her mother what it meant. Mollie presented her mother with the picture and explained about the heart; Alana welled up with tears but said nothing about the picture to Mollie.

At such an early stage of our relationship with the family, we may note things that are hard for them but if we think this would be too challenging for the family to hear at this time, we would not yet comment.

The Work with Mollie and Her Family

The second session was for the adults. Early sessions are often separate for parents and children to enable us to give children a voice and allow us to develop relationships with both parents and children. Without Mollie being present Lara was able to ask about the picture and help Alana reflect on her relationship with her child. Alana said that she was delighted to hear from Mollie that she loved her, as she felt that, when Mollie was angry, Mollie hated her. Lara did not seek to reassure Alana but instead empathised that it must be hard to feel that about her child. Alana's eyes filled with tears and she looked away and began tidying up; Lara noted these strategies to avoid or distract from the strong emotions she was feeling.

We use reassurance sparingly as it can cover over real opportunities for learning and often springs from the need of the professional rather than the true need of the family (see also Chapters 5 and 10). Supervision for practitioners is vital to help them manage their own distress in the face of the anguish being faced by families in order that they can convey compassion for the family's suffering without closing down opportunities for growth. At this early stage of an intervention, we would typically keep challenge low and warmth high but this would be discussed in our team meeting in which the team provides a reflective space, keeping our work safe and open to ideas. While challenge is important it needs to be done with care and at the right time to keep the family engaged.

Lara showed Alana a picture diagram called the Circle of Security (Hoffman *et al.* 2006) and explained that all children need their parents to help them to manage their emotions. However, due to the early separation, Mollie needed extra support in managing her emotions. Lara used the example of the feedback from the last session and said that she had noted how Alana had been able to look at Mollie's picture and tell her how well it was drawn. Lara linked this with the image of a parent delighting in her child shown in the diagram. Alana agreed that 'being nice' to Mollie (as she saw it) would make a better atmosphere in the home but also said that the problem of Mollie's behaviour could not be ignored and needed to be resolved. Lara accepted what Alana was saying and the need in Alana to 'do something'.

We work collaboratively and alongside parents and so it is important for the success of the work for the goal to be defined by the parent.

Lara asked Alana what was the most important thing for her to be able to manage. Alana identified the bedtime and night-time eating difficulties. Lara asked Alana to describe the last time that this was a problem and tell her in detail what had happened. Alana explained that at bedtime Mollie would say she was hungry and go into the kitchen and snack, ignoring her mother telling her to go to bed. Alana would end up shouting and finally would give up and 'let Mollie get on with it', taking her to bed when she went to bed herself. Lara recognised how tired and desperate Alana felt at these times and how her anxiety about Mollie's eating made it difficult for her to see the issue clearly.

In clinical supervision Lara and I thought together about how parental anxiety to 'do something' to solve the problems they are experiencing can make workers feel they need to act to provide solutions. This risks encouraging a narrowly focused behavioural approach: giving parents something 'to do' (e.g., filling out charts) that makes them feel they are actively dealing with the problem. However, this can miss opportunities to help parents deepen their understanding and learning about themselves and their child that would help them to be able to make changes on their own. We need to tread a fine line between action, thinking and reflection. Lara and I explored ideas about the language Alana used ('sending' Mollie to bed) and how this time represented a separation for Mollie, unconsciously taking Mollie back to the original trauma of separation from her mother (see also Chapter 7). The huge need Mollie still felt at this time was unbearable for Alana and so she used strategies such as physical distance and time to avoid this, shouting at Mollie from another room and letting Mollie become too exhausted to demand closeness.

We began our work from the description that Alana had given us. In the simplest terms, Mollie was in the kitchen when she was supposed to be in her bedroom, and Alana remained in the lounge throughout. Neither mother nor daughter was in the same room as each other, again suggesting avoidant ways of relating. Lara playfully asked what would happen if the kitchen was closed, and how would people know this. Together they decided that the kitchen could be 'closed' an hour before bedtime. Alana expressed concern that Mollie may be hungry at night and decided she could offer Mollie supper before the kitchen 'closed': they could make a 'closed' sign for the kitchen together. Mollie enjoyed decorating the sign and showed none of the anticipated anger at this boundary being placed upon her. We wondered whether this was because she saw it as a fair rule, as it applied to all in the house; Alana noted that Mollie now looked forward to her supper-time.

Unsurprisingly, this did not lead to Mollie going to bed when asked but it did reduce tension, as Alana felt she had achieved a success in stopping the evening snacks. This small triumph was used as a way-in for talking about short-term separations such as bedtimes. Lara began a conversation designed to prompt Alana's attunement to her daughter's feelings and needs, using curiosity to wonder how Mollie may be feeling at bedtime. Alana showed self-awareness and insight into her daughter's needs, saying that, as the day was filled with conflict to which she responded with screaming, Mollie probably went to bed feeling upset and angry. She said that, since having supper, Mollie seemed a little happier but Alana expressed frustration that she was still not going to bed. She admitted, however, that she was glad that Mollie seemed happier, saying that she was not arguing as much with Mollie and so was not feeling as tired and stressed.

Although Lara wanted to explore further what separation may mean for a child with Mollie's attachment pattern, she decided that there were things that Alana and Mollie could do together to increase good times during the day that would help promote a more secure attachment. Lara asked Alana what activities they might both enjoy and Alana said that Mollie liked art but she did not. Lara accepted this without judgement, acknowledging that it was important that they find something they both enjoyed but Alana could not think of anything she liked to do. Lara understood this in terms of her likely attachment style, where Alana had learnt to be independent and avoid close contact: therefore thinking about her own needs was potentially difficult (painful) for her (Ainsworth *et al.* 1978). Lara noted with empathy that it was difficult for Alana to choose an activity and playfully complimented Alana, saying that she always looked well turned out. With this, Alana suggested painting nails and doing hair as things they both enjoyed and agreed to try this with Mollie during the week. These times proved very successful, with both Mollie and Alana saying how much they enjoyed them. Mollie also told Lara that her mum seemed happier. Lara told Alana that the activities she had chosen were perfect as they involved touch and that this is known to deepen the parent–child bond. Alana was delighted and discussed with Lara other ways she could increase touch, such as making the morning routine of hair-brushing and braiding more special.

In her individual work with Mollie, Lara used the medium of art to explore her feelings and concerns. One concern that emerged was a recurring nightmare Mollie had about someone taking her away; apparently unable to comfort her, Alana tried to reassure her by dismissing her fears as 'silly'. Sharing this issue with Alana, Lara coached her gently to recognise that Mollie had been 'taken away' before (to live with her grandmother) and that subsequently Social Services had been involved: with the real possibility that Mollie might be 'taken away' again. Alana now trusted Lara enough to be able to tell her that she had used the threat of Social Services taking Mollie away to try to get Mollie to behave.

Lara noticed that Alana looked both defensive and confrontational as she made this admission: possibly expecting critical judgement. Instead Lara reflected back to Alana how she was presenting and invited her to reflect on what this could mean. Alana's response was immediate and dramatic, explaining that she feared that she could not cope and could not see a way of 'getting things right' with her daughter. Lara explained sensitively how in increasing Mollie's insecurity, as a response to the insecurity she herself felt, Alana was likely to increase her daughter's difficult behaviour. Lara discussed the positive work Alana and Richard had been doing together as parents to increase predictability and security, for example by establishing a good bedtime routine, but also explained that what Alana said and did needed to match to be effective.

A family meeting was held where Alana was able to be responsive to her daughter's fears, reassuring her that she had not meant it when she threatened Mollie with being taken away and that Mollie was home for good. Richard was present and although he said little, he was consistent in articulating that he found his relationship with Alana and Mollie incredibly hard but he loved Alana and cared for Mollie and was in it 'for the long term'. At this point in the work we recognised that the adults needed more time and attention paid to their own needs and we made an internal referral to our Family Therapy Clinic run by systemic psychotherapists. This is not a time-limited intervention; it can continue after the Family Intervention Team has finished its 12-week intervention. Alana and Richard were offered appointments to talk about how the difficulties with Mollie affected their relationship as a couple. Alana also began to attend a Wellbeing Group for women with post-natal depression run by two members of our Parent Therapy Service.

At the mid-way review meeting that I attended with the FSP I noticed visible differences. The living room itself had been rearranged so that the room was lighter and the beautiful views were visible. Alana and Richard were relaxed and smiling and although they acknowledged they still had a way to go they felt they had made big changes. They told me that they needed to 'keep' Lara and although their tone was a joking one, there was a seriousness in their eyes. I felt it was important for them to understand that just as they had already made changes themselves, they could continue to do this after Lara had left. We needed to emphasise that these changes had happened in just six weeks and maintaining changes was just as important a goal as adding new ones. Getting the family to name their recent actions and the reasons behind them helped them see how much they had achieved and how simple steps could lead on to other strategies to improve the relationships at home. As the home situation became more secure Mollie's nightmares stopped.

Over the next few weeks, Lara worked alongside Alana using principles from Dyadic Developmental Psychotherapy (DDP; Golding and Hughes 2012). DDP (see also Chapters 5 and 6) proposes that security needs to be increased within the relationship and environment and that a Playful, Accepting, Curious and Empathic (PACE) attitude from the caregiver can help children regulate their emotions. We continued to look at ways of increasing security and predictability. We focused particularly on creating opportunities for Molly and Alana to have fun together and for Mollie to have frequent and regular time with her mother, so that separation at bedtime could be part of a calm and caring routine and hence experienced as less scary.

Lara continued weekly home visits so that Alana and Richard were able to ask questions about concerns they had. These conversations were increasingly positive and at the same time provided a safe space for Alana and Richard to explore their new ways of behaving that were not yet completely natural to them. Lara used these opportunities to offer some psycho-education about realistic expectations of Mollie's behaviour from a child development perspective, such as not expecting Mollie to perform simple tasks without needing ongoing reminders. This is common for children in the primary school years and when parents realise this, it can become a routine parenting task rather than a source of conflict. During the second half of our intervention, we reflected on the cycle of change, helping parents to expect setbacks and looking at their resources for getting 'back on track'.

The final family meeting (the end-review) took place in the family home and was a celebration of what had been achieved, as well as a reminder of the support systems around the family. For this family, who had begun thinking about their own relationship and how this impacted on the parenting dynamic, fortnightly meetings with the parent therapist had already begun, and therefore a high sense of optimism prevailed. Mollie expressed how much she had enjoyed working with Lara, and shared with us that she felt able to seek support from her mother and feel confident that she would receive it. This reciprocity is an inherent part of secure attachment (Howe 2011), signifying a deep and enduring connection established between child and caregiver. In facilitating more consistent and nurturing caregiving Alana was able to develop confidence in her ability to parent Mollie lovingly and, in return, Mollie was able to develop a sense of herself as lovable and worthy.

DISCUSSION

Early intervention work such as ours is sometimes seen as less challenging than work with families needing intervention from statutory services. However, this underestimates the complexity of these families' lives and the challenges they face. The focus of our work is to create a safe space for healing. The skill lies in the ability of practitioners to develop meaningful and empowering relationships with families who often feel overwhelmed, disengaged and powerless to effect change. In creating a secure base for parents and children we are able to communicate and transform complex, psychological concepts into ideas and activities that make sense to the families we work with and that fit their individual needs and style.

Chapter 9

'SLOWLY UNDOING'
A Case Study in a Residential Setting

JONNY MATTHEW AND TRICIA SKUSE

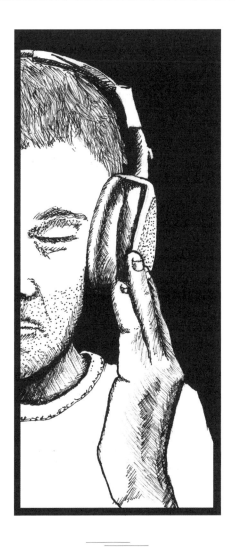

INTRODUCTION TO THE CASE AND THE CONTEXT

At the time of this case study we were employed as deputy manager of a secure children's home and clinical psychologist, acting as clinical lead for interventions.

During our tenure working in the secure children's home we came upon a young person who challenged and changed our practice. It was a positive change and has lasted from that day to this. This chapter explores the case through the lens of attachment and child development theory. We will show how we started from scratch to formulate the case, plan the interventions and work closely together across disciplines to help this young man.

Attachment is a central organising theory of child development (Siegel 1999). It speaks to the way that infants and their parents interact. The nature of this relationship is key to the child's growth psychologically, emotionally, socially and physically (Bowlby 1980, 1988). If a parent is abusive or neglectful this impacts the child's well-being adversely (Gaskill and Perry 2012; Levy and Orlans 2014). If a parent is safe and offers consistency of responsive care and affection, the child's development will reflect this.

BACKGROUND ON TIM'S EARLY LIFE

Tim was born into a very troubled home. His father had a criminal history, and was well-known in the area. He died when Tim was seven years old and became something of an absent idol for his son. Mum was a drug user whose mental health problems meant that her parenting was neglectful. Rumour had it that she earned extra money through sex, with a succession of different men passing through the home. It was reported that some of these men were violent to Tim and to his mother. Tim spoke about the concerns he had for his mother. As a much younger child he had become aware of a number of suicide attempts; he had been the one to find her on more than one occasion following deliberate overdoses. Tim had called the ambulance at other times too, for example when he found his mother lying on the settee in her own vomit and urine, having a seizure.

Later, Tim spoke of the abuse that occurred at his home. He spoke less of what happened to him, but of the sexual abuse he witnessed towards a little girl. She was his cousin and was abused at the hands of Tim's older half-brother, a young adult. He described hearing the girl crying and calling for help upstairs, and his own sense of anger and helplessness at being unable to stop it. This lack of appropriate care and the risks presented by his parents and various visitors to the home were of concern to social services. As a result, Tim was placed on the child protection register. He was accommodated by the Local Authority from the age of seven years old and experienced a number of foster placements. His history in care was one of instability, placement breakdown and absconding to return home. While he recalled one placement as being positive, and clearly had affection for the carers, Tim never settled for any sustained period. He roamed the streets, staying with friends and miscellaneous others who took him in.

The drift into criminal behaviour began early, through petty offending with other children. Tim's drug use and the associated need for cash meant that he became well known to the youth offending team and had been subject to a number of community sentences. Eventually, in 2009, aged 15, he received a three-year custodial sentence for a number of sexual assaults against adult women. This is when we first came across Tim and began our work with him.

TIM'S PRE-TREATMENT PRESENTATION

Clearly this kind of developmental history has a profound effect on a child (Perry 2009; Levy and Orlans 2014). Here are the main points of Tim's presentation at the outset of the work:

- *Unkempt.* He had no good habits of washing, changing his clothes or caring for himself. His skin was dirty, scabbed and scratched.

- *Anxious.* Tim was pacey, fidgety and struggled to sit still. He picked at his skin, fingernails and hair, as a result of that he had a small bald patch on the crown of his head. His lips were red and raw because he constantly licked them.

- *Hypervigilant* (see Chapter 3). Any sound in the corridor outside would send him to the door to try to find out what had caused it. He would turn his head at even the slightest sound and ask what we thought it was.

- *Disturbed sleep.* Tim slept lightly and stirred a lot during the night. He would use objects to anally masturbate and would pick at his anus with his fingers. He wet the bed consistently and would smear faeces in the morning while trying to clean himself.

- *Volatility.* Staff at the children's home had to weather some very difficult behaviour as Tim's anxiety and fearfulness tipped over into aggression and, occasionally, into violence. Rarely was there an identifiable cause for this. Tim seemed to be on a hair-trigger that could give way to anger at any moment.

Clearly Tim was a very mixed-up child, socially, sexually and emotionally. At first he lurched from one mood to another at lightning speed and seemed almost completely unregulated (see Chapter 3 for more on dysregulation). Despite this, there were occasions when he was lucid, polite and considerate. He would enquire how we were and wish us a good weekend. But this was not sustained for any appreciable period, before the sociability gave way to emotional lability once again.

Tim's case bears many of the hallmarks associated with maltreated children, although it is perhaps quite an extreme example, given the numerous damaging factors involved. As we progress through this case study, we hope readers will benefit from the lessons we learned in employing attachment theory to case formulation (Johnstone and Dallos 2014), intervention planning and the therapy process. As usual, our work with Tim began with assessment. We were required to produce a specialist sexual behaviour report to inform sentencing in the Crown Court and a clinical assessment to support and inform his care in the secure children's home.

CASE FORMULATION

The gathering together of all the known information about an individual in order to make sense of their life so far, the problems they are experiencing and the way they see themselves. This then informs the intervention.

However, it became immediately apparent that Tim would not be able to engage in such processes in the usual way:

- His speech was disconnected: more a stream of consciousness than a series of related sentences.

- He would ask questions but rarely waited for answers.

- When asked a question he would begin to answer and then divert away on to something completely unrelated, often about drug use, his life before custody or the antics of his friends.

- He shifted constantly in his seat, frequently jumping to his feet to check on some sound outside the door. On other occasions he would be sat staring at the floor, saying very little. The potential for anger and aggression, even violence, never seemed far away.

Such was the degree of emotional damage to Tim, as displayed in his presentation, that we decided to use this, and the file information, to produce preliminary assessments. His need for help was obvious: this was an extremely needy child. The lack of stable engagement for the more focused and detailed assessment did not preclude the need for a lot of work to mediate the effects of Tim's history.

Tim's anxiety, hypervigilance (see also Chapter 3), lack of social skills, volatility and constant sense of threat, spoke of a child who had suffered serious trauma. He had not attached securely to anyone and so had not enjoyed the safety and stability of care he needed to develop optimally. Tim could not regulate his emotions and thoughts, so he was constantly at the mercy of his current subjective state. Hence our attempts to impose a structure to our discussions were fruitless.

Key decision: We would work only with what Tim brought to sessions.

A mainstay of attachment theory is the crucial role played by primary caregivers in responding to infants. When children cry, they are calling for help. 'Crying is a baby's intense bid for you to help her with her overwhelming feelings and frightening bodily sensations because her brain is not yet developed enough for her to manage these on her own' (Sunderland 2007, p.36).

It is the caregivers' responsiveness and their efforts to ameliorate the causes of distress that enables babies to begin to learn to regulate their distress for themselves (see Figure 9.1).

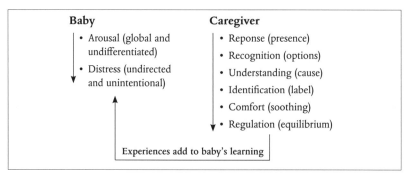

FIGURE 9.1 LEARNING CYCLE – SUMMARY
Source: Copyright © Jonny Matthew

Tim had clearly experienced little, if any, healthy, responsive care. Therefore, to make in-roads towards helping Tim, we would need to respond to whatever he offered. In this way we hoped to help him to 'unlearn' his neglectful past and begin experiencing safe and responsive care. We understood that this would take time, a long time, but we hoped it would form something of a foundation upon which to build. We spoke to the staff at the home who did most of the day-to-day caring for Tim, and explained our plan. We would respond to him as we would to a very young child: by taking what he offered, (through his observed feelings and behaviour) and working with this to help him through.

DEVELOPMENTALLY SENSITIVE CASE FORMULATION AND INTERVENTION PLANNING

The great advantage of a secure residential setting is the ability to regulate and order all aspects of the young person's daily life. With Tim we went back to basics: he needed to be listened to, responded to and to experience co-regulation.

Key decision: To respond consistently with concern and care, rather than with rebukes and demands for compliance.

Good enough caregivers (Winnicott 1958) do not punish infants and toddlers for crying, since they are merely responding to, and communicating, their internal states. The caregiver's job is to identify the need, meet that need and then help the child back to a place of emotional equilibrium. This is what we set out to do with Tim. See Figure 9.2 for an illustration of this.

- **Arousal** – to stimulus from within or without
- **Response** – crying
- **Caregiver attention** – proximity, picking up
- **Caregiver regulation** – checking out, options, action, amelioration
- **Equilibrium** – back to calm state via the carer's response – arousal has been co-regulated

FIGURE 9.2 FROM UPSET TO CALM AGAIN...
HOW A BABY LEARNS ABOUT FEELINGS
Source: Copyright © Jonny Matthew

Tim's arousal behaviour – anger, aggression, violence, shouting, swearing – were adapted to help him to cope when he lived in constant threat and danger. But what had worked to keep him safe on the streets or in an abusive household was anti-social anywhere else. So, if we offered to listen, communicated understanding and were patient and caring, his behaviour may calm.

Over time this process was followed consistently by staff. Tim learned that he could ask for help, rather than be aggressive and swear at people. He was told off less and was listened to more. Very slowly, his behaviour began to be less turbulent and volatile.

Although young people are clearly different from infants, the arousal–response–co-regulation–calmness cycle is equally vital. Troubled teenagers need to experience the same process in order to make sense of strong and difficult feelings and learn self-regulation skills.

SEQUENCING OF CARE AND TREATMENT

In recent years, great progress has been made in understanding the impact of violence and trauma on child development. In no area is this more the case than in the child's developing neurobiological systems, brain growth and organisation (Gaskill and Perry 2012). Children who live in conditions of persistent threat and danger experience high levels of stress: they are over-exposed to the toxic effects of neurochemicals such as cortisol, which maintain them in a heightened state of emotional arousal. If sustained over long periods, as in Tim's case, children's neurobiological systems, including their brains, become over-sensitised, perceiving threats where there are none and living perpetually in a stressed state of fight, flight or freeze. This explains why Tim seemed to have a hair-trigger for his anger and aggression.

In 1949, Hebb, a pioneering psychologist in the field of neuroscience, wrote that neurons (brain cells) that 'fire together, wire together'. In other words, the repeated operation of neural networks associated with danger consolidates these networks and suppresses those that would bring balance through the intervention of a safe caregiver. The only way to mediate this is to expose the child to repeated responses that do not spell danger but bring empathy, help and calmness. Over time, the stress-associated neurobiological responses will be balanced by those linked to good caregiving. The attendant release of neuro-hormones, such as oxytocin, associated with a return to equilibrium and a sense of well-being (Shemmings and Shemmings 2011) begins to 're-balance the chemical equations' moderated by the autonomic nervous system and create healthier neurobiological networks.

Through the process of sensitive co-regulation with caregivers, children learn that their internal somatic (bodily) and affective (emotional) states are not permanent, do not spell catastrophe and can be mediated. After several years' experiencing co-regulation, they acquire the capacity for self-regulation. Since Tim had lacked this help during the critical early developmental period (Schore 2001b), he needed to experience it now, over a protracted period, in order to achieve the capacity for neurobiological re-balancing.

Diving into work to address his offending at this stage would have been untimely: he just was not ready for it. Cognitive approaches assume a degree of affective stability and meta-cognition that Tim did not have. We had to start at the beginning and work up from there.

THE FOUNDATION OF TRUST

Over time, Tim began to trust us. This came out in the little things at first: being calmer for slightly longer, some improvements, for example, in his attentiveness, increased focus in his speech, eye contact and sitting still. He also began to initiate conversation on topics he was interested in: the chief one being music. This remained the case throughout; Tim responded to our enquiries about the artists he liked. These were mainly rap and hip-hop performers – not our preference at all, but this was not about us! As we attended to Tim's thoughts, asked him questions and listened to his views, he began to grow in confidence and increasingly set the direction during sessions.

Tim's main focus was relating the lyrics of songs to life experiences. He knew an immense amount about the life of the artists and helped us to see that the words of the songs reflected real-life events. He played us the songs, repeated the lyrics for us and then expanded the story to set them in context. The subject matter ranged from social exclusion and poverty through to parental drug use and interpersonal violence.

Key decision: Despite the obvious potential for parallels with his own life, we did not seek to press the pace. We continued to talk about what *he* wanted to talk about. This pattern continued, with minor variations, for some months. The benefits of this process for Tim, developmentally, were:

- being listened to – unconditionally and repeatedly

- having others listen to, and validate, his thoughts and opinions

- being in control of the session

- learning to explore sensitive issues at a distance and without the pressure to 'process' them at someone else's pace and in someone else's way.

Throughout this process, Tim was learning to trust. We asked him if there were particular things that he wanted to discuss. Although we also raised issues that had come up for him in between sessions, such as his assault of a member of staff, we never pushed our own agenda or insisted on a particular approach. In this way, Tim was treated with respect and afforded the status of an equal. We were there for him, not the other way around. Eventually, it seems, he came to believe this for himself.

HOLDING OUR NERVE

Over a period of about 15 months, we held to this course. There were times when pressure came to bear that tested our resolve. For example:

- *Pressure from ourselves* – to be more 'proactive'. We decided that this was our professional insecurities kicking in: trying to persuade us we were not best serving Tim by being so passive. Yet he clearly was not cognitively ready to change tack.

- *Pressure from other professionals* – answering the questions of the case managing youth offending team and social workers, who were rightly expecting that we would be 'addressing the offending' and doing all we could to minimise the likelihood of re-offending. We *were* addressing these issues but we were doing so developmentally: from the bottom up.

- *Pressure from colleagues* – this was a time-consuming case. Twice-weekly therapy time involved a significant commitment of resources. In addition, Tim's behaviour continued to be problematic on a regular basis. Assaults of peers and staff were still a risk and personal hygiene was a daily challenge for Tim's care team. There were some in the organisation who wanted him moved elsewhere, to a young offender institution (YOI). We resisted this robustly, but felt the pressure nevertheless!

In short, our hypothesis was being challenged. We had set our course based on the view that Tim was a traumatised child. His presentation and behaviour bore the hallmarks of problematic attachment patterns and impaired neurobiological functioning. This extended to his offending behaviour, which we also believed had its genesis in the traumatic abuse and neglect trauma he suffered during his early years.

If we were right in thinking that Tim needed to learn to manage his physiological and emotional internal states through co-regulation with trusted adults, this would take some time to resolve. We found ourselves turning back to the writings of Bowlby (1958, 1980, 1988) and Ainsworth *et al.* (1978), and to the later work of Perry (2009), Teicher *et al.* (2003) and Creeden (2005). This allowed us to see Tim's case clearly and we found the resolve to stand our ground, hold our nerve and keep going. Although holding our nerve sounds resolute and determined now, it was a lot scarier at the time!

DISCLOSURE...BUT NOT AS WE KNOW IT

Over time, in truth after more than a year, Tim began to open up. He began to allow us to help him explore his early experiences. Once again, this was usually in connection with his musical musings. We did not ask him directly, but slowly, as time passed, he made the connections himself. He started to write lyrics for us, giving expression to his own thoughts, feelings and experiences. Sometimes he did it in an impromptu way and just started rapping then and there. At other times he would write lyrics in between sessions and bring them for us to read.

He showed pride in what he wrote but was also tentative and desperately seeking reassurance. We gave him this in spades! We thanked him for letting us share his work. And he wrote more and more.

This rather indirect and creative method, accessing the right hemisphere of the brain (Siegel 1999) gave way to conversations about his life, a left hemisphere function (Siegel 1999). Eventually, we were able to ask him about specifics, but this came slowly. For the most part, we kept to our strategy of passive facilitation of whatever Tim brought with him to the sessions. If he mentioned something and seemed open to being asked, we would ask; otherwise we let him lead.

Tim's growing awareness of his own history and its relevance to his offending behaviour became increasingly apparent. But he was also aware of the size of the challenge that lay ahead of him, if he was to get himself 'sorted', as he would say. Here is one of the poems Tim wrote around this time: 'New Beginning', which we use with his permission.

I am changing fast

I hated what I done

I caused harm to people by doing drugs and crime.

I ain't proud of it – I just needed a bit of a wake up call…

…I still got problems I need to get them sorted

But I am still a better person than ever before

I got a lot of targets and goals I need to reach

Before I am fully sorted

Sometimes I feel overloaded

But then I think 'What's the point of giving up?'

Here there is a real sense that Tim is beginning to see hope for himself. He also acknowledges the immense struggle he is embroiled in as well as the impact he has had on others. 'New Beginning' gives a sense of the complexity and challenge of Tim's journey in therapy – but he's moving at *his* pace, not ours. He is using his *own* means of expression and clearly making significant progress.

BREAKTHROUGH

The true test of all this, of course, was how Tim would respond as the going got really tough. Could he cope with the realities of the damage he caused? Could he confront the gritty and sordid truth of what his family was like and what it had made him?

From our perspective, as those trying to help him, would the time in custody allow sufficient opportunity for us to build trust? Would he have the insight required to make links between his own frightening history and the fear and distress his behaviour caused others? If not, would we have wasted this golden opportunity in a secure setting and would Tim just revert to his old adaptive behaviour once he was released?

The answers came during our later sessions. I recall one session when we were discussing his mother's behaviour and the ambivalence this caused him. One minute he despised her drunkenness, her suicidality, her passivity during his abusive experiences and the violent men she had introduced into his life. The next minute he was desperately concerned about her welfare. 'Was she safe? Did she have enough money? What about her health?' In the throes of all this, he stopped speaking. He sat very still, staring at the floor. Then, in a quiet voice, he said, 'I can't believe what I did to those people.' A simple enough statement: nine words but jam-packed full of insight, empathy and regret.

Tim went on to talk about his offences. He spoke of how painful and humiliating it was for the adult women he punched and grabbed. He worried about how frightened the children must have been as they saw what happened. He shook his head and went quiet again. This kind of insight does not come easily. It certainly does not come from 'offending behaviour work': at least not when the young person concerned has never dealt with his own history. True empathy comes when someone has first learned to empathise with themselves: 'How can I appreciate the feelings of others if I have no appreciation of how my own experiences have impacted me?'

These were key moments – moments during which Tim needed to be held with special care. He required lots of reassurance and often asked if we felt differently about him, knowing what he had done. Of course we had known all about this but he was just beginning to see it for himself and was now reappraising himself in light of it. During these sessions, our work became more directive as we helped Tim to explore his past and gain insight without becoming overwhelmed.

MORE THAN THERAPY

It is important to emphasise that it was not the twice-weekly therapy sessions alone that helped Tim. On the contrary, the 24/7 care he received from the residential care staff, particularly his keyworker and case manager, built the foundation upon that this emerging trust and insight were based. Before young people like Tim can begin to make anything of therapy, they have to establish something of a secure base (Bowlby 1988). Just like an infant, Tim needed a physical and emotional 'place' where he could feel safe and from that he could then begin to explore. He found this in the routine of the secure children's home, the predictable responses of the staff and the consistency of the care they offered Tim, despite his pushing them away. And he pushed hard! He assaulted, he verbally abused, he threatened, he smeared and he rejected. But still they cared and, eventually, he felt safe enough to engage with his past and begin moving forward.

When young people have not experienced positive attachments, they are not equipped to gain the self-insight they need to function in the world. They struggle to relate and see their place in relation to others. This is compounded even further when, as in Tim's case, those caring for children are abusive. Children learn that people are a threat: their behaviour adapts to cope with this. Survival is the priority. Such was the story for Tim. The structure and care of the environment 'held' him for long enough to help him feel safe. From this place of safety our therapy allowed him time, space and the means to start the process of exploring his childhood and who he was now. This was a slow process. Tim described it in terms of unravelling. He wrote a poem about it called 'Slowly Undoing':

> You people wanna see the real me
> You people will have to dig deep
> The problem of me is I never really show my true emotion
> I only swear and shout
>
> I hated being a kid.
> I forgive my mum and family for my past but my heart is still ripped.
> These people think they know me and the truth but you all don't
> I only show my defensive side.
>
> Slowly I will undo but it's hard to.
> I hate what I became.
> I ain't blaming nobody but myself
> But fuck I want to be me
> But it ain't easy.
>
> To everyone who reads this
> I ain't a bad boy.
> I am just a kid.

EDITORIAL DISCUSSION

By the time severely traumatised children reach adolescence their troubling emotional, behavioural, perceptual and thinking patterns may seem 'set in stone'. As with Tim, many have experienced neglect and abuse in their earliest years and often have histories of frequent moves within the care system. Frequently in their teens their behaviour becomes increasingly anti-social and they become involved with the criminal justice system. Management approaches are predominantly aimed at addressing offended behaviour and some, as in Tim's case, culminate in a custodial sentence in a children's secure unit or in a YOI.

While a custodial sentence may provide a measure of 'containment', the concept of providing a secure base within which young people can begin to feel safe, held and understood is often sidelined (see Chapter 10). For adolescents like Tim there have been few opportunities to acquire this essential sense of feeling safe, being comforted or having their needs recognised and met consistently. Early traumatic experiences establish 'trauma normal' (see also Chapter 7) physiological, emotional, perceptual and cognitive neurobiological patterns and maintain children and young people in perpetual hyper- or hypo-aroused and hypervigilant or dissociative states (see also Chapters 2 and 7).

Only by 'going back' and providing the consistent, attuned dyadic attachment experiences (Hughes 2012) they missed can we help children to 'move forward' and 'move on': to gain self-regulation, self-awareness, insight, self-control, resilience and well-being (Siegel 2007). The work undertaken with Tim, although sometimes painfully slow, provided him with just those reparative developmental attachment experiences he needed to begin creating new, healthier neurophysiological response patterns and 'get back on track'. Thanks to the almost infinite power of the body, brain and mind to heal (Siegel 2007, 2010) this will allow him to 'find himself', alter his behavioural and relational patterns and reach his full potential.

PART 4

LEGAL NARRATIVE

Assessments and Court Reports

Chapter 10

BEYOND FEEDING AND WATERING

Trauma and Attachment-based Court Assessments

CHRISTINE GORDON

INTRODUCTION

I have been a social worker for over 35 years, more than 20 years of which have involved working with adopted or fostered children and their families: first at Family Futures Consortium in London and latterly as an independent social worker with Adapt Scotland. This includes working with children and families in care proceedings where the courts are asked to make 'best interest' decisions. Here a 'Letter of Instruction' is issued, outlining the questions the court wishes to be addressed, accompanied by a 'bundle' of documents varying in length and collated by the lead solicitor.

The aim of this chapter is to consider factors that should be taken into account when making 'best interest' decisions. In addressing this we need first to consider the unique characteristics of children who are subject to court proceedings.

CHILDREN SUBJECT TO CARE PROCEEDINGS

Generally, children in the care system today have suffered the trauma of neglect, abuse and/or abandonment at the hands of the very people who should have cared for and protected them: their parents. They may have experienced the chaos and unpredictability accompanying a drug-abusing or transient lifestyle. 'Best interest' decisions for these children, therefore, need to start with an understanding of the impact of trauma on children.

Trauma has long been acknowledged to have a powerful emotional and psychological impact on children: in recent years this has been supported by growing evidence of the neurobiological impact of trauma (see also Chapters 2 and 7), highlighting that children develop neural network patterns in line with their early lived experience. Children born into safe and secure environments develop 'neurotypical' biological patterns reflecting these experiences; traumatised children develop markedly different 'trauma-normal' neurobiological patterns that reflect their experiences (Schore 2001b).

It is a popularly held belief that older children are most impacted by their traumatic experiences since they have lived with trauma for longer than their younger siblings; this may be inaccurate. Parents who barely managed to parent their first child may have their parenting capacity and financial resources stretched to breaking point with the birth of subsequent children. Drug and alcohol abuse is often progressive, with parents becoming increasingly dependent on these substances: parents' capacity may therefore deteriorate from being 'adequate' to neglectful as their drug abuse intensifies. Since the greatest growth in brain development occurs during children's earliest months (Schore 2001b), it is their earliest experiences that have the greatest impact on children's neurobiological, and hence socio-emotional, development. Reduced parenting capacity may therefore have a more profound impact on younger children.

The question of what 'good enough' parenting means for traumatised children is often foremost in 'Letters of Instruction' from courts. Frequently, the primary focus is on whether parents can adequately feed the children, clothe them and get them to school. While these things are undoubtedly important, 'good enough' parenting from an attachment and trauma perspective means much more than this. It means focusing on the impact that trauma has had on children at a socio-emotional and neurobiological level as well as a physical one, that is, an attachment-focused assessment process for both children and parents. It also means recognising that Looked After Children often have differing parenting needs from their less traumatised counterparts.

Traumatised children entering new families carry with them distorted internal working models (Bowlby 1988) that make them susceptible to misinterpreting caregivers' benign intentions in light of their previous abusive experiences. They need parents who understand this and who can develop the therapeutic parenting style that reflects their children's trauma history. As this demands greater than average parenting skills it has relevance when assessing the viability of children returning home to birth parents, contact arrangements, sibling relationships, and what children need from alternative caregivers if a return home is not viable.

BEST PRACTICE IN TRAUMA AND ATTACHMENT ASSESSMENTS

Trauma and attachment-focused assessments should begin with a detailed consideration of children's history, including careful assessment of what happened to children *and* what it did to them as exemplified in their current perceptions, cognitions and behaviour.

Assessors must consider not only what is included in court bundles but also what is not. Social work and police reports detailing recorded incidents may be the tip of the iceberg in terms of the trauma suffered by children. Numbers of caregivers listed in children's records may not include the myriad changes and types of care within, for example, drug abusing and chaotic families. Smyke, Dumitrescu and Zeanah (2002) found that the total number of staff caring for institutionalised children in Romania correlated directly with the number of indicators of attachment disorders they displayed. Educated extrapolation from the known to the likely reality of children's care histories should therefore become an integral part of any assessment of the trauma they suffered. In practice, health visitors, nurseries and schools often contribute usefully to this picture.

Alongside experiences within their birth families, we need to consider children's in-care experiences. Frequent attempts at rehabilitation are common; being returned from a safe foster home to an unsafe birth family can increase children's fear and lack of trust that adults can meet their needs. Frequent moves in foster care can exacerbate these feelings. Often children are accommodated in emergency foster placements, only to be moved within a few days; they are often subject to respite care and further moves of foster care placement. Every move within foster care should be considered as potentially traumatising to children. It can add to their fear of abandonment and reinforce their perceptions that the world is an unsafe and unpredictable place (see also Chapter 5).

Siblings may be kept together when their needs are so great that separate placements would be optimal; conversely, siblings may be separated for logistical rather than needs-based reasons. The needs of one child in a sibling group may differ from those of another so that being separated may be in one child's interests yet not in the interests of another. Such experiences, over which children have no control, can further traumatise them; while separation from a sibling may be in a child's interests it also represents another loss.

Assessors need to consider children's behaviours in light of their past. Archer and Gordon (2013) speak of children's behaviour as the 'language' they use to communicate their understanding of themselves and the world they inhabit. Assessors need to obtain a clear picture of how children present behaviourally in the here and now, taking into consideration differences between descriptions offered by caregivers and schools. While some differences may reflect caregivers' issues, most can provide a more in-depth picture of children's inner worlds and their beliefs about themselves and others.

Understanding children's behavioural language (see also Chapters 5 and 7) and their 'dictionary' (derived from their trauma and attachment history) allows assessors to determine what a particular child or sibling group needs. It gives clues to what happened to children, how it affected them and their particular care needs. For example, neglected children who steal or hoard food in a foster home where food is plentiful may be unconsciously reacting to their early neglect and using the survival strategies they developed to manage hunger and fear in their birth family. An awareness of the underlying reasons for this behaviour can help workers and caregivers devise parenting plans to meet children's needs; providing written (and illustrated) daily menus of food and clear, dependable meal times, can help children develop a sense of security and predictability.

While each child is unique there are often themes that predominate traumatised children's way of understanding themselves and their world. These include:

- The world is a scary, crazy place.

- I can't trust that adults will keep me, or keep me safe.

- I'm not worthy of having my needs met.

- I need to be in control of everything.

- I can control nothing.

- I need to be really good so my foster carer(s) won't give me away.

- I hate myself and know that if 'they' really knew what I was like then they would hate me as well.

- I know they are going to give me away so I may as well act 'bad' to have some control over this.

- It's my fault that I was abused, neglected or abandoned.

- It's my sibling's fault that I was abused, neglected or abandoned.

- It's my fault that my sibling was abused, neglected or abandoned.

It is important to recognise that fear underpins these beliefs and motivates traumatised children's actions and responses, whatever their behavioural presentation. Since early intra-familial trauma is the most potent source of fear, children's traumas are often held in their bodies at pre-verbal or non-verbal, and therefore pre-conscious, levels (see also Chapter 7): making the task of helping children heal from developmentally based trauma more difficult. Traumatised children need caregivers who can acknowledge their history of abuse, neglect and abandonment and who can (with support):

- 'read' children's behavioural and body language

- work with and through the defences that children developed to survive their trauma

- recognise the way that children interpret adult/caregiver actions in light of past experiences

- acknowledge the blame and shame that children feel for what has happened to them and work towards altering their distorted cognitions.

Clearly, therefore, 'good enough' parenting is much more than being able to feed, dress and get children to school. Traumatised children require parents/caregivers who can:

- be honest about the nature and extent of children's traumatic experiences

- accept appropriate responsibility for their part in these experiences and offer apologies

- work hard to repair their relationship with their children

- accept that their children will continue to feel unsafe for some time.

Assessors working with birth parents must address these crucial issues, challenging parental defences and assessing whether parents can step into their children's shoes and recognise both what happened to their children and what it (and they) did to them. Assessors need to take parents' attachment history into consideration, as inter-generational levels of abuse and neglect are often a major factor. Parents who did not receive 'good enough' parenting as children can struggle to recognise that their parenting is not 'good enough' or change parenting patterns that were the 'norm' in the cultural milieu within which they were raised and on which they continue to depend.

Archer and Gordon (2006, 2013) adopt the terms 'developmental' or 'therapeutic' reparenting to describe the style of parenting required by traumatised children. Developmental reparenting begins by understanding children's histories and how this is demonstrated in their sensori-motor responses and behavioural language. It recognises that children 'can't do' rather than 'won't do': that traumatised children are doing their utmost to manage the fear and belief that they will be further abused, neglected and/or abandoned. Developmental reparenting provides a safe and consistent environment where children's attachment needs are met; it helps children begin their neurobiological, socio-emotional and cognitive repair process. These strategies may differ widely from more commonly used approaches. Employing a 'traditional' stance of rewarding 'good' behaviour and punishing 'bad' behaviour can further traumatise 'hurt' children, ignoring the negatives can lead to escalation, in order to be 'heard'; the 'naughty step' can be experienced as abandonment.

Empathy and understanding must be cornerstones of developmental reparenting, as should treating children at their functional and emotional age, rather than their chronological age. Aggressive children need help to express their anger and fear in less challenging ways; 'good' children need to recognise that 'all of them' is acceptable and practise being playful, over-independent children need to experience being safely dependent: 'going backwards to go forwards'. Maltreated children need endless opportunities to change and develop their physical and emotional, as well as cognitive, literacy. Caregivers can transform understandable feelings of disappointment or frustration into motivation and even elation when their children struggle with self-care tasks, such as cleaning their teeth or tying their shoelaces, or seem unable to do so at that time, despite having the skills. This may appear counter-intuitive but allows caregivers exactly the opportunities they need to offer the understanding, nurture and support their children missed in their early years. Encouragement and opportunities for caregivers to provide 'baby and toddler care' is a vital step to 'fill in the experiential developmental-attachment gaps' and move children towards self-belief and true independence (Archer and Gordon 2013).

CONTACT

Observation of contact is often viewed as a crucial part of assessing how well parents respond to their children's needs and therefore as a precursor to rehabilitation. Missing contact or arriving late is seen as a lack of commitment and as a contra-indication that rehabilitation is realistic. While contact may provide such information, my experience has been that it is often less than helpful to the assessment process or to planned rehabilitation. Often contact is conducted in environments that are far from ideal, with limited privacy and a dearth of toys and equipment. It is frequently supervised by workers who see their role as observing and note-taking rather than supporting and enabling parents and children to develop meaningful relationships. Moreover, contact frequently appears to meet parents' needs and to be used as a 'bargaining tool', rather than meeting the needs of children who may love their parents but are fearful they will be abused and/or rejected again. Parents may undermine a child's feeling of security, as can be seen in this foster carer's words:

> My foster daughter enjoys meeting her birth mother, but her appetite before and after contact is enormous and her behaviour becomes very challenging. This was especially noticeable after one contact supervised by a social worker she didn't know. We later discovered that her birth mother had talked about a weekend overnight stay that was not part of the care plan.

This child had been neglected by a birth mother with drug and alcohol issues; she had also experienced several failed rehabilitation attempts prior to a 'best interest decision' that her foster carers should apply for a 'Permanence Order', a decision that reflected the child's growing attachment to them and her anxiety that she might return to a mother who could not meet her needs. I assessed that the child's need to 'fill' herself before contact reflected not only her body's memory of being hungry in her mother's care but also concern that her mother could not meet her emotional needs.

The inter-generational nature of parents' attachment and trauma histories needs to be recognised by contact supervisors who must be proactive in helping parents develop their parenting skills in ways that reflect their children's needs. Meeting parents in advance of contact and discussing issues from previous contacts, *and* what parents could do differently, can give support and opportunities to assess parents' ability to make the changes that would facilitate rehabilitation.

Contact is rarely used to help children make sense of their past: instead it is seen as a forum for children to play and interact with their parents, usually at a superficial level. I have already highlighted the messages that children need to hear from their parents. If children and parents are not helped to ask and answer questions such as 'Why am I in care?' or 'Why did you hurt me?' children will be left to provide their own answers, which rarely reflect the reality of their experiences. Since it is terrifying to feel that a parent cannot 'get it right' children are more likely to blame themselves than to recognise parental responsibility. Self-blame feels far safer for children, as it gives them a (false) sense of self-efficacy: 'If I can figure out what I did wrong, Mummy might not hurt me, neglect me or abandon me.' The inevitable outcome is the development of the belief that 'I'm a "bad" kid and don't deserve to be kept, or kept safe.' This is contrary to the messages children must receive to begin the process of trauma resolution, the development of healthy attachments and healing.

Consideration of continuing contact with other 'safer' family members such as grandparents requires careful exploration of issues around kinship care and the competing needs of parent and child. For example, assessors need to consider whether a grandmother can recognise the possible deficits in her parenting that may have led to her daughter struggling to parent well. They may have to assess whether grandparents can realistically help their grandchildren explore the reality of family life. Moreover, grandparents may have divided loyalties and minimise their own child's responsibility for the grandchild being in care: often blaming the grandchild's other parent. An in-depth assessment of intra-familial relationships and clarity of expectations for all concerned are vital.

SIBLINGS

There are statutory requirements on local authorities to keep siblings together; it is seen as a protective factor in maintaining placements. Eighty to 90 per cent of children coming into care are part of sibling or step-sibling groups, where typically they share a mother but have different fathers (Lord and Borthwick 2008). Many of today's adults are likely to have been part of sibling groups, but these similarities may disguise significant differences. Many childcare professionals have been raised in stable, functional families as part of sibling groups. Children raised in neglectful and/or abusive families, where both food and love were scarce, may have developed dysfunctional sibling relationships where attention to one child may have felt overwhelmingly threatening to a sibling. Hence, making 'best interest' decisions for children in sibling groups may create heightened or conflicting emotions, making realistic assessment of sibling relationships more difficult. Current literature (Lord and Borthwick 2008) promoting the maintenance of sibling relationships for children in care may reflect professional experience rather than the needs of cared for children. It is vital that children's individual and sibling needs are assessed in the context of their intra-familial trauma, attachment histories, family reconstitution and often enmeshed sibling relationships.

Assessors must distinguish between sibling groups who were raised in (relatively) non-traumatising environments and those raised in traumatising environments. Sibling rivalry is likely to be much stronger in abusive or neglectful families where, for example, food given to one child meant another child going hungry. Skewed sibling relationships are also likely to exist in families where one child was regularly scapegoated. 'Parentified' children may need to know that the siblings they cared for in their abusive families are safe and well looked after, while needing individual space to be children. Children who have primarily looked to a sibling for care and protection may struggle to attach to adult caregivers if they continue living with that sibling. Children within a family may hold different perceptions of who constitutes their sibling group; some of these may not conform to biological status or adult perceptions. Assessors need therefore to consider psychological, alongside biological, factors, recognising the importance of considering each child's needs individually.

PLACEMENT FOR FOSTERING OR ADOPTION

Assessing children's individual needs provides the essential stepping stone to offering caregivers opportunities to look at similarities and differences in parenting approaches. Children in sibling groups do not need to be treated the same; they have different needs and interests and need to be treated uniquely (Crittenden 2005; Perry 2009). If these needs differ too widely it may be impossible for one set of parents to meet each child's needs appropriately. All parents have their strengths and vulnerabilities. All were children and will have been affected by the way they were parented, internalising this as their parenting model and informing their parenting and attachment relationships. Hence, effective assessment of children's needs must also include assessment of the attachment and parenting styles (see Introduction) of prospective alternative families.

If the decision is made that children cannot be adopted together, their need for ongoing contact should be considered and explored with potential adopters. For example, in a family of two children aged seven years and 15 months, the older child was placed with a relative and the younger placed for adoption. The elder boy had acted in a 'parenting' role to his younger sister and was very anxious that she be placed in a family who could meet her needs. To reassure him that his sister would be safe and well cared for it was important that he had information about the adoptive family; this was not so important for the younger child at the time. However, in later years the fact that the girl became aware that she had a brother who cared so deeply for her became significant in terms of her identity and self-esteem.

CASE STUDY: THE JOHNSTON FAMILY

The Johnston family comprised six children (age range five to 15 years), all with the same mother. The eldest two had the same father, the third a father whose identity was unknown and the youngest three boys shared the same father with whom the mother was currently residing. The elder two children had half-siblings on their father's side, with whom they sometimes lived. The children were accommodated due to drug use and neglect by their mother and her co-habitee. The eldest boy was placed on his own, the eldest girl and the third child were placed together and the three youngest children also placed together.

The reasons for this were unclear but seemed to reflect both logistical and perceived sibling relationship factors.

Assessment suggested that the two eldest children had a close relationship and a quasi-parenting role to the three boys. The third child was largely ignored by her parents and siblings: her sister expressed puzzlement that they were living together when their relationship felt so tenuous. The three youngest boys were highly disturbed and presented major challenges to their skilled foster carers; they looked to their oldest sister for comfort rather than their parents during contact.

Contact for the family was held in a busy contact centre. The family used two rooms, one of which was the main thoroughfare through which other families passed for contact. The toys in the room were primarily for under fives. The contact supervisors sat taking notes and sometimes talking to other families. The parents struggled to engage with their children and primarily focused on the youngest three: also the focus of attention of the eldest two. The eldest boy tended to play-fight with his younger siblings or spent time on his mobile phone; the eldest girl moved between mothering her younger brothers and whispering to her elder brother. The third child was on her own for most of contact. She spent the time drawing but when she tried to gain attention for her efforts, her mother's attention was quickly drawn back to the younger boys.

The parents were seeking the return of all six children. However, the mother denied drug use, despite heroin having been found in the house and the children disclosing that they had seen their mother injecting and demonstrating the mechanics of this. The parents could not acknowledge that they had struggled to care for their children, blaming social services and the father of the two oldest children for the current situation. The mother spoke about the three younger children as if they were one child and was unable to acknowledge the scapegoating of her third oldest child or that this child was impacted by not knowing who her father was.

It was clear from the assessment that the children had very disparate needs. The eldest boy's loyalties lay with his mother and he intended to return home as soon as possible. The oldest girl was the most parentified, worrying not only about her younger brothers but also her father's children who were living with him and his new partner. A Care Plan needed to incorporate both, allowing her to be a teenager and continuing contact with her siblings.

The third child demonstrated major self-esteem issues. She worked hard in foster care to be the 'good kid' (see Chapter 7) and, throughout contact, to gain her parents' attention. She needed foster carers who could spend time with her, notice her even when she was quiet and unobtrusive, emphasise her good points, encourage her to be playful and even risk being 'naughty', so she could begin to feel that 'all of her' was acceptable. A single placement could have been the ideal, although this might have increased her sense of isolation.

While the most tenuous relationship was the one between the two girls currently living together, keeping them together could allow the older sister to develop a healthier sibling relationship and the younger sister to feel she had one sibling who was there for her. This would require skilled carers who were aware of the wider sibling dynamics and who would be pro-active in supporting the sibling relationship between the two girls.

Care planning for the three youngest boys was difficult. The foster carers believed that they had close relationships, but acknowledged that it was well-nigh impossible to meet their individual needs in one foster family, however skilled. There were concerns about finding an adoptive family who could meet the individual and sibling needs of all three.

Contact between the children was also a concern. The eldest boy's plan to return home was a contra-indicator that contact with his younger siblings would be in their best interests, yet his parenting role meant contact was important to him. The third child needed a contact plan that gave her opportunities to connect with her siblings in ways that meant she was not side-lined: ideally one-to-one contact. However, this was difficult to manage for the three youngest children and placed strain on their foster carers. The eldest girl needed contact not only with her siblings in care but also with her half-siblings living with their father in ways that minimised her role as quasi-parent.

CASE STUDY: THE MOORE FAMILY

The Moore family comprised two children, a girl aged six years and a boy aged three years; they shared a mother but had different fathers. The elder child had never met her father and regarded her brother's father as hers: the Moores had met when she was only three months old and Mr Moore had since filled the parenting role in the girl's life.

The couple's relationship was permeated by domestic violence and they had separated; the children remained with their mother while the father had contact. Contact arrangements were difficult since the acrimonious parental relationship persisted during contact handovers.

The children were accommodated after the mother threatened suicide; there were also concerns about her ability to budget. She struggled to get her daughter to school and it was felt that the children were subject to physical and emotional neglect.

Contact was arranged with both parents. The children's contact with Mr Moore appeared more positive than contact with their mother, who struggled to relate emotionally with her children and seemed unaware of safety issues: for example, not noticing when her young son put toys in his mouth. Each parent blamed the other for the children being accommodated; they seemed preoccupied with their couple relationship and did not recognise the impact that this had on the children. Initially, rehabilitation was thought to be unlikely with the mother, although possible between the boy and his father.

Work with both parents started with an exploration of their respective histories and the impact this had had on them. Mr Moore struggled with this; attempts to discuss the children's needs were impossible since he turned any conversation into a tirade against his ex-partner and social services. Ms Moore struggled to prioritise the children and focused on her partner relationship. However, gently challenged, she was enabled to talk about her early history and recognise that her children had been traumatised by their experiences of domestic abuse and the ongoing parental difficulties. She was also able to acknowledge her difficulties with budgeting and worked well with social services on this. Independently, she sought therapeutic support for herself. She agreed to meet Mr Moore to discuss contact and, unlike Mr Moore, was able to focus on the children. She successfully managed a situation where she had contact with her daughter in the same building as Mr Moore when he was having contact with their son. She gave her son a kiss as he left with his father and said she hoped he had a nice time; Mr Moore did not respond to, or acknowledge, Ms Moore.

Contact began to improve. The venue for contact was child-friendly with a garden and kitchen where Ms Moore was supported to practise safety issues while baking cakes with her daughter. During this intimate mother-daughter time she was helped to apologise to her daughter, acknowledging to her that she understood how much parental arguments had scared and upset her. Ms Moore also encouraged her daughter to share the cakes they had baked with her brother and Mr Moore at the end of contact, giving her the message that she could love both her parents. As work progressed rehabilitation with the mother became increasingly viable.

DISCUSSION

Assessors concerned with 'best interest' decisions must move beyond mere 'feeding and watering' issues towards recognising that children in court proceedings require parenting that embraces their neurobiological, socio-emotional, cognitive and educational needs. Clear acknowledgement that traumatised children require better-than-averagely good reparenting to repair the developmental-attachment interruptions of their earliest years is vital. Social workers should become more proactive with birth parents, making it clear what 'good enough' parenting 'looks like' and offering sustained support to make change possible. This information must be passed on to the court through clearly written reports supported with case examples and interpretations. Criteria for what is not 'good enough' and realistic timescales for change must be clear to all parties. Children cannot wait five years, moving within the care system and in and out of rehabilitation, while the viability of permanent return is considered. Children's timescales are quite different from adults: six months to a toddler, or two years for a five-year-old, can represent half their lives and feel like forever.

Adopters and foster carers also need help to recognise the impact of trauma on children. They need training and support to recognise both what happened to children and what it did to them; they need help to explore what developmental reparenting means in theory and practice. This support needs to be both part of the assessment process for foster carers and adopters and ongoing. Training, while crucial, must be supplemented by continued support that allows caregivers to consider these general principles, alongside the individual needs of the children in their care, and remain available until adulthood.

Training also needs to extend beyond front-line practitioners. The judicial system plays a crucial role in making 'best interest' decisions for the most vulnerable children in our society. Without a thorough understanding of the impact of trauma on children, judges may be hampered in their role as advocates for children. While these proposals have clear cost implications, this needs to be considered against the long-term costs of acts of professional omission. For example, less than 1 per cent of all children in England are in care but Looked After Children make up 30 per cent of boys and 44 per cent of girls in custody. The average annual cost of a prison place in England and Wales for the financial year 2011–2012 was £37,648 (Ministry of Justice 2012). Working with accommodated children and both their short- and long-term caregivers to help children heal from the trauma of abuse and neglect would reduce long-term economic costs and benefit both the most vulnerable members of our society and the community as a whole. Maintaining the status quo should not be an option in 'The Big Society'.

PART 5

PERSONAL NARRATIVES

Pain, Persistence and Growth

Chapter 11

THROUGH PRISON WALLS

Strengthening Adult Attachments from the Outside In

HANNAH FRYER

Our son Owain experienced repeated physical and emotional trauma during his early years, which was not acknowledged by the adoption agency that placed him with us or the educational, clinical and independent support services we consulted over subsequent years. He was placed with us approaching his second birthday having been diagnosed, after many clinical examinations and periods of hospitalisation, with a rare genetic disorder affecting his face and extremities. Gradually the doubts about his physical development receded while his emotional and behavioural difficulties increased. It was years before it was acknowledged that Owain's initial inability to smile and strange reflex movements were due to early traumatic experiences and his facial characteristics were related to foetal alcohol exposure.

Owain's behaviour swung from gentle and clingy to aggressive and rejecting with predictable unpredictability. He was, however, a bright 'little angel' in school: adding to our sense of frustration, inadequacy and self-blame. Over the years we sought help from statutory and independent psychological services, which proved of limited use. Finally, aged 12 years, Owain was diagnosed with conduct disorder at a leading London hospital, with the advice that he should be immediately accommodated: the implication being that we were responsible for his challenging behaviour. Owain's reaction was to smirk and rub his hands in apparent glee, followed, as we left, by terrified screams of 'Don't let me go!' Fortunately, no action was taken to remove Owain from us. Our growing awareness of Reactive Attachment Disorder (RAD), through PPIAS (now Adoption UK), led to Owain's clinical diagnosis by experts in the field; access to up-to-date information and literature strengthened our stubborn determination to support him and prove 'them' wrong.

By the time that Owain reached adolescence we felt that we had 'tried everything'. We were struggling to protect ourselves and our possessions and provide basic safety for him or his siblings within our home. His teenage years are a blur of 'lost' or damaged confidence, possessions and peace (ours and his); we inhabited a war zone. By mid-teens he was absent from our home more than present and was supplementing his income in illegal, dangerous and self-harming ways. Only with time did we realise the extent of Owain's substance abuse, despite items and cash going missing and his excuses, aggression and unexplained disappearances.

When Owain was 20 years old, with grave misgivings and heavy hearts, we asked him to move out so as to protect his younger sibling and ourselves. Shortly after this he was arrested and subsequently convicted of a serious, violent offence. We became increasingly certain during his trial that Owain had not committed the offence, despite his presence at the crime scene. Unfortunately, the law of 'joint enterprise' was enough to secure his conviction, despite evidence that his early traumatic experiences meant that he 'froze' and was unable to think rationally or intervene.

Owain's patent mental ill-health and his shame and fear of rejection led him to withdraw from family members and other would-be supporters. This hampered our ability to provide vital information to his defence counsel about the impact of his early trauma. Neither a teenage clinical diagnosis of RAD nor our recognition of his chronic dissociation (see also Chapters 2, 6 and 7) and Post Traumatic Stress Disorder (PTSD) could be submitted in mitigation without Owain's permission and he was too psychologically and cognitively distressed at this time to consider this. As with mental health services, once individuals turn 18 they are deemed to be competent adults, and assured of complete confidentiality. This takes no account of those adults whose early traumatic experiences continue to affect their everyday socio-emotional and cognitive functioning adversely (Perry 2009). If such difficulties were recognised this could lead to them being deemed 'vulnerable adults' and offered the protections afforded to adults with other more readily identified learning difficulties; it should include the involvement of families, who could provide invaluable information and support.

Justice seems blind to the lasting effects of the early experiences of abuse, neglect and chronic pain, contributing to the disproportionate numbers of previously Looked After and adopted adults within the prison estate. Statistics from Young Minds (2014) show that 72 per cent of children in care (excluding those from the same cohort subsequently placed for adoption) have behavioural or emotional problems and that 95 per cent of imprisoned young offenders have mental health disorders. Moreover, children experiencing periods in care (that would include most adoptees) are more than twice as likely to become involved with the criminal justice system and more than 25 per cent of young men in young offender institutions have spent periods in local authority care (NACRO 2012). Risk factors discussed in the report include vulnerability due to past abuse, neglect or unstable living arrangements.

During Owain's total of 11 years in seven prisons, some hundreds of miles away, we struggled to establish and maintain contact with him. He telephoned so infrequently that we retained and treasured his answerphone recordings for many years. He found it well-nigh impossible to write or to send us Visiting Orders (those precious 'invitations' without which we were unable to visit) due to a toxic combination of poorly developed attachments, weak Object Permanence (OP; see also Chapter 7), chronic developmental trauma, pervasive shame, undiagnosed dyslexia and a stubborn, survival-based, refusal to engage with the prison system.

OBJECT PERMANENCE (OP)

OP plays a vital role in the developmental-attachment process (van Gulden 2010a). During their first year infants learn that objects, including their home, do not disappear when out of sight, hearing or touch. Once established they apply this principle to people (van Gulden 2010b), allowing them to perceive the world as increasingly predictable and consolidating their secure base. Object Constancy (OC) evolves from OP: when young children grasp that first objects, then people, remain substantially the same despite apparent changes: for example, shape, colour, facial expression or mood.

If caregiving is inconsistent, neglectful or abusive, or children experience repeated separations, multiple clinical interventions or chronic pain, opportunities to acquire these vital concepts are compromised. As a consequence, children's ability to trust that the world is a secure and predictable place and that their caregivers are reliably 'there for them' is compromised: with potentially long-term negative effects on their capacity to feel safe, form healthy relationships, acquire vital cognitive skills, such as reflection and self-control, develop resilience or experience well-being.

With maturity, weak OP and OC are often hidden. Children and adults come to 'know' that things and people should always be there and remain the same while appearing on the surface to differ. However, their words or actions can indicate the uncomfortable dissonance between what their heads tell them 'should be' and their 'gut feelings' (including irritability and digestive problems). Persistent difficulties with 'losing and finding things' or dismissal of their value, and repeated changes in relationships, employment or dwelling can result from uncertainty about the persistence of things and people in time and space.

Owain continued to struggle with isolation, depression, ongoing dissociative episodes and the ever-present knowledge that by maintaining his innocence he risked indefinite extension of his original sentence. The 'system' did not provide us with relevant information regarding visiting; it prevented us from making the first move in contacting him; it precluded us from exploring reviews of his sentence; it limited 'gifts' to him of simple personal items like underpants, skin cream or stamps. It denied us our role as parents to reach out and help him feel loved, safe and cared for and it denied Owain the restorative parent–child experiences he still needed.

In spite of what sections of the media claim, the British prison system is no holiday camp, nor should it be. However, if, as successive governments contend, one of the main aims of our prison system is to rehabilitate, helping offenders to move out of offending and become useful members of society, then enabling prisoners to remain connected to their families and communities is critical. Figures for 2010–2011 (Sapouna *et al.* 2011) show that reoffending is reduced where prisoners maintain 'quality ties' with family and community and hence feel there is a place for them 'at home' on release. We found the prison system's approach to facilitating the maintenance of these vital connections far from helpful: I suspect ours was the experience of most prisoners and their families. Even basics relating to costs of visiting, mailing and supporting inmates seem excluded from consideration when decisions about prison placements and prison regulations are made. While perhaps justifiable in economic terms, they are ultimately costly in weakening the lifeline between vulnerable inmates and their families – their principal emotional and financial supports.

From the point of his arrest, communications with our son were restricted, discouraged and controlled almost to the point of impossibility. While he was held in custody, communication with Owain was only possible at the discretion of the police. For the next six months while he was on remand, 30 miles from home, we made only one visit to the 'local' Youth Offender Institution. For us to visit, Owain had to make an official formal application. His physical and emotional health was extremely poor, meaning that his ability to engage with and navigate the necessary processes was severely compromised. Owain had no personal possessions other than the clothes he wore at the time of his arrest but his emotional fragility, depression, alienation and fear prevented him asking us for more.

The prison system requires prisoners to provide their families with the regulations relating to prison visits and supplying personal items and cash. Moreover, the procedures relating to visits, personal items and cash differ for each prison and frequently alter over time. The 'system' presumes that prisoners will be emotionally, mentally and physically equipped, and sufficiently skilled, confident and competent, to retain and supply this information to their families and follow it through by telephone or letter. Our requests for this vital information to be provided directly to us were always refused by prison staff on the grounds that inmates had access to the relevant forms and were responsible for passing them on. It is worth bearing in mind at this point the high incidence of mental health issues (Young Minds 2014) and low rates of basic literacy among the prison population (Clark and Dugdale 2008).

Prison rules varied over time in relation to what items we could provide for Owain; over the years they became more difficult, restrictive and expensive. With few exceptions we could not take clothes, cash, toiletries or other possessions into prison, even if offered for examination by prison officers. In the early years we were allowed to buy things for Owain and post them to him, as long as they were in their original packaging. This did at least feel a little personal, although postal costs made it expensive. As rules became stricter we were no longer permitted to send Owain parcels, this remaining personal element being lost as we were allowed only to send money. He then needed to order what he required from the prison canteen: tricky with executive function difficulties. Sending postal orders was costly; cheques required detailed knowledge of the specific rules current in any one prison at any one time about how, and to whom, to address the cheques; there were often long delays in the transfer of money into Owain's account.

It was painful to feel unable to provide for even the most basic needs of our child. How much worse this felt when we needed desperately to spell it out 'in actions of one syllable' to Owain that he was always in our minds and in our hearts; this was particularly poignant since we knew he was severely underweight and often depressed. Celebrations such as birthdays and Christmas, part of the ritual of family life, for our son were loaded with pain. It meant so much more than the giving and receiving of gifts. How could we change Owain's long-held associations of these events with rejection and loss into a true sense of belonging if we could not engage in them: knowing instead that he was spending these times alone and, in terms of Christmas, more isolated and 'banged up' than 'normal'?

No prison visits can be arranged over the Christmas period as most staff take leave: the thought of our son solitary and ruminating over past and current losses almost broke our hearts. All I wanted to do was to be able to take him in my arms and cuddle him, laugh with him, play Monopoly and let him win the 'get-out-of-jail-free-card'. Sending him a home-made Christmas cake was a poignant but unattainable luxury. In time this became a standing joke; when asked what he would like for Christmas, after his first painful reply, 'You know I hate Christmas,' Owain would always add, 'Cake – and don't forget the ladder and the file.'

The principle of denying offenders their liberty is understandable, hence at one level limiting telephone contact appears a reasonable part of 'denial of liberty'. However, it makes vital day-to-day connection with family impossible and is contrary to every citizen's right to family life, as laid down in the Universal Declaration of Human Rights. Access to the 'wing' telephone is restricted; further limited by demand and the effort and costs involved. For Owain this was compounded by a deep sense of shame and, no matter how much we reassured him otherwise, a sense of being the cause of hurt, making him 'unworthy' of belonging in our family. Moreover, if he couldn't see us he couldn't be sure we were there (let alone 'there for him'), so why bother?

Owain's developmental-attachment issues led to difficulties with organisation and executive function, attention, memory and dyslexia. The requirement that phone cards should be purchased at weekly intervals following completion of order forms, and submission of completed forms to prison staff on a designated day, created further barriers. The cost of telephone calls from prison is significantly higher than from normal domestic landlines, leaving prisoners with the dilemma of spending precious resources on phone cards they must 'fight' to use or purchasing 'luxuries' such as soap or coffee. Beyond the practical difficulties, exorbitant cost and prohibitive bureaucracy in prison, Owain's *modus vivendi* was to remain 'invisible' and avoid interactions with prison officers: rendering it well-nigh impossible for him to make calls. There are no facilities for families on the outside to make calls to their relatives within.

The budget provided for prison food is low, allowing for only the most basic of diets. Our son has always struggled to eat and has been persistently underweight. We became aware that Owain often avoided prison food: eating only a limited number of items purchased from the prison 'canteen', provided he remembered to complete the necessary forms and submit them in the prescribed way. His physical health was therefore poor, in turn negatively impacting his already poor mental health. Food is such an essential part of experiencing nurture, regulation and comfort: experiences that were in short supply in Owain's early years of abandonment and abuse, overlaid by the constant pain and discomfort of Irritable Bowel Syndrome (IBS). When he came to us as a child we tried to provide regular tempting, healthy food, and vitamin and mineral supplements. However, on the rare occasions we were able to visit Owain it was hard to access freshly brewed hot drinks, let alone healthy, nutritious and comforting food we could share: albeit within the stark, strained environment of prison visiting rooms.

Prison access to health care is not easy. Whether founded in fact or not, Owain was suspicious of prison medical staff, unable to trust their confidentiality; he believed that asking for medical help would impede his progress towards release, or result in a return to a more secure setting. As a result, a number of illnesses and medical issues (including severe tinnitus) went untreated: reinforcing his perception of the world as a pain-filled place where he could not expect to be cared for or learn the essential capacity to self-care. Counselling and psychotherapy were almost non-existent or, where available, short-lived. Our intermittent contact with Owain meant that the help we could offer was sporadic and restricted. We felt unable to help and comfort Owain in meaningful ways, again increasing his sense of turmoil, isolation and lack of belief that he deserved love and care. The distorted perceptions and cognitions that were the legacy of his early traumatic experiences persisted (Schore 2001b; Perry 2009).

Prisoners are allocated a 'personal officer' responsible for their well-being. As Owain was an adult, we were never made aware of their identity or how we could make contact ourselves. Moreover, because of his mistrust of the 'system', Owain actively discouraged us from making contact with staff. Individuals struggling with attachment issues have not achieved basic trust in even their nearest and dearest, let alone those perpetuating their incarceration: asking for the help and support they need from 'strangers' is well-nigh impossible. On the one occasion we did try to share our concerns with a prison governor about Owain's physical and mental well-being our worries were ridiculed and dismissed. The only accessible resources were prison chaplains: most of whom were approachable and helpful but possessed limited powers within the 'system'. On the death of the great-aunt to whom Owain felt close (expressed as 'She's just crazy!'), we had to trust an unknown chaplain to inform him. When prison authorities denied his request to attend her funeral (not a close enough relative) the chaplain enabled him to select a poem for me to read out at her memorial service.

Nevertheless my tenacity, determination and disaffection with officialdom, honed by the endless search to get the support we all desperately needed, stood me in good stead. This, combined with my husband's patience, diplomacy and boundless optimism, enabled us to circumvent some of the endless obstacles standing in the way to nurturing and strengthening the connections with our son that we knew were vital to improving his resilience and well-being. Given Owain's poor OP and OC, we needed endless opportunities to reach out to him and refuse to allow him to reject us in order to establish new patterns of perceptions and cognitions. The only weapons available to me, apart from my determination, were pens and postage stamps.

Throughout his incarceration I fought tooth-and-nail to beat the 'system' and let Owain know that he was always in our hearts, we were 'there for him', and always would be. I wrote to him daily; I knew every last posting time at letter boxes within several miles of our home. On holidays I bulk-bought stamps and postcards to keep up regular dispatches. We never expected, and rarely received, replies but it was obvious during occasional, stilted conversations in inhospitable prison visiting rooms just how important this daily contact was. We later learned that Owain displayed some postcards on his cell door!

Gradually, we nurtured stronger attachments, recognising that, despite years of being offered commitment and love within our family, Owain had been unable to 'feel' loved (Perry 2009) or internalise, at the gut level, that we existed when he *could* see, hear and touch us, let alone when he could not. Since he did not feel 'held' in our hearts and minds, he could not 'hold' us during separations. His interrupted neurobiological development resulting from early trauma experiences meant that his feelings, sensations and perceptions of the world did not match his apparent understanding at an intellectual level: he had been unable to benefit sufficiently from the 'later love' we offered (Perry 2009). Slowly, 'love-snail-mailing' reached the parts others could not, until Owain finally accepted that he was stuck with us, so he may as well get used to it! He now seeks us out when distressed and often tells us how lucky he is that he is our son; we reply wholeheartedly, 'And we're so lucky to be your parents.'

Friends and family often asked me what I found to say in my daily letters. It was never a problem for me: it was not about what I said but that Owain could 'hear my voice' as I wittered on about the rain (of course) or what I needed to buy for dinner. My aim was to maintain the consistency and predictability of loving, everyday interactions that Owain had missed during the vital months of his infancy. Although I often asked him how he was and what he had been doing, I did not expect a response, reasoning that few teenagers willingly tell their parents about their day when asked. I tried to resist the urge to request visiting orders or telephone calls from Owain since I felt that if I 'poked too hard' he would curl up defensively like a hedgehog. I found postcards easiest to write and tried to find humorous ones. They were posted in envelopes to afford Owain some privacy, although we both knew that all mail is opened and 'vetted' internally before delivery: another reason to stick to the mundane. The shared intimacy and relationship-building lay in the ongoing contact not the content: just as with infants. It was comforting to know that Owain's 'nutty' great-aunt also wrote regularly (and idiosyncratically); some good friends also sent cards, or good wishes for me to pass on.

Prisoners are allocated a probation officer (PO) within the prison alongside an external PO responsible for preparation for release and after-care. Owain had little trust or respect for the in-house POs, seeing them as part of 'the system' rather than being there to support him. As he approached the end of his mandatory tariff his focus was on the Home Office Review that was his gateway to freedom. A previous Review laid down requirements for Owain's release: including undertaking voluntary, full-time work in the local community and identifying full-time paid employment and accommodation on release. Our attempts to liaise with ever-changing external POs to clarify plans and offer our support were rebuffed, presumably on the grounds that our son was a competent adult and that full confidentiality should be maintained. This contributed to several months' distressing delay before his eventual release.

HAPPY EVER AFTER?

It was not until the time of his release approached, after years of our 'refusal to be rejected', that Owain was truly able to trust in our ability to support him and feel he belonged. Although it has been a hard and painful struggle for him, and it continues to be so, he is a survivor and we aim to enable him to thrive. He is a beautiful person, almost too sensitive for his own good. He has become a wonderful son and a responsible, caring uncle. Now, almost three years since his release on licence, Owain has a comfortable flat and undertakes regular voluntary work with a local charity 'sorting out' and updating their IT software and website. His criminal record still stands in the way of finding paid employment but Owain is making plans to establish his own website development business. He has established a stable relationship with a delightful, caring Asian woman. He remains, at times, impulsive, anxious and disorganised, but endearingly lovable and loving..

We visit several times weekly on 'food-and-hug-runs' (continuing the nurturing phase of attachment) and offer emotional and financial support (providing co-regulation, safety and protection; Crittenden 2005). Daily text-messaging keeps us in close touch when we, or Owain, check in: 'Are you still there?' (encouraging the exploration checking back developmental stage; Bowlby 1988). Life is never a bed of roses but when life starts in a bed of thorns, requiring painful grafts on to another bush, it poses additional challenges. But Owain is beginning to wake up and 'smell the roses': with plenty of watering, pruning and TLC, the buds are opening to reveal an awesome plant.

DISCUSSION

Practitioners throughout the criminal justice system, including police officers, barristers, judges, prison governors, probation officers and 'hands-on' prison staff must be made aware of the impact of early traumatic experiences on children's developmental attachments. Failure to do so is an indictment of society as a whole. Without thorough understanding, and recognition, of the implications of early trauma for the vulnerable adults they may become, they will continue to be over-represented within the criminal justice system. Their difficulties with relationships and struggles with self-organisation and education, and their impulsive, chaotic, often addictive behaviour and disaffection with society will repeatedly bring them into the prison estate. These difficulties may well serve to keep them there: they may repeatedly challenge authority, react violently to provocation or make use of readily accessible drug supplies. Conversely, prison may become their 'safe place': the place they know, with predictable routines, clear expectations, containment and a sense of community. Hence the rehabilitation system will for many remain ineffective and ultimately costly to both offenders and society.

Many of those incarcerated have experienced abuse and neglect and have passed through the Looked After system, being fostered, adopted or in residential care (NACRO 2012). If we are serious about preventing the social, economic and human costs to society and individuals, offending and re-offending must be prioritised. Restorative justice should cut both ways: applying equally to the victims of crime and the victims of childhood who commit them. If we are serious about a healthier, happier society in the long term, our growing awareness of the dynamics and long-term effects of distressed developmental attachments (Perry 2009) should guide education, support and interventions to protect its most vulnerable members in their earliest years (Howe 2005) and throughout their lifetime. It is never too late to make good the hurts of the past (Schore 1994, 2012).

Chapter 12

MENDING HEARTS
The Lasting Effects of Clinical Trauma

JANE MACNAMARA

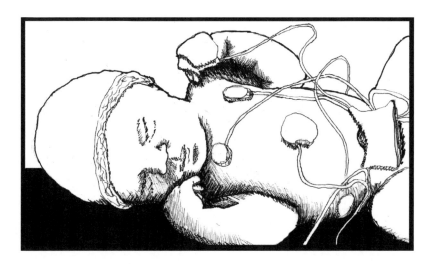

I am a mum of five children, the eldest of whom was born with a serious heart condition. Over the years, as a family, we have fostered children of all ages, all with attachment difficulties, and I now work therapeutically with children and their families. I have become increasingly aware of the impact of trauma on children's development through my therapeutic practice. As a family we muddled through the effects of my son's early medical trauma: I was a young mum and he was my first child. I wish I had the knowledge I have now when he was younger and we needed help. We felt very confused as to what we were doing wrong, when he failed to respond to the love and support we were giving him. What worked with our subsequent children rarely worked with him; it was hard for us all as a family. With hindsight I believe our son was suffering from Developmental Trauma Disorder; (van der Kolk 2005; see also Introduction) but this was unheard of in the 1980s when he was born.

Over time I have worked with adopted children, Looked After Children and children who have experienced loss through parental death or divorce. Initially, I used person-centred counselling, play therapy and art as means for children to explore their underlying feelings: placing them at the core of the whole process, seeing them on their own and maintaining complete confidentiality. Gradually, I found that working inclusively with children *and* their caregivers proved much more effective, in line with Hughes's developmental trauma approach (Golding and Hughes 2012). It makes sense for families as a whole to be included, as the caregivers are the ones 'on the frontline'. They need to know what is happening, why it is happening and how to deal with it. As a foster carer I know only too well how alienating it can be if children trot off to therapy alone. Without personal involvement, primary caregivers can feel excluded, invalidated and less effective in supporting their children. Moreover, vulnerable children may conclude that they do not truly belong, or that their caregivers are not valued. I feel an inclusive approach would have been most effective in helping my son and us all as a family.

SERIOUS ILLNESS

My son was born in our local hospital after a long, difficult labour culminating in a stress-inducing forceps birth (Gitau *et al.* 2001). He was pronounced healthy and we took him home, full of the usual trepidation and excitement new parents have. We called him Joe. At three weeks old, Joe was rushed by ambulance to the nearest cardiac hospital when a common cold pushed him into heart failure. As a new mum I had made an unconscious pledge to my child to protect him and keep him safe, yet here I was in hospital, witnessing him having tubes forced down his tiny nostrils into his stomach. My soft, tender, new baby was fighting for his life, his tiny arms flailing and his body arched. My instinct was to grab him and run to a safe place, away from the pain. I had to fight against these protective urges throughout the series of gruelling medical tests and treatment that lasted a week. I insisted on staying in the room as they were being carried out: I did not want to abandon him even further.

We were told that Joe had a major heart condition: transposition of the great arteries, plus a hole in his heart. The good news was that Joe could be operated on at about 12 months and, if the operation were successful, he would lead a 'normal' healthy life without further operations. For my boy, visits and stays in the cardiac hospital and our local one soon became normal, while we waited until he was big enough to be operated on. Joe's dad and I became used to surrendering our son to whatever was needed as his progress was monitored and he was prepared for surgery. I always stayed in hospital with Joe, even if it meant sleeping in a chair; thankfully the cardiac hospital had a special room where parents could stay. This made all the difference, as we could take it in turns to be with him and I could prepare all his meals, since the hospital food was poor.

At home we tried to mend our small son with lots of love and nurture. We were still working out how to be a family, establishing the routines and rituals that form part of childhood and would be crucial as Joe grew up. We did our best as he developed into a lively, sociable one-year-old. It was the hardest year of my life and at the same time the most precious. I wanted to live each moment fully with my son. He was a cheeky character, full of laughter and mischief, adored by all our friends and family. Yet some days a tiny coffin would come floating into my mind's eye and I just could not shift it. My husband dealt with it by refusing to even discuss the possibility of Joe dying but there were days when that's all I thought about, as if my mind was trying to prepare me in some way.

At one point we stayed on a children's cancer ward; it was so overcrowded that Joe had to sleep in a cot next to the reception desk without even a curtain around him. He was very fretful and distressed in such a noisy environment. Hospital was such a contrast to being at home, with lots of high-pitched noises and constant activity. Joe would 'perform' for the nurses, enjoying the attention one minute yet becoming distressed and crying the next, when the inevitable procedures had to be performed by the same people who were being so kind to him. I realise now that Joe would have been unable to remember a pain-free existence and would associate us with these distressing interventions, rather than protecting him from them. He was becoming 'hard-wired' to pain, confusion and chaos and we felt that there was nothing we could do about it.

I breastfed Joe for six months; I wish I had persisted for longer. I fed my subsequent children for up to two years but I was too exhausted after six months with Joe, as a result of the stress I was under. At home I made friends with other mums and we would get together with our babies. We had so much in common until they asked, 'What are you doing for Joe's first birthday?' and I could not reply. The truth was I did not know if Joe would have had his operation by then, or would even be alive. He became more blue and breathless as his first birthday approached, reminding us of just how ill he was.

By strange coincidence, Joe had his operation on his first birthday. He was unconscious for his special day but we were told that the operation had gone well. We stuck his birthday cards to the monitors stacked around his hospital cot. After a couple of days he came off the heart–lung machine and breathed independently. He sat, propped up with hospital pillows, a dressing on the gash down his chest, his face puffy with fluid, staring at us. His eyes had no sparkle at all and he had the air of a weary old man. I had never seen a depressed baby before. He did not look like Joe or respond in the same way to us. The worst thing was not being able to pick him up and give him cuddles because of all the tubes and wires attached to him. We tried talking to him in our usual way to get a response but he just stared at us. After a couple of days his humour started returning; he pointed to something and spoke in a small croaky voice, with a little smile. I knew then that underneath the battered exterior Joe was still there. However, we felt as though we had fundamentally betrayed him as parents and knew on some deep level that Joe felt this, too.

Eventually, we were allowed to go home. 'He will be fine,' the doctors and nurses assured us. 'It's natural to feel nervous,' they said. 'Go home and enjoy your healthy little boy.' Unfortunately, just days after being discharged, Joe was not at all fine; he nearly died because of a build up of fluid around his heart that had not been detected in hospital. I ran from one end of our local hospital to the other with him in my arms, his head lolling into unconsciousness, his lips going black. I knew that he was dying. Minutes later I watched as a team of doctors and nurses worked manically on him. I became rooted to the spot with shock. Eventually, I fought through the crowd to get to the head of his bed and shouted at him, 'Hang on, don't give up after all you've gone through.' He survived. The next day the paediatrician was still shaken by the whole experience, seemingly as traumatised as we felt. He told me that he had never seen a child in such a collapsed state before and that if he had been an adult he would have died. I am not sure if that made me feel better or worse but those words stuck in my head like a splinter.

There was no follow-up support in the community when Joe was discharged following his heart operation: looking back I find this shocking. The GP had dismissed his strange crying as teething the day before Joe collapsed and if I had not followed my maternal instincts and rushed him to hospital he would have died, just like that. Yet here we were on our own again. Once home, it felt weird just being with my baby, doing normal things that mums and babies do, suddenly having a future together. Joe had not felt completely like my baby in hospital. He became incredibly clingy, following me around crying, desperate not to 'lose me'. He would follow me to the toilet and I just let him. He did not want to let me out of his sight and I did not want to let him out of mine.

CHAOS

I started attending our village toddler group to meet other mums and for Joe to socialise. One day he ran in, pushed one child over, bit another and grabbed a toy from a third. He seemed to find it hard to enter the room and was overwhelmed by the chaos of bikes and noisy toddlers around him. When incidents happened I would take him into a quieter room and try to calm him down before going back in, holding his hand and explaining, 'This is how we behave here.' A few mothers complained about Joe's behaviour, which made me not want to go back, but I persisted and he made some friends. I'm sure Joe would have benefited from a calmer environment to socialise: he felt compelled to join in and then did not know when to stop. Any sort of chaotic movement triggered a similar response in Joe, as if he were embodying it on a sensory level (see also Chapters 2, 5 and 7). He was much calmer on his own turf, seeing children he knew well, although even then could whirl out of control at times.

I needed to talk about what we had been through but most people could not handle it and looked away or changed the subject. 'He's all right now, so why dwell on what happened? He's a baby; he will soon forget all about it.' I found friends who would listen but there was no real understanding at that time about early trauma and how things might unfold for Joe. I was constantly told, 'Oh, they all do that,' in relation to his behaviour but when our three eldest girls were born, when Joe was two, four and seven years old, I realised that actually they did not, or at least not to the extent that Joe did.

Joe had the 'all clear' health-wise when he was two years old. He appeared very robust and he rarely became ill after his operation. It felt as if he did not dare give into minor childhood illnesses, the rites of passage that all children have. However, once every few years he collapsed with something serious but unrelated to his heart. We ate wholesome food and went for long walks: I did my best to ensure he became a fit child. As he grew up, not many people knew he had had heart surgery. To look at him it was impossible to tell.

We established strong routines at home and Joe liked that. Meal-times and bed-times were predictable: he liked to know 'where he was'. We lived in a cottage by the sea and it was a peaceful place to raise children. Joe was a sweet, magical little boy who could suddenly erupt into head-banging tantrums when things did not go the way he felt they needed to. I thought they were normal toddler tantrums but they were extremely severe and it was difficult to know what to do with him when he got in such a state. We were not punitive with him and would try to reason and be consistently loving but he was a hard child to console.

SEPARATION

Starting school nursery was a huge step for Joe and it took him a long while to settle (see also Chapter 4). He did not speak as well as most other three-year-olds and I was concerned that he would not be understood by the teachers. He was referred to a speech and language therapist, and ended up an articulate little boy but, like all things with Joe, it took time. Full-time school was even harder. It was a small village school but quite pressured academically; Joe struggled to pick things up as quickly as some of the other children. Often children become stuck developmentally around the time of their traumatic life events and then slowly catch up in some areas. I think Joe was mostly functioning at two or three years old when he started full-time school, not his chronological age of five years. He found it hard to sit still and pay attention, so how could he learn?

He took years to learn to read: finally being diagnosed with dyslexia at ten years old. He often shut down emotionally when he came home, as if it was the only way he could cope. He would be uncharacteristically quiet and less responsive to our hugs and reassurances, or, conversely, would come home extremely frustrated and tearful (see also Chapters 1 and 4). He could not always tell us why. He would lash out at his sisters and shout to vent his frustration. I encouraged Joe to talk about his feelings; but he found this hard to do: to this day he hates discussing his feelings; his actions still tend to do the talking.

Joe also took time to catch up physically; he was small for his age. He was bullied by some of the older kids and it frightened him. One big boy would swing him around by his head every playtime until I intervened when I learned what was happening. Joe was easily led: if the older boys at school told him to do something, however silly, he would do it just for the thrill of it. He got into trouble with school staff and as he grew older was labelled 'naughty' and 'stupid'. Joe was incredibly bright but had difficulties with attention and following instructions, so found it hard to get ideas on to paper or develop them properly. I now understand that his dyslexia formed part of his self-organisation and executive functioning difficulties, almost certainly related to his underlying early traumatic neurobiology.

Joe found it hard to empathise: it was as if he knew it was something he should do but could not access. Sometimes he would sob with frustration but as he got older he would act as if he did not care even if he did underneath. He was constantly in survival mode; he progressed from bullied to bully. He bullied one of his younger sisters, telling her she was ugly and stupid. He bullied a girl on the school bus; when confronted by the girl's parents he could not see what the problem was. He could, however, see it upset us: this obviously made him feel bad, yet I knew it would happen again because he still did not 'get it' – and it did. Asked about his behaviour his first instinct was to deny it, then minimise it and then become really angry because we had brought it up. I now understand his anger was his way of managing feelings of shame that would otherwise overwhelm him (Schore 1994).

DYSREGULATION

Similarly, growing up, Joe would often 'lose' it, becoming out of control emotionally. He progressed from 'normal' toddler tantrums to 'flying off the handle' when asked to cooperate or when challenged about his behaviour. We made allowances for him because of his history, always trying to listen and reason with him, with plenty of reassuring hugs. This worked sometimes but at other times I felt I could not get through to him at all. I remember people in our local shop staring at the sight of a ten-year-old screaming over the amount of sweets he had. Nothing ever seemed to be right or to be enough. Where I could reason with his younger sisters I could not with Joe. I now realise that he became dysregulated when he 'got in these states': he needed help to recognise and manage his bodily and emotional feelings. Ironically, this is something we have learnt to do with the children we have fostered.

I clearly remember, at a party we had for one of our daughters, Joe running around and pushing every child over in a frenzy of excitement. He was discharging his emotions in the only way he knew. Sometimes I would become cross and I could see this frightened him more than it did the girls. He hated the word 'no' and would do anything to take control; it felt like he hated us because we were the ones in control. Life became a battle of wills. I had other children to consider but at times his extra emotional needs dominated the family. His sisters often just had to 'behave' as we had no energy left to deal with more friction. If Joe went away I noticed that my eldest daughter, two years younger than he was, would start acting up, filling the rather large space that he had left behind. Looking back, I can see I relied on her to be the well-behaved one, the healthy child with no problems, but like all children she had her own struggles. The difference was that the girls' 'default' seemed to be a sense of well-being that Joe lacked.

MANAGING CHANGE

Joe had major problems shifting from one place to another and this continued into adulthood. If we wanted to go to the beach to play he screamed and shouted in outrage at being disturbed; once on the beach he did not want to go home and would refuse to get into the car; once home he did not want to go anywhere else – and so it went on. If we went on holiday he would make the girls cry and become extremely argumentative and difficult in the car. His anxiety levels were spinning out of control, although I did not realise this at the time: I did however recognise he had big problems with change of any kind and tried to smooth any transitions.

If things grew stressful at home, with one of the younger children crying, or some minor family drama, Joe whipped things into a frenzy, almost whooping with joy because at last here was something that he could understand: chaos. I often felt overwhelmed by the relentlessness of his behaviour: always coming back to a point of love and acceptance yet not knowing what to do, since none of the normal pieces of advice regarding children's behaviour seemed to work. Believe me, we tried it all, from star charts to timeout, some of which we were unhappy using but we felt that we had to do something.

ADOLESCENCE AND TRANSITION INTO ADULTHOOD

Joe started taking risks as a young teenager. He would grin as he related how he had taken big chunks out of his legs on his skateboard, show me quite serious wounds and appear impervious to the pain. Other days a small scratch could cripple him with anxiety.

When Joe was fourteen we began fostering and Joe got seriously into dope. He would smoke on the way to, during and after school. He became angry and violent when challenged; his mood swings were frightening. He found it hard to find a direction in life and make decisions for his future. He did not drink at all until he was 18, then drinking took over and that was just as extreme. It was all or nothing with Joe.

Joe left school with one GCSE. However, driven by his passion and thirst for knowledge about animals, Joe found a residential 'bridging' course that led to his gaining a place at a prestigious university to study Animal Sciences. This period away from home increased Joe's separation anxieties but, following a series of ups and downs, he completed his two-year course and moved on to study for his BSc. He was thrown out of halls of residence for accidentally setting fire to them, after he left food on the cooker and went to bed drunk. 'It wasn't my fault,' was his stock reply, followed by a look of bewilderment at how people had over-reacted. Cause and effect still seemed hard to compute. While at university he intervened in a fight involving four men kicking and punching one guy on the floor. He stopped the fight because he thought it was wrong, which it was, and they turned on him and his friend. He still has the scar on his cheek from that experience. I dreaded him going out and something happening to him because he drank so much and put himself in vulnerable situations. In between these episodes Joe often became very down about his life and how it did not seem to flow like everyone else's.

Joe continued to take one step forward and two back but obtained a good degree. We were thrilled but he still struggled to accept how capable he was. Not long after that he finished with his girlfriend of two years and became very down. The emotional pain he was experiencing was awful to watch and completely overwhelming for him. He seemed ashamed of the way he had treated her, although there had been issues on both sides. He was distraught for three days and we were concerned at how low he became. We did not leave him on his own until he recovered. I'm sure he was connecting with what he went through as a baby: abandonment coupled with difficulties distinguishing between emotional and physical pain. The pair had been very close and separating physically and emotionally from his girlfriend opened up a chasm of self-blame, helplessness and loss. Re-centering himself was hard. He avoided close relationships for some time, saying it had 'all just done my head in' and he wanted to focus on work instead.

I really believe that the saving grace in Joe's childhood was living by the sea. Joe spent hours exploring rock pools, absorbed completely by his passion for wildlife. We encouraged that passion by allowing him to keep snakes and lizards, which he read up on and looked after well. He only ever read factual books, never anything remotely right-brained, and became an expert on reptiles. This gave him a place in the world (Griffiths 2013). As a family we always had lots of animals and they became a fantastic source of unconditional love from which he could draw. The beauty and rawness of where we lived gave him a sense of peace and belonging: a different type of attachment. We spent many happy family days outside, making fires, going for moonlit walks or playing on the beach. Fishing became Joe's way of connecting to stillness, and he still enjoys it today. This strong sense of place, relating to the first stage of Object Permanence (see also Chapters 4 and 11), was an extremely calming and healing base for Joe to return as a young exploring adult.

I had so many hopes and dreams for Joe but I have had to reshape them. I am still incredibly proud of what he has achieved. He is who he is. His current job is fundraising: he is very good at chatting to the public and raising their concerns for wildlife. He is carving an interesting career out for himself. He will never be a nine-to-five man but travelling and working intermittently have opened his horizons in ways that no single job ever could. His passion for wildlife has found him work and given him a more secure place in the world. Joe has many friends and is a popular young man. We are very close and try to keep in touch wherever he may be because we know he still needs us.[1]

EDITORIAL DISCUSSION

For valid reasons, clinicians focus primarily on effective medical interventions, treatment and outcomes. However, there should be equal focus on managing the invisible pain, distress and longer-term difficulties caused by pain and clinical interventions in very young children. Moroz (2005) allies medical procedures with more widely acknowledged causes of childhood trauma; in particular, there has been recognition of the traumatic impact of painful procedures on neonates and very young children.

Czarnecki *et al.* (2011) list among the immediate and long-term harmful effects of procedural pain physical, emotional, behavioural, cognitive and psychological issues typically associated with early traumatic experiences. These include fear, anger, aggression, difficulties with concentration and overall reduction in economic, social and spiritual well-being. Mitchell and Boss (2002) discuss the structural and physiological changes within the nervous systems of infants, affecting their reponses to pain and self-regulation. Grunau *et al.* (2006) explore the adverse cognitive and psychosocial effects of early painful experiences in pre-verbal children, despite their lack of conscious memory of the events, related to the close proximity between brain areas processing pain, emotion and attention. They connect the susceptibility of infants to experiences of pain to their developmentally immature communication skills.

---

1   Postscript: Joe is now working for a well-known animal charity and is thinking of taking a mindfulness course. He is beginning to recognise what he needs to do to help himself, for example staying away from certain situations and in general trying to lead a calmer, more peaceful life.

Systemic changes in the management of care and treatment on maternity wards, neo-natal intensive care units (NICUs) and paediatric wards should be based on a full understanding of the interactions between trauma, attachment and development in children. Primary caregivers provide vital somato-sensory neurobiological co-regulation in the early months, allowing their infants to feel comforted, nurtured and protected. Clinical interventions pose major challenges to these dyadic interactions, comparable to separation, loss and maltreatment. Parents may feel distressed and powerless to provide essential nurture, comfort and protection to their babies due to prioritisation of clinical over parental care: including, for example, incubation. Similar difficulties can arise from facing the barrage of machines and wires surrounding infants, limiting direct physical contact, or tube feeding and reducing the soothing opportunities of suckling. It is noteworthy that Grunau *et al.* (2009), in their study of cumulative procedural pain in neonates, report the modulating effects on cognitive outcomes at 18 months of lower parental stress levels.

Ludington-Hoe (2008) cites evidence that 'Kangaroo Care' (involving long periods of skin-to-skin contact between infants and parents) enhances pre-term infants' regulatory capacities, feeding and longer-term outcomes over comparable babies placed in incubators. Boyse (2007) proposes a number of ways in which parents can actively mitigate their children's traumatic experiences of clinical interventions, including holding and skin-to-skin contact, rocking, singing, talking, suckling and sucking on sweetened pacifiers. She also discusses how parents can identify behavioural signals indicating their babies' suffering, including high-pitched crying, body posture, movements and irritability. Parents should be actively encouraged to communicate their concerns to nursing staff so that effective pain management can be implemented immediately to achieve positive health outcomes for infants and young children (Mitchell and Boss 2002).

There has been burgeoning awareness of developmental trauma in adopted and fostered children and effective therapeutic interventions are gradually evolving (Archer and Gordon 2013; Golding and Hughes 2012; Levy and Orlans 2014). However, less attention has been paid to the deleterious effects of medical trauma on young children's attachment and development, or on how these can be mitigated. In clinical settings children and parents are often encouraged by medical staff to 'move on' and 'get over it', without acknowledgement of what 'it' is or how this can be achieved. This may relate to a culture of stoicism and objectivity in clinical settings; staff members certainly need support to protect themselves from being overwhelmed by the suffering they witness daily. Children need narratives that make sense of their early traumatic experiences and permission to act their 'sensori-emotional', rather than chronological, age in order to grow up healthily 'from the bottom up'. It is primarily parents who co-create these narratives with their children: they can only do so if they are provided with the information and support they require to achieve this effectively.

Moroz (2005) provides a list of recommendations for agencies to combat the unresolved effects of childhood trauma on behavioural, social, emotional, cognitive and health difficulties over the lifetime, including:

- increasing public awareness of the epidemic nature of trauma and the enormous costs to individuals, families and society

- making small changes, at no or low costs, to increase public and interagency awareness of the effects of trauma

- investing in prevention and early intervention programmes

- improving identification and treatment of at-risk children using specific screening tools.

Identification of the short- and longer-term effects of clinical interventions on children's neurophysiological and socio-emotional functioning is essential. Specific systemic changes to address these issues include:

- encouraging and facilitating the full involvement of parents in the care of their children

- acknowledging the sensori-emotional needs of infants and young children and the emotional needs of their parents

- creating greater opportunities for parents to have skin-to-skin contact, even when babies and children are seriously ill

- increasingly 'family-friendly' wards so that parents feel relaxed and 'held': allowing them to soothe and co-regulate their children

- designated nursing staff 24/7, not only to make vital moment-by-moment clinical observations but also to support parents through stressful times and take on the role of secondary attachment figures when parents cannot be present

- providing more information to staff on the potentially lasting post-traumatic effects of hospitalisation on children and their families

- education and counselling for caregivers while their children are in hospital

- ongoing support for families within the community following discharge

- designated therapeutic facilities for children displaying significant behavioural indicators of trauma

- education and counselling for medical staff around the protective role of available attachment figures in early traumatic experiences and the effects of secondary trauma.

Chapter 13

HOLDING ON AND LETTING GO

Bereavement and the Bonds of Attachment, An Adoptee's Perspective

TAMARA GORDON

I was born Charmain Michelle Brown and placed at birth, as pre-arranged, immediately into a family where I would become Tamara Rose Gordon. It was a transracial adoption, as was my adopted brother's four years before me. I had a highly successful adoption and a carefully handled and successful reunion with my birth parents 27 years later. Now, aged 44 years, I have met many adult adoptees who are able to convey the direct experience and consequences of attitudes and policies made by others in the late 1960s. I am contributing to the book in a very personal way with the hope of encouraging professionals to listen to the lived experiences of 'experts', the adoptees themselves. I thank the editors for including this too often silent voice.

In this chapter I wish to explore some unexpected effects from a successful 'attachment' story: effects that occurred later in my life, but are connected to the success of the connection and bonds we formed in our family. Most important to me is reflecting on the impact of successful attachment at the time of death.

Death has become my most recent teacher and so this is where I start. My adoptive mother died ten years ago of pancreatic cancer. For the short six months between diagnosis and death I was her main carer. At the moment of her death I became acutely aware of a paradox. It felt to me that natural parents and children, from birth on, are gently experiencing a letting go, from cutting the umbilical cord onwards until the children fly the nest. For adopted children it feels like the opposite. There is a lifetime's work in attaching and bonding – a tightening rather than a letting go.

For someone adopted, with successful attachment, death and the inevitable grief can be a brutal severance of a lifetime's work. My experience of an ongoing process of attachment over 37 years makes it more than just a habit to break. In the last ten years it has felt like I am holding my breath to keep her with me, rather than breathing out and letting her go. This is partly through fear that with losing her there will be no legacy of a bloodline. It is also a fear of losing myself as I look at my identity now she is not here. My adopted identity feels under threat.

But to return to the beginning. When I first came to my new home, family folklore tells of my mum leaving me out in the garden crying in the rain. On relating the story Mum would chuckle, saying she had simply forgotten she had a new child. Shocking though we both found this later, when I had been pregnant myself, I thought of the nine-month long period of adjustment and preparation that my mum had never had. I remember my feelings as my body was taken over by 'another'. The joy, fear and shock of my interconnectedness with my unborn child, knowing that everything I ate was affecting my child and that every emotion I felt could potentially affect her future. My mum never had this. She had to learn it with me outside and alongside, learning and adjusting on the job. As we attempted to bond there must have been feelings of delight and surprise at my presence and demands.

From the time that I arrived there was a morphing of identity, the forming of bonds through love, ritual, home and community. Attachment is not only to a mother but, I believe, to the extended family, the community, the culture. Sometimes my mother's desire for total absorption and acceptance as one family was so strong that our obvious differences, through colour and race, were overlooked. This could lead to a dissonance at times between my experience within my adopted identity and what I was experiencing outside of that and wishing to explore and celebrate. For example, as an adult at my brother's wedding I was told I should not wear a sari (that was the smartest item of clothing that I had) as it would be seen to be a 'political statement' and therefore not really appropriate for the occasion. Acknowledging and drawing attention to our differences was seen as threatening to the family we had created. For me the sari was not political but expressed a newfound pride in my racial identity that I would have liked to have had accommodated into the majority culture. I wanted to be accepted with my difference acknowledged and celebrated rather than it being seen as political.

After Mum died I felt able to look at things from different perspectives without the concern about how Mum may feel. As children we had always been told that we had the right to a good, loving home just like any other child. In reality, however, I felt that my adopted brother and I were just not 'like any other child'. I was not the same as those who were related by blood. Laudable though these ideas of rights are, my experience was different. I was given up first before I was rescued. Yes, I was comforted by stories of being the 'chosen one' through adoption, but I was also aware of the initial rejection that the fairytale of adoption, maybe because of embarrassment or unease, often leaves out (see also Chapter 5). In fact for me it felt good to be honest about the rejection if only because it helped me really treasure how lucky I was in my adoption. The truth is that I could have been an orphan and, as such, I didn't feel that I had the same experience or rights as a child born of parents who wanted her. I had an important, separate story of my own. I was different, but no less equal.

When I confessed how I felt about this, about being so different, to my brother, he seemed shocked, and I felt guilty, as if I had been disloyal in acknowledging our separate starts. But when my mother died she too seemed at last to acknowledge our difference. In the letter she wrote to me as she was dying she spoke of our 'incredible good fortune in having found each other'. This was an acknowledgement of fate's hand in our destiny, an acknowledgement of difference and separation, and an understanding that this need not threaten our close relationship or create a stifling attachment. Where in life we rarely spoke of our differences, in the separation of death our separate starts were acknowledged and so it felt that my identity was a stage in my life rather than being fixed and immortal.

For me it has been profoundly important to face these awkward truths around attachment as I believe it has often, unconsciously, dictated my behaviour. As I grew up I became adept at 'acting out', testing out whether they would still love me, whether their love was really unconditional, whether my parents would really never abandon me. I was afraid that, unlike blood relatives whose genetic connection is physical and enduring, the bond between me and my mother would not exist unless we kept creating and re-creating it. It would not be an invisible line that kept us linked even if we never spoke to each other again. However, despite this testing behaviour I never really rebelled. Real rebellion would have felt too much like really letting go and that was far too scary. I rocked the boat only to be reassured of my parents' recommitment, not for me to truly spread my wings.

My mother was always there, but perhaps her long-suffering patience with my testing behaviour has not always been helpful to me in the long run. In adulthood and after her death, I have had to break these habits and re-learn ways of relating to people in my closest and most trusting adult relationships so I do not push people away and test them way beyond acceptable limits. These have been some difficult life lessons and have made me think about my relationships with those closest to me. I now question how my experience has shaped, and continues to shape, my relationships, not only as an adopted child, but as a friend, a lover and, most importantly, as a mother myself. I question whether it has meant I stayed in unhealthy relationships longer than I should; I was busy with the work of attachment. And I question where I have deflected my attachment habit to, after the loss of my family unit through first divorce and then death.

Seven years on, my adoptive brother was diagnosed with pancreatic cancer. This is a rare form of cancer and so it was a horrific coincidence that it struck our family twice. It felt to me that my brother's diagnosis with the same cancer that our mother died from was another connection they shared. To me it was like an umbilical cord that had not been, and could not be, severed. It felt like a psychic wound that bound them from beyond the grave. Proof of the connection and attachment between my mother, my brother and me had been revealed privately during her illness. It felt as if we had become physically connected. I physically felt her pain reflected in my own body and so did my adoptive brother. The pain we felt told us when she was in pain and when she was at peace. When we admitted these phantom symptoms to each other we silently understood the invisible lines of attachment between us, and we also realised how strange this may seem to others. This idea of a psychic bond beyond death became so all-consuming that I performed rituals of letting go, desperately trying to find a way to resolve my need to remain emotionally connected while also letting go.

When my brother died I was left absolutely devastated. To some, my grief seemed huge, exaggerated, disproportionate. It has taken me time to understand that it has been amplified because I was experiencing my original fears of abandonment. I felt like the orphan that my mother and brother had sheltered me from ever being before. I felt insecure about whether the family relationships and connections could exist beyond the grave without the invisible, yet somehow tangible, bloodline connection. I had always struggled with the concept of 'ancestors' and for the same reason I struggled with the idea of 'legacy', and wondered then if I had a right to claim my mother's ancestry, and to be her legacy beyond the grave. If attachment within an adoptive family is created and a constant process of re-creation, then I questioned how it could be kept alive after death. 'I will always be your mother,' my mum had said in a card she left for me. She seemed to know I would ask these kinds of questions later and she had left me her reassurance.

However, I believe Mum must also have felt this insecurity over the immortality of the attachment and identity, too. For during her whole illness, while she never felt self-pity at her situation or fear of death, in her only moment of openly acknowledged pain and fear she said, 'Try not to let your children not know who I was.' I did not have children then but her comment upset me and I responded by assuring her that my children, of course, would know her. As I am of her, so of course they will be too. I think now we were both skirting round issues of her legacy and our attachment when not sharing DNA in the unknown territory of death.

Now I feel I am practising at being an orphan. As I watch my dad get older and his memory fade, I feel his is the last connection to our shared history. I am scared. I am avoiding him. I feel like a child learning to step out into the world alone. I am afraid that once he has gone my fears will be realised, that I am of no consequence to anybody, that my well-being and my struggles will be solely my own. There is no back-up or context and the grounding of my own identity feels shaky. There is little history to hang on to. Everything my mother spent 30 years building has been dismantled. This grief and loss, I am sure, is shared by all who lose their parents but, for me, as an adopted child, I feel the absence of that blood-link keenly and I am afraid that, without it, I lose my right to my part in a family history and a family future without the family members to help me create and re-create it moving forward in time.

I am reflecting on who I am – my identity and my place in the new order of things. Identity is not, after all, something that is given and fixed but is constantly changing and evolving. I find it interesting that the human body recreates itself completely every seven years. Every seven years we have a complete new set of cells from those we had at birth. It makes me question whether I really am the identity that I cling to but feel is threatened as our collective histories dissolve and change around me. For me, I think the answer to that question is 'no'; this body is just what I rent for this lifetime. As someone adopting an identity, I should have known that. As much as I am Tamara Rose Gordon, I could also have been Charmain Brown. Today I have other, new choices: I could run to my birth parents and ask them to become a new family. I could cling to my old family through distant relatives, although, like Chinese whispers, this may just give me mis-told stories, recipes that do not taste quite right, rituals that do not feel the same. Or I can just accept myself as me, the woman I have become – not other's names, the relinquished baby Charmain Brown or the chosen adopted daughter Tamara Gordon but just me: free of all these outside connections. Believe me I am grateful, and I know how incredibly fortunate I am, to have loved and lost with such intensity. But I also want to remember and embody what my adoption therapist once told me, 'Define yourself from the inside out, not the outside in.'

What has attachment meant for me? There has been love, connection and support as well as the fear and pain of loss. It has given and then it has taken away. Perhaps this is just the natural order of things, but with the lifetime's work of building the bonds of attachment I felt that I was not ready for the inevitable severance and separation.

As an adoptee I have raved against others taking charge of my destiny, and the lack of control I experienced as I was swapped from one family to another, from one identity to another. I became very busy trying to regain control, bind relationships and mend bridges. Now I am learning to let go, to have faith that in easing my attachment I will still be OK. I have spent a lifetime accumulating attachments to shape an identity and create my place in the world. Now I feel I am in the years of shedding: identities, roles, jobs, homes, possessions. How many people do this before death: strip away all external identities to learn to accept themselves, face themselves?

And one day soon I hope to see the whole journey, the attachment and the letting go as an interacted journey.

EDITORIAL DISCUSSION

Attachment and development are life-long processes: journeys 'from cradle to grave', often with many unpredictable potholes, crossroads and steep gradients along the way. Thus, everyone's life experiences are unique: yet there are often patterns discernable on closer study. It is inevitable that adoptees' experiences will create markedly different patterns from 'born to' children and there is much still to learn about their unique, yet shared, perceptions and thoughts. Experience-based knowledge is essential to our understanding of complex social phenomena and the experience base of adoptees, both children and adults, offers unrivalled insights into their innermost lives: from the 'inside out'.

The 'primal wound' of adoption (Verrier 1993) cuts deep into the psyche of adoptees: setting them on their life's journey, bearing the painful scars of loss (Levy and Orlans 2014), rejection and abandonment (Archer and Gordon 2006, 2013). This is still frequently overlooked in the enthusiasm of matching and placing infants and children in adoptive families: in the creation of new families (see also Chapter 5). Adopted children carry with them 'old scripts' (Archer and Gordon 2006) that drive their life narratives: even when their early histories seem straightforward and they are embraced wholeheartedly by their 'forever families'. The adoption experience is predicated on loss, beginning at the visceral level (Porges 1998): loss of the original mother–infant bond, loss of self-worth and self-identity (Levy and Orlans 2014), and the loss of blood links and a natural feeling of connection.

Attuned, caring parents create, through consistent, reliable 'holding on', the secure base (Bowlby 1988) from which they encourage their infants to explore and become independent, through timely and gradual 'letting go'. The dynamics and trauma of adoption, of losing and 'being let go', imprints an unconscious script of fear, of 'being let go' and 'being let down', that primes adoptees' expectations of further loss, abandonment and rejection. There is a tendency for adoptees to 'hold on too tight', push to be 'let go' prematurely, or 'let go' first, to avoid anticipated pain. The developmental process of 'letting go' becomes more complex when 'holding on' was interrupted 'the first time around', when the experiences of traumatic loss and abandonment have the most critical impact on developmental attachments (Archer and Gordon 2013; Levy and Orlans 2014; Perry 2009) and internal working models (Bowlby 1980). This premature 'letting go' interferes with the developmental-attachment process of moving from a secure base, through the exploration phase, towards individuation and autonomy; it is likely to affect adoptees' capacity for self-regulation, self-reliance, relationships, well-being and resilience (Levy and Orlans 2014).

It is important to recognise and respect the courage and tenacity of adoptees, as with all those who experience early attachment trauma, in 'hanging in there', in continuing to practise 'holding on' and 'letting go' through the lifecourse. This personal account provides an invaluable, insightful account of the 'drama of adoption' (Vaughan 2003). However, there is still a distance to travel for many social work practitioners and politicians in changing their 'positive' perceptions of adoption as 'happy solutions' (see Chapter 5) and identifying the possible 'blind spots' that provide them with a degree of insulation from the traumatic pain, fear, confusion or anger that many adoptees carry with them. Post-adoption support services for children and adults, such as Adoption UK, After Adoption Wales, Adapt Scotland and independent adoption services, for example Family Futures™, already perform a vital role in providing information, support and counselling alongside community forums (real and virtual) within which adoptees may gain a greater sense of 'belonging'. Such support systems must be made accessible to adoptees of all ages (and their families) as a priority. Across health and education service provision, acceptance of the implications of adoption for emotional health and widespread availability of appropriate services must also become the norm, rather than the exception as at present.

PART 6

CLOSING NARRATIVE

Expression and Exploration

Chapter 14

'AND IF YOU HAVE NO WORDS FOR IT?'

An Exploration of Attachment Issues through Art Psychotherapy

HELEN JURY

INTRODUCTION

Working through art psychotherapy with children who have issues of attachment, abandonment and emotional and psychological abuse can bring up many issues around how relationships function for both therapists and patients when confronting such a complex fabric of associations. In my experience, for children with attachment issues it is useful to work in the context of a secure base within their lives. This may mean working with them in their most familiar context: the home or the environs where they feel some sense of control over their circumstances (see also Chapters 7 and 8). Or it may mean working with them in a way that allows them to access a sense of a more secure part of the self within a safe environment. It may include working with other members of the family to broaden the understanding of any issues and problems facing the child at that point. However, working with innovative approaches and methods may at first feel awkward. Wilson (2005) talks of the 'discomfort' in trying something new and different but how this can also enable practitioners to develop new skills. He argues that if we are prepared to try out new, safe ways of practice then this may allow us to 'tap the creativity that may be resting in the child's mind if only we could make a move towards them' (p.92). I believe that this also requires a strong appreciation, belief and trust in the integrity of the child in context.

THE ART PSYCHOTHERAPY CONTEXT

> Art enables the object to be created in imagination, to be grieved, attached, separated from or transformed in a way that was impossible in the course of abusive or constrained development. (Holmes 2001, p.111)

The beginnings of engagement in art psychotherapy are a process during which the nature of working with the materials, combined with the newly emerging relationship with the art psychotherapist, establishes an area where the exploration of sometimes difficult, and often non-verbal, matter can be facilitated. It becomes a space where the child finds permission to question and sometimes discard old ways of being, to try out a new understanding of self and explore the more complex feelings that are difficult to voice, or express safely elsewhere. These emotions tried out, checked and named in a confidential and safe space can allow the child to better comprehend their capacity for attachment to others. What they have felt to be their more 'loathsome selves' can be safely explored and deposited with the art psychotherapist, through the art materials and the manner and process in the creation of the artwork.

By keeping safe these elements of discovery and the manner of their exposing, the art psychotherapist can then explore with the child the potent and emotionally charged vehicle of the artwork, while maintaining a safe boundary around the very concrete and actual feelings that the child may be experiencing at the time. This allows the art psychotherapist to develop with the child a sense of enhanced engagement, both for exploring any attachment issues, and to facilitate a deeper understanding of the child's inner world. As Holmes says:

> We discover who we are through our actions and artefacts. Initially, a parental presence is needed to shape the ability of the child to use first his body as an instrument and then to offer the tools of self-expression… Later an internal dialectic is created in that part of the self interacts with the medium of artistic expression, which, in turn, is scrutinized and shaped by a more reflective part of the self. (Holmes 2001, p.11)

Before working with Tommy, I made the conscious decision to base the work in his school. Having newly arrived in the area, it was not going to benefit Tommy to feel any further sense of estrangement from peers and the new surroundings he was trying his best to fit into. Being brought to another location for therapy would have significantly subtracted from his school day and marked him out as 'different'. Therefore, it was agreed with his class teacher that as soon as he became confident to do so he could make his own way to therapy. This would enable him to leave and re-join his class in a way that formed part of the routine timetable of classes and was less conspicuous.

TOMMY

Tommy was eight years old when he was placed in kinship care, and contact with his mother was restricted. The court order also stipulated that he should receive a creative and therapeutic intervention. The court concluded that Tommy's mum was not capable of understanding or meeting his needs. She was described as lacking in empathy, with impulsive and unpredictable behaviour traits, and unable to separate out her own needs from those of her child. Her own adolescence had been disturbed, with a diagnosis of personality disorder alongside undiagnosed psychological difficulties. His mum left home aged 16 to live in supported accommodation but elected to return shortly afterward.

At the time of the art psychotherapy sessions taking place, the impression formed by agencies involved with Tommy and his mum was that Tommy's mum was seeking to punish her parents, now Tommy's carers, through behaving in what was thought to be a manipulative and obstructive manner. Referring to the 'incoherent narrative' that can occur in families, Barratt and Harris (2005, p.146), discussing Dallos (1997, 2005), talk of the 'fragmented and incoherent' sense of the overview of life history that can result for the child as a consequence of the 'dominant discourse' being 'the adult discourse'. Here, stories can be presented as being both competing and at odds with one another. This, Dallos suggests, can be potentially frightening as well as being very destructive for the child. Certainly in Tommy's case, he expressed through the art materials confused fantasies that were chaotic and dramatic concerning stories of his life as he had experienced it in the past, and his recent transition, thereby demonstrating his understanding of the complex and bewildering worlds he was witnessing and felt himself to be involved in.

Background

Prior to the agreement to be placed in kinship care with his grandparents, Tommy had been in a closely monitored placement with them and they were in the process of filing for a Special Guardianship Order. Simultaneously, Tommy was struggling with strong negative emotions around betrayal, psychological abuse and the constant negation of his feelings from his mother. This was accompanied by the lack of a sense of his own identity and worth, due to a lack of any psychological patterns of a sense of self, which should have occured through care and nurturing, having been laid down in his early years.

Tommy's father had been in the army and served away from home and consequently Tommy had neither seen him frequently, nor spent any significant time with him during his formative early years. After the relationship between his parents had broken down, Tommy's father moved away and contact with him had been lost. However, Mum would at times suggest that not only was she in contact with Dad, but that he was in the room with her when she was on the phone to Tommy. Both these factors fuelled Tommy's heightened sense of abandonment and aroused feelings of insecurity and jealousy. He felt taunted by her apparent refusal to let him speak to his father, although it was doubtful that Dad was actually there. This feature was to be played out in the relationships in the art psychotherapy sessions, in a demonstration of a damaged sense of self on Tommy's part, as well as in his desperate, angry and humiliated sense of worthlessness. Inevitably, Tommy clung to those memories of his father that he did have with an anxious longing. He brought into one session a crumpled photograph, the only image he possessed of his father, which he now guarded fiercely and kept hidden in his bedroom. It was understood by both of us that I was privileged to have been shown it.

Tommy's low self-esteem and the psychological cruelty, emotional abuse and neglect he had suffered with his mother had contributed to leaving him academically and socially challenged, with a limited vocabulary for his age and speech delay. He had had little emotional and academic investment in his early years, with no sense of a secure base or a facilitating environment. When he began sessions of art psychotherapy, Tommy was extremely challenged linguistically and in his pronunciation. He often remained silent, lacking the language skills to articulate complex emotions and also, perhaps, not wishing to risk what might be a further sense of humiliation and lowering of his self-esteem. Fundamentally, however, he was a bright and naturally cheerful child – traits that developed over time as he came to feel more secure.

Stern talks of linking the intersubjective self to individuation, showing that 'by forming physical and sensory distinctions of self and other' (1985, p.125) the infant begins to develop and understand an essential sense of *the self*, as distinct from *the other*. This allows for an appreciation that others can hold a different awareness of the outside world to his own, which eventually allows for the possibility of relating to this individualised experience of the world that the other person possesses and demonstrates. The development of this intersubjective self, Stern argues, is a strong and innate desire on the part of the infant, giving him the potential to develop a sense of the presence of another person as a complete individual. It follows that the infant can then develop the social self in relation to another's experience, essential for survival in a social world. Ultimately, Stern argues, this assimilation allows for 'psychic intimacy', in addition to the infant's already integrated understanding of physical intimacy.

However, for this to happen, the infant needs to understand how this can be done from an early age; the quality of that sharing needing to be maintained and invested in, usually by the caregiver and those close to the child. In Tommy's case, he had had little or no understanding of such intersubjective experience in the caregiving he had received from his mother. Indeed, his experience of interaction with *the other* had been based upon pain, and a curtailment, or worse a wounding, of his feelings. Therefore, Tommy's way of demonstrating the nature of social relatedness in the art psychotherapy sessions was expressed in terms of fantasy: injuries, entrapment, and, to a lesser extent, being a saviour and defending the self and others from attack.

Tommy would often arrive for the session physically injured in playground tussles. At times the wound itself was not visible, but the wounded response on Tommy's part was all-preoccupying for him and would indicate his general overall feeling of pain and suffering, mixed with murderous feelings toward his apparent friend and aggressor. At such times, Tommy appeared vulnerable and very young. He would retreat into listlessness, hiding himself behind a barricade of art materials: paint bottles, a bag of clay and other objects, or peep out from behind his hands. At other times it was difficult for Tommy to distinguish between a sadistic response to a situation and the introjection of humiliated anger, which then became a self-inflicted and, at times, indulged sense of injustice and furious grievance, mixed with shame and self-pity. At such times risk may become a factor to be explored through the art materials and played out in the session.

Tommy needed to explore risk-taking to understand the potential for feeling safe and he would do this through complicated games with the art materials (small balls of clay, flickings of rolled-up paper, art tools), flicking these, or projecting them around the room – never enough to hurt either me or him, but always with calculation of the situation being precarious enough to *potentiate* harm, the 'what if…' Tommy needed to be able to safely externalise what it felt like to have risky feelings and experiment safely with these in a contained and safe environment. What if the ball of string twirled round hit him on the head? Or a flicked clay tool hit him – would he be hurt? Or would he be able to survive and recuperate? What would happen if I were to be hurt? Would I retaliate and hurt him in return, or would I be irreparably damaged, beyond repair? Would I be angry and punish him in revenge, as he had been used to? Would I reject him? Was this risk-taking dangerous, or proportioned to his feelings and his need to explore safely? At other times, the risk would be in arranging a precarious montage of materials and implements to see if they would balance. If so, then how, and for how long? This felt suggestive of the need to understand how far he could steady things and be in control of his own life balance – what the equable point of understanding of his situation may be, and, conversely, what the tolerable sense of collapse and its consequence may be.

Sometimes, however, Tommy needed to use the sessions simply to manifest his feelings of being embattled. At these times he did not explain his actions, use words, or wish to interact with me verbally, although he would listen carefully to any narration proffered and any suggestion of the significance of his activities. In short, Tommy demonstrated a sense of embattlement that he needed to explore and experiment with and that he had to survive to enable him to finally emerge as victorious and successful: a winner, a survivor, an individual with his own identity. By doing so, he would be able to begin to understand and introject a more positive experience of the self and of his own capabilities in supporting both loss and gain in feelings. As Stern says, 'the point is that intersubjectivity is...crucial for creating experiences of being with a mentally similar other and for furthering individuation and autonomy' (1985, p.127).

The Artwork in Practice

Tommy's use of the art materials was prolific and varied. At times he would produce several pieces of artwork in one session, not all of them possible to keep, as some were transient and incidental montages within the room through assemblages and positioning, much like installation work: temporary in actuality, but significant in the moment and important for the process that has led to that point.

When feeling most threatened, but also in need of exploring his feelings in a safe environment, barricades were built, behind which Tommy would hide: the bag of clay opened up tall and wide; the paint bottles ranged in a row with the clay tools ranged along the tops in the gaps between them, like guns or cannons on turrets ready to fire and defend the area behind. When these were placed facing outwards, I would check with Tommy whether he felt that he needed to defend himself against me as well. This was always denied, as well as the potentially murderous direction of the aim of his 'armoury', too, but it was evident that even the safest environment may hold dangers for him and he needed to understand his own ability to defend himself. However, a gap was always left in the barricade nearest to me, to enter – or escape. I would request permission to enter these barricaded areas and, while entry was always given and I was sometimes invited in, it was evident that this was not always easy for Tommy, as he would then feel vulnerable and evidently unsure as to whether or not allowing another person into his internalised space had breached his psychological defences. Through time and integration of the experience, this became more tolerable for him. At other times, Tommy talked about traps and secrets; these became his defence: wily systems were put in place in his bedroom, trapping those who entered – even the cat; he was ever ready *in case* an attack was imminent.

The longer we worked together, the more complicated it became for Tommy, as I came to represent the good parts of the self that he felt he needed, but as he was working entirely on a representation of self through the materials – a beleaguered self – he constantly needed to remain on the alert and well-defended in case an unexpected attack occurred from some quarter, especially one that he had felt that he had trusted. Occasionally a password was needed to enter the barricaded areas, which would then give me access inside the fortress to see the world from Tommy's point of view. Sometimes, having acknowledged that I did not know the password and having given it to me, Tommy would then say that he may change it. Rules were invented and changed at whim so that he could remain safe if necessary and anyone invited in, should they prove dangerous, could then be swiftly ejected. I was not to feel too secure, especially when he himself did not.

When, in one session, I suggested to him how vulnerable and under attack it may feel being on the other side of the barricade, Tommy at first grinned and nodded enthusiastically, but later invited me round to his side. I checked whether I had permission from him to be there, and he stated that I had. However, although it felt less exposed and safer on Tommy's side of the barrier, there were traps here, too, in case any enemies broke through: cut up straws covering the plastic animals contained a poison (harmless to animals but deadly to baddies) that would kill the invaders. The implements and art materials were ranged towards me even on this side and when I commented to Tommy that this might feel uncomfortable, he made no comment and I was left to understand that I could not enter the inner areas of his safe zone without him scrutinising me and being ready to defend himself once more against a possible surprise attack. Unconsciously, he needed me to know just how intolerably uncomfortable he felt both emotionally and psychologically, for much of the time.

After 40 sessions of working with Tommy, I was only considered safe to a certain extent, such was his need to remain highly defended. I commented to Tommy that his art structures felt very powerfully organised; it was evident that he did not feel powerful or in control. I suggested that he had set up a very safe and defended place over which he had control. Tommy held eye contact and studied my face, smiling when it was evident that the eye contact had lasted longer than was needed to simply read my expression. He then commented that he had been able to change phoning his mum from Monday to Friday, and that he had asked to see her only in the holidays. This was very significant for Tommy: he was now able to assert his own needs over his mother's demands, which he had never previously had the opportunity to do. This experience of being heard, witnessed, and having his needs understood and acted upon was for Tommy a confirmation of his usual sense of attack and embattlement. This needed to be acted upon for him to begin to trust and engage with future potential attachment opportunities and to feel that it was safe to invest in these.

Such violation of personal and significant attachments as Tommy had lived had made him very fearful of his own personal defences being breached. In ensuing sessions, when it emerged that Tommy's mother was suggesting that she was going to move away, Tommy closed the gaps in the wall of paint bottles with smaller items such as the glue-sticks, thereby preventing any further leakage of himself into the outer areas of the room or, conversely, of the area outside into his carefully constructed personal space. However, the baddies were inside in the form of wooden figures, alongside the goodies (animals) that were protected under bits of straws that Tommy now referred to as having 'an electric current running through them'. When I was invited inside, Tommy showed me how the baddies could be repulsed and ejected from the area by flicking them over the barricade with the clay tools.

As I talked to Tommy about the constancy of the art psychotherapy sessions, reiterating the purpose of them and how he could use them for himself, his aggressive destruction of the baddies changed and he stood them up to simply be blown over. At times, the animals would be sentinels. At other times they would live inside Tommy's fortified house. Tommy was so alert to needing to be defended that he could not appreciate the complexity of the psychological defences he was representing through the physical defences of the art materials. At one point when his social worker was changed without warning for the third time in a year, Tommy expressed consternation and an internalised sense of disturbance and insecurity by encasing in string all the assembled animals behind the fortress of paint bottles, telling me that it was 'wire to protect the animals from the baddies'. Tommy was once again feeling the sense of nameless, all-encompassing threat and instability. While he could not express for himself where this sense of danger may be located or where it may have originated, he was exploring being prepared for any possible attack and being prepared to create a safety zone where he and those he considered 'friends' were secure from 'baddies'.

COMMENTARY

Witnessing Tommy's interaction with the art materials could have felt overwhelming in the same way that Tommy was accustomed to feeling: foolish and stupid; impotent while being beholden to others. These were experiences so loaded with depressive, sullen loathing and anger that I would feel useless and a waste of space, just as he felt at times in the presence of his mother. Fish (2009), with reference to Jung, talks of 'Harm's Touch' and how what we are witnesses to in the therapy sessions can affect us adversely, potentially causing us to carry around and enact the traumatised feelings we are experiencing. As effective practitioners, we need to ask ourselves how our own understanding of attachment becomes affected, and to what extent those close to us also become unwitting recipients of these feelings, too. As art psychotherapists, to practise safely and to remain capable of sensitivity, empathy and good judgement, we have the possibility of calling upon the artist self (Allen cited in Fish 2009) to be able to process the more difficult and complex feelings that we sometimes find challenging to process in words.

At times, in the fullness of feeling created by complicated and undigested emotions and material resulting from a challenging session, I find myself turning to the art materials to produce artwork and work with the discovery and the experience of these feelings through the physical non-verbal actuality of art making. Both the process and the result I may not recognise either as me, or mine. However, I can understand that the value of the experience is about handling and making apparent the relationship with my patient. What can result is a manifestation of the dynamic attachment issues apparent in the engagement with my patient at that particular point in the therapeutic process. Calling for the therapist's self-care, Fish (2009) calls us 'intentional witnesses in our own work', urging us to continue to process our feelings, so as to benefit from both the clarity of an informed understanding of the patient, as well as to avoid the 'festering' of unprocessed material. This is especially important when working with the damaged sense of being that can be exhibited by children who have not been able to make secure attachments in family life.

As practitioners, we are able to process the unpalatable clinical work and the feelings it arouses. Wilson suggests that our connection with children and young people is not just about this engagement, but that it is aided by 'a sensitised connection with the context in which the meeting between client and therapist occurs', arguing that allowing ourselves the space and time to reflect enhances the potential of the work that subsequently takes place (2005, p.93). He suggests it is essential that as practitioners we are prepared to 'enter the playground of ideas and activities familiar to most children: art, music, play, pretence, storytelling, games and playful ritual' (p.94). Indeed, we cannot necessarily expect the children we work with to express themselves and their burdened feelings non-verbally through the art materials and the art-making process if we do not actively keep in touch ourselves with the process, and what can result from it.

On occasions, when working with Tommy alongside informed and explorative supervision, this process was especially important to guard against becoming subsumed by his feelings of shame and worthlessness; of not feeling loved or wanted, of potentially losing a sense of proportion of my own internalised sense of good attachment models. In relation to the process of using the artwork Holmes writes:

> Art enables the object to be created in imagination, to be grieved, attacked, separated from or transformed in a way that was impossible in the course of abusive or constrained development. (Holmes 2001)

The child faced with a mother who cannot reciprocate feelings has little or no opportunity to internalise a positive interpersonal experience as takes place in the maternal gaze (Hart 2012, p.150). In the case of Tommy, he had had no validation of a positive sense of self through mirrored response from his mother. Without this, Green (cited in Hart 2012) suggests that the experience of the emptiness of this relationship can be devastating and 'carries in its wake, beside the loss of love, the loss of meaning'. Without such meaning, this experience can only be replaced by a punishing object. Such was the case for Tommy who, early on in our work together, felt very little sense of self-worth, manifesting this through his artwork in which he wrote phrases too painful to vocalise, such as, 'I have no brain.' At other times, the clay artwork that Tommy produced appeared to represent an un-nourishing breast: flattened, rounded shapes that he would flip and flop from hand to hand, the wet thwack dull and unresponsive, there being no volume or body to the forms however much he kneaded or shaped them, like an infant searching for sustenance from the breast and finding none. Ambivalence in his maternal relationship was evident and without any nurturing connection with the mother figure, there was a destructive void inside him leaving him feeling emptied out and unnourished – a truly terrifying state. Conversely, to allow the maternal figure to enter inside him, or for him to be able to feed upon what it offered, was to potentially ingest something that might destroy him from the inside. In this way, his ambivalence about allowing me to enter into his barricaded areas can be further understood. As Holmes says when considering the therapeutic process of artwork:

> Art in therapy can help the discovery and strengthening of the sense of self. Art is always communicative…it is always an attempt to get in touch with the self, through an external medium. That in its origins requires the presence of another. The artist is attached to his artefact as though it were a person, but can play and experiment with a relationship that both has a life of its own and is completely under his control. (Holmes 2001, p.111)

Hart (2012, p.150) also suggests: 'Children who have never had the experience of being heard and responded to, may find it both easier and safer to project a persona that doesn't care, rather than risk forming an attachment.' Initially, Tommy was such a child. Confused, wretchedly bewildered and hurt by a mother whom he had never been able to internalise as a good object that would nourish his needs: who was at times unresponsive, at others absent, and sometimes actively withholding of love and any sense of affection, Tommy's response in art psychotherapy was to physically represent his feelings by protecting himself from his symbolic sense of unbearable emptiness, pain and bewilderment by physically barricading himself in behind the art materials. From here he could attack the enemy, apparently unfeelingly, demonstrating his feelings through the materials and simultaneously using the safe space to attack any sense of attachment to me in a quasi-maternal role.

My role was to hold his experience for him and to contain his painful feelings of rejection, at the same time as allowing him to explore a new – and for him potentially overwhelmingly risky – feeling of positive attachment to his kinship carers. He was filled with unconscious doubts about whether he was both worthy of the care they could offer and whether they would continue to care for him, as he needed to be cared for, if he was so lacking. As Holmes continues:

> Through looking at himself, with the help of a therapist…a patient may understand preoccupations previously hidden from his conscious understanding…and feel a strengthened sense of worth and self-esteem as his creativity becomes more accessible…the very act of artistic production creates the container for feelings that may have been lacking in childhood and puts the patient into a state of relatedness to himself and the world that may have been stunted in the traumatic environment in which he grew up. (Holmes 2001, p.111)

Through the two years of weekly art psychotherapy, Tommy was able to lodge his uncomfortable feelings of anger, emptiness and despair in me via his exploration of his feelings through the artwork. He was able to consider a meaningful interpretation of his relationship and its potential with his grandmother, with whom he formed a strong attachment, and who had also been consistent in representing his needs and understanding the possible negative implications of his early experiences. Constancy of sessions, and maintaining the space and boundaries, were for this reason all-important to a process of reparation for Tommy, to allow him the opportunity to begin to understand more completely the nature of interpersonal and intersubjective relationships and to appreciate a healthy and positive sense of subject and object, eventually allowing him to assimilate a strong sense of reparative attachment to his new family and environment.

EDITORIAL DISCUSSION

A major theme running throughout the book has been the emphasis on creating safe space, a secure base, for children, caregivers and families: enabling them to explore new concepts and conceive and effect positive change. Yet providing this 'holding environment', within which individuals can explore their deepest fears and express their sometimes terrifying feelings, can feel extremely challenging. The theoretical constructs of attachment provide the secure foundations from which practitioners can garner knowledge, confidence and trust in themselves to build, in conjunction with children and/or adults, a framework for communication through shared experience. Likewise, professional supervision and shared safe space within the Attachment Network Wales,[1] based on developmental attachment principles, can offer confirmation and essential support when confidence or new ideas flag.

The experience of being seen and heard, of having their actions and feelings contained and reflected back to them, enables babies and young children to gain a more complete sense of self and others and trust in their environment, both physical and social. Conversely, children who have been repeatedly exposed to abandonment, loss, abuse and neglect (emotional and/or physical), serious illness, medical interventions or unavoidable protracted separations, internalise that the world is not safe, that they live under constant threat; they lack

---

1   The Attachment Network Wales (ANW) is a network of professionals and individuals based in Wales with an interest in attachment-based issues. ANW works to promote understanding of the importance of attachment in bringing about better outcomes for children, young people, adults and families, through practice exchange sessions, training, research, lobbying and the raising of knowledge and awareness in both policy and practice.

self-regulation, self-awareness and self-belief and have little or no sense of belonging.

In Chapters 1 and 7 these issues are discussed in terms of the underlying neurobiology: the development of the 'triune brain' and the neurobiological 'networks' that are moulded according to experience, especially in children's earliest years. The concept of 'bottom-up' development is introduced to explain the 'whole-systems' disruption that occurs following early traumatic experiences: in particular to the sequential 'coming on line' of specific, influential brain areas in the 'middle layer' (limbic areas) of the triune brain. Having 'no words for it' is a fundamental characteristic of early adversity, especially intrapersonal adversity. The 'dance of attunement and attachment' (see Chapter 1) is founded on repeated dyadic interactions between caregivers and infants within which infants find themselves reflected in caregivers' facial expressions, prosody, gestures and timely, consonant responses (Trevarthen 2001).

Paucity of caregiving leaves children feeling 'unseen' and 'unheard', without having had their sensory and emotional feelings acknowledged or contained (Roth 2010). Their arousal levels remain high and their survival responses primed for action (fight, flight or freeze). Early adversity is pre-verbal and remains non-verbal unless caregivers are able, through sensitive reflection, to provide children with 'the words to say it' and, through consistent co-regulation, the means to 'work it out' (Siegel 2010). In recent years the concept of reflection has been validated by the identification of 'mirror neurons' (Iacoboni *et al.* 2005; Rizzolatti *et al.* 2001), through which humans create 'mirrored sensori-emotional feelings' within themselves and learn to 'read' others' facial expressions and intentions (Iacoboni *et al.* 2005). This ability allows them to empathise and modify their own feelings and responses appropriately (Siegel 2007). Interestingly, brain-imaging studies indicate that a significant linguistic area (Broca's) is activated during observation of others' gestures, suggesting direct links to the mirror neuron system (MNS; Nishitani and Hari 2000). Hence poor early caregiving becomes inextricably linked to a weakened ability to articulate sensory and emotional input from outside and inside (visceral or 'gut' feelings). Moreover, poor sensory experiences, particularly of movement, involving the vestibular system (see Chapter 7) and through eye contact and facial expression (Baron-Cohen 1999) are known to lead to poor facial muscle control in young children, affecting their ability to produce speech with clarity (dysarthia) and fluency (Archer and Gordon 2013; see also Chapter 7).

However, children have an indomitable capacity to 'show and tell' (Archer and Gordon 2013; Bombèr 2007): to communicate through their behaviour, their play, and artistic expression, their innermost needs and fears *if* we are prepared to observe and 'decipher' their non-verbal communications. Tommy slowly began to learn to use the safe space he shared with the therapist to enact and play out his traumatic experiences of maternal abuse and neglect and paternal abandonment. Very gradually he began to let go of his survival-based defences and make eye contact with the therapist. While Tommy continued to deny the therapist's reflections on his actions, and hence his feelings, it appears that they were being 'taken on board': hence they could influence his future perceptions and responses. This principle, of reflecting back what they perceive, is invaluable for caregivers. Rather than asking their children how they feel, what happened, or 'why they did what they did', caregivers can learn to infer this from previous experience and what they are being shown (via their MNS), and develop the confidence to provide sensitive feedback. 'Best guessing' can become 'best practice' in giving children awareness and the ability to connect the past with the present, their feelings, perceptions and cognitions with their actions, thus creating a more coherent narrative and greater attachment security.

GLOSSARY

Terms appearing in italics appear in the Glossary in their own right.

ADHD Attention deficit hyperactivity disorder, a medical term describing a cluster of symptoms: primarily poor attention and impulsive and over-active behaviour. Diagnosis of ADHD is contra-indicated where there is history of childhood *trauma*.

Adrenalin Neurochemical messenger (neurotransmitter) produced by adrenal glands in response to *stress*, preparing individual for fight or flight.

Amygdala Area of *limbic system* essential for processing emotion, including pre and non-verbal memories. Develops more dynamically in right hemisphere than in left.

Arousal Physiological, emotional and psychological functions involving vigilance and readiness to respond to internal and external environment. Includes activation of *brainstem, ANS* and endocrine systems to transmit information to *limbic* and *neo-cortical* areas, promoting appropriate responses and returning body systems to equilibrium (*regulation*).

Asperger's syndrome Disorder on autistic spectrum; individuals can be very 'high-functioning' yet still have socio-emotional deficits.

Attachment Enduring shared relationship created between two individuals. Since human infants are unable to care for themselves, attachment facilitates physical survival. It is the matrix for emotional, social and intellectual development, leading to health, resilience and well-being.

Attachment-trauma Impact of early adversity, such as distressed or disrupted intra-familial relationships, affecting *attachment* and neurobiological development.

Attunement Harmonising process of getting in touch (in synch) with another's sensations, rhythms and feelings and resonating or empathising with them.

Autistic spectrum disorder (ASD) Neurobiologically based grouping of disorders characterised by poor sensory integration, social awareness and 'mindreading' capacities (also referred to as autistic spectrum conditions (ASC)).

Autonomic nervous system (ANS) Part of nervous system; consists of network of glands producing neuro-hormones responsible for involuntary responses e.g. *fight, flight or freeze.* Characterised in traumatised children by high *arousal* and/or low arousal.

Brainstem Developmentally one of the 'oldest' parts of the brain, regulating basic bodily functions such as heart rate, respiration, body temperature, sleep and elimination (beneath consciousness). Forms the 'bottom layer' of *triune brain.*

Central nervous system (CNS) System of neurons and *neural networks* creating links to all areas of the brain and body.

Circle of Attachment Attuned parenting construct: within that caregiver provides *secure base* from that child can explore the world: watching over, supporting, encouraging and taking delight in child's actions and discoveries. Subsequently, child is welcomed back to a secure haven, feeling protected, comforted, 'felt and understood'.

Circle of Security Visual explanation of *attachment* used as part of evidence-based group intervention for caregivers and their children. It is designed to help caregivers understand their own past and their children's communications to develop more attuned parenting patterns.

Coherent narrative Explicit memories (stored in *hippocampus*) that can be accessed, recalled and interpreted in a consistent, sequential, organised manner, creating a meaningful 'self-story'.

Co-regulation Essential developmental process within that infants' *arousal*, sensations and emotions are modulated by primary caregivers. Facilitates infants' capacity for *self-regulation* and thus healthy physical and emotional development.

Cortisol Neuro-hormone allowing individuals to respond to *stress*, including immune functions. In moderation cortisol releases energy within the body and promotes healing. Excess cortisol due to *toxic/chronic stress* leads to the destruction of specific brain areas, nerve cells and connections and compromises long-term health and well-being.

Dance of attachment (attunement) Active, synchronous inter-relationship between parent and child, providing essential security and containment and creating reciprocity and mutual feedback.

Developmental trauma disorder (DTD) Diagnosis proposed by van der Kolk (2005) to define more accurately the altered neurobiology and constellation of symptoms resulting from early *attachment-trauma* and to develop more focused therapeutic interventions.

Disorganised attachment patterns Dysfunctional *attachment* patterns, normally resulting from early childhood maltreatment, that adversely affect developmental neurobiology and interfere with individuals' capacity to form healthy relationships based on security, predictability and trust. Typified by states of high/low *arousal*, poor ability to *self-regulate*, and inability to use caregivers for *co-regulation*. There is a high correlation between disorganised attachment patterns in childhood and serious adult mental health problems.

Dissociation Adaptive survival response maintaining separation between senses, emotions, awareness, behaviour and memories; occurs on a continuum and can be partial or total. Affects sense of self and can inhibit learning, through temporary loss of awareness and inability to integrate experiences.

Dopamine 'Feel good' neurotransmitter enhancing glucose uptake, thus stimulating neural growth in the *prefrontal cortex (PFC)*. Contributes to the maturation of *neo-cortical* 'top-down' controls, positive expectations, resilience and well-being.

Dysregulation Disturbance in ability to monitor and modulate neurobiological arousal and feelings. Highly correlated with poor early caregiving and ongoing socio-emotional difficulties.

Emotional lability Prone to constantly changing emotional states and mood swings.

Emotional literacy Capacity to identify, 'read' and make sense of one's own emotions and identify, 'read' and make sense of others' emotional world.

Empathy Ability to 'get in tune with', or share, another's sensations, emotions, thoughts or needs. Requires *emotional literacy* and involves *mirror neuron system (MNS)*.

Executive function Acquisition of ability to evaluate situations, plan, organise and execute actions appropriately. Essential to optimum learning, relationships and well-being.

Fight, flight or freeze response Primitive survival mechanism available in response to perceived threat. Limbic areas override reasoned neo-cortical responses (see Figure I.1) to prioritise movement (root of term limbic = 'limb'; emotion = moving outwards).

Good enough parenting Winnicott (1958) introduced this concept to describe the pattern of predictable, attuned caregiving that conferred on children a sense of security, trust, self-awareness and self-worth.

Hippocampus Area of limbic brain involved with verbal memory formation, storage and retrieval and hence *coherent narratives*. Greater development occurs in left hemisphere of brain; comes 'on line' at three years plus. Adversely affected by excess *cortisol* secretion.

Hypervigilance A state of heightened awareness, being constantly alert to potential threats, acting as if in imminent danger – even where no threat exists.

Internal working models (IWMs) Internalised 'road maps' of self, others and 'how they work', affecting future perceptions, expectations and responses.

Life story book Small, personalised book, usually prepared by social workers, providing factual information for children who have been, or are being, adopted. Ideally should be prepared prior to placement and is intended to provide a brief explanation of their lives to date, to help children make sense of their lives and the decisions taken about them. May be prepared as part of life story work with children.

Life (story) work Direct work with child, through expressive therapies, for example, play, art and drama, relating to the child's early experiences (both positive and negative), alongside age-appropriate discussion of their meaning in terms of current feelings and perceptions. Should actively involve current caregivers. May or may not include preparation of life story books.

Limbic system Areas of *triune brain* associated with *attachment*, emotional connections, motivation and memory (both non-verbal and verbal).

Metacognition Awareness and understanding one's own thinking and cognitive processes; the ability to, and activity of, 'thinking about thinking'.

Mind-sharing Provides reciprocity and co-regulation (Siegel 2007), encouraging children to feel 'the same as' rather than 'different from' and hence unacceptable and 'not-belonging'. Only when 'me-and-you-togetherness', developmentally appropriate dependence and OP are firmly established can safe exploration of separateness, separation and independence begin.

Mirroring Act of attuning to, and reflecting back, another's sensations, emotions or thoughts. In doing so, parents provide awareness and insights for their children that enable them to make sense of themselves and others. Now identified as involving *MNS*.

Mirror neuron system (MNS) Neural circuits playing a major role in imitation, predicting and understanding others' actions, empathy and acquisition of new skills. Traumatised individuals tend to 'misread' vital actions, gestures and visual cues, and hence respond inappropriately.

Motherese Form of language instinctively adopted by *good enough* caregivers to communicate with their babies – using distinctive pitch, sounds, patterns and rhythms (prosody).

Neo-cortex Most recently evolved area of brain that enables mature reflection, social communication, language development, 'top-down' controls, decision making and inter-personal negotiation.

Neural networks Complex connections between neurons (nerve cells) of brain and body that are organised developmentally according to experience.

Neuro-biochemicals Chemical 'messengers' carrying information around the brain and nervous system (both *CNS* and *ANS*).

Neurobiological Relating to the structure and function of the brain and nervous system.

Neuro-development Sequential formation and inter-connection of nervous systems and brain according to experience: with developmental 'windows' providing opportunities for optimal maturing and healthy development.

Neuro-hormones Neuro-biochemicals carrying information within the brain and nervous system.

Neuro-physiological Relating to the functioning of the nervous systems, rather than to their structure.

Neuro-plasticity Ability of neural networks to create new connections and, at least in part, 'fill in the gaps' in terms of physical, emotional, social and intellectual functioning. Most effective in early years but remaining possible throughout the lifetime.

Neurotypical Cartwright and Morgan (2008) use this term (rather than 'normal') to remind readers that children with *ASD* have neurobiological difficulties; we use it for the same reasons to distinguish between 'normal' children and those who have experienced *attachment-trauma*.

Object Constancy (OC) Expands the development of permanence so that people and objects are perceived as fundamentally the same through numerous variations, such as expression, emotion, position or shape. Permits an integrated perception of self; its absence leads to continuing *dissociation* of behavioural and feeling states.

Object Permanence (OP) Plays a major part in establishing a *secure base*. Acquisition allows infants to learn that they, and others, persist through time and space: that their attachment figures are 'there for them', even when temporarily absent, and can 'hold them in mind' during separations.

Oxytocin 'Altruistic' neuro-hormone. Promotes caregiving in mothers, bonding between individuals, pleasurable feelings and well-being.

Prefrontal cortex (PFC) Provides vital neurobiological connections between the *brainstem* and *limbic* areas and the *neo-cortex*, or 'thinking brain'. Facilitates cognitive competence, top-down controls and executive functioning.

Primary caregiver Child's main source of physical and psychological security; main *attachment* figure.

Proprioception The unconscious sense of body position and motion from skeletal, connective tissues and muscle neuro-receptors. Alongside *vestibular system* (see separate entry), proprioception is the primary organiser of the nervous system, arousal and movement and hence self-awareness.

Psychologically held Children's sense of 'being held in mind' confers on them a comforting sense of security, safe containment and self-confidence as they explore their environment (see also *Object Permanence (OP)*).

Regulation Ability to monitor, sustain, or return to 'normal' comfortable levels of physical, emotional and cognitive *arousal*. Infants and young children are unable to *self-regulate* and depend on primary caregivers to help them develop self-regulation through repeated, consistent *co-regulation*. Development is from the bottom up – leading to top-down *neo-cortical* control.

Relationship-based social work Model of social work starting from the position that human behaviour and professional relationships are part of any intervention and so practice must be inclusive, collaborative and respectful.

Secondary trauma The impact on body, brain and mind of caring for a traumatised individual (see also Chapter 2).

Secure base Primary *attachment* figure to whom infant can turn for reassurance, warmth, comfort and safety at times of anxiety: allowing them to explore their environment with confidence.

Sensori-motor Sensations, perceptions and responses relating to the body and/or movement.

Serotonin 'Feel good' neuro-messenger (neurotransmitter). Excess *cortisol* (due to stress) reduces serotonin levels that in turn is associated with aggressive behaviour and/or depression.

Shame-rage Unconscious survival response created in early life to limit overwhelming sense of helplessness and hopelessness. The 'normal' *neurophysiological* response of 'shame socialisation' is experienced as temporary loss of connection to significant others that is swiftly repaired. Without immediate repair or resulting from repeated humiliation, criticism, abuse or neglect, shame is experienced as an existential threat and externalised (in anger and blaming others).

Social engagement system (SES) Provides flexibility in communication and regulates areas of the body used in social interactions, for example, facial, middle ear and pharyngeal, head and neck muscles. The mature, adaptive response of SES facilitates rapid alteration of heart rate and allows swift engagement with the environment and in social relationships.

Somato-sensory Relating to physical (somatic) sensations.

Stress The demands and pressures of daily living are essential to healthy life. Healthy individuals have the capacity to 'bounce back' (resilience), to get back in balance, once the immediate stress recedes or is dealt with. However, excessive or chronic stress overwhelms the system and makes recovery problematic: stress responses become normalised (*trauma-normal*) and have long-term health implications.

Toxic stressors Can be chemical, for example, tobacco, alcohol, toxic metals, adverse events, for example, hospitalisation, or inter-personal, for example, abuse, neglect, loss of, or breaks in, significant relationships.

Transitional object Familiar, tangible item (such as teddy) representing the caregiver and providing sense of security and comfort to child during periods of anxiety and/or separation.

Trauma An injury to body, brain or mind due to excessive *stress*. The lasting distress of abandonment, loss, maltreatment and lack of 'containment' of affect in the early years adversely affects neurobiological development and hence ongoing perceptions, responses and relationships. Leads to persistent feelings of terror, panic, loss of control, powerlessness, anger and/or numbing.

Trauma-normal Describes individuals whose neurobiology is geared to anticipate and react to perceived threat (see *stress* above).

Trigger Sensation/Perception or event setting off a pattern of (inappropriate) responses, beneath awareness, derived from previous traumatic experiences. Involves *limbic* areas and *ANS fight, flight or freeze* reactions.

Triune brain Simplified conceptualisation introduced to highlight the bottom-up evolution of the brain from *brainstem*, to *limbic* areas, to *neocortex*, culminating in top-down *regulation*.

Vestibular system Located within the inner ear it provides information about the position of the body in space, controls the sense of balance and is involved in auditory and visual functions.

Vestibular system functioning Flow of information from neuro-receptors within *vestibular system* concerning the body's gravitational relationship to the earth, informing bodily responses – including *neurobiological* arousal and movement. Primes entire nervous system functioning. (See also *proprioception*.)

REFERENCES

Ainsworth, M.D. and Bell, S.M. (1970) 'Attachment, exploration and separation: Illustrated by the behaviour of one-year-olds in a strange situation.' *Child Development 41*, 1, 49–67.

Ainsworth, M.D.S., Blehar, M.C., Waters, E. and Wall, S. (1978) *Patterns of Attachment: A Psychological Study of the Strange Situation.* Hillsdale, NJ: Erlbaum.

Ahmond, A. and Betts, B. (2003) *My Life Story CD-ROM.* Northampton: Loggerhead Publishing Ltd.

Archer, C. (1999) *Parenting the Child Who Hurts: Tiddlers and Toddlers.* London: Jessica Kingsley Publishers.

Archer, C. (2003) 'Weft and Warp: Developmental Impact of Trauma and Implications for Healing.' In C. Archer and A. Burnell (eds) *Trauma, Attachment and Family Permanence: Fear Can Stop You Loving.* London: Jessica Kingsley Publishers.

Archer, C. and Burnell, A. (eds) (2003) *Trauma, Attachment and Family Permanence: Fear Can Stop You Loving.* London: Jessica Kingsley Publishers.

Archer, C. and Gordon, C. (2006) *New Families, Old Scripts.* London: Jessica Kingsley Publishers.

Archer, C. and Gordon, C. (2013) *Reparenting the Child Who Hurts.* London: Jessica Kingsley Publishers.

Axline, V. (1947) 'Play Therapy.' New York, NY: Ballantine Books.

Axline, V. (1964) *Dibs: In Search of Self.* New York, NY: Penguin Books.

BAPT (2014) 'Play Therapy.' Available at www.bapt.info/play-therapy, accessed on 20 February 2014.

Barnes, A. (2007) 'Integrative work with children in long-term placements.' *British Journal of Play Therapy 3*, 40–51.

Baron-Cohen, S. (1999) *Mindblindness: An Essay in Autism and Theory of Mind.* London: A Bradford Book, MIT Press.

Barratt, S. and Harris, R. (2005) 'The Changing Context of Permanency.' In A. Vetere and E. Dowling (eds) *Narrative Therapies with Children and Their Families: A Practitioner's Guide to Concepts and Approaches.* Hove: Routledge

Bentovim, A. (2011) *Trauma-Organized Systems: Physical and Sexual Abuse in Families (The Systemic Thinking and Practice Series).* London: Karnac Books.

Bifulco, A., Jacobs, C. Bunn, A., Thomas, G. and Irving, K. (2008) 'The Attachment Style Interview (ASI). A support-based adult assessment tool for adoption and fostering practice.' *Adoption and Fostering 32*, 3, 33–45.

Bombèr, L.M. (2007) *Inside I'm Hurting.* London: Worth Publishing Ltd.

Bombèr, L.M. (2011) *Inclusive Strategies to Support Pupils with Attachment Difficulties Make It through the School Day.* London: Worth Publishing Ltd.

Bonin, E.M., Beecham, J., Dance, C. and Farmer, E. (2014) 'Support for adoption placements: The first six months.' *British Journal of Social Work 44*, 6,1508–1525.

Booth, P. and Jernberg, A. (2010) *Theraplay: Helping Parents and Children Build Better Relationships through Attachment-Based Play* (Third edition). San Francisco, CA: Jossey-Bass.

Booth, P. and Lindaman, S. (2000) 'Theraplay for Enhancing Attachment in Adopted Children.' In C.E. Schaefer and H.G. Kaduson (eds) *Short-Term Play Therapy for Children.* New York, NY: Guildford Publications.

Bowlby, J. (1944) 'Forty-four juvenile thieves: Their characters and home-life.' *Journal of Psychoanalysis 25,* 19–52, 107–127.

Bowlby, J. (1951) *Maternal Care and Mental Health.* Geneva: World Health Organisation Monograph, Series 2.

Bowlby, J. (1953) *Child Care and the Growth of Love*. London: Penguin Books.

Bowlby, J. (1958) 'The nature of the child's tie to his mother.' *International Journal of Psycho-Analysis* 39, 350–373.

Bowlby, J. (1969) *Attachment and Loss: Volume 1. Attachment*. London: Pimlico.

Bowlby, J. (1973) *Attachment and Loss: Volume 2. Separation: Anger and Anxiety*. London: Pimlico.

Bowlby, J. (1980) *Attachment and Loss: Volume 3. Loss: Sadness and Depression*. London: Pimlico.

Bowlby, J. (1988) *A Secure Base*. London: Routledge.

Boyse, K. (2007) *Pain and Your Infant*. University of Michigan Health System. Available at www.med. umich.edu/yourchild/topics/paininf.htm, accessed on 7 January 2015.

Bratton, S., Ray, D., Rhine, T. and Jones, L. (2005) 'The efficacy of play therapy with children: A meta-analytic review of the outcome research.' *Professional Psychology: Research and Practice 36*, 4, 376–390.

Brisch, K.H. (2004) *Treating Attachment Disorders: From Theory to Therapy*. London: Guilford Press.

Bromberg, P.M. (2011) *Shadow of the Tsunami: And the Growth of the Relational Mind*. London: Routledge.

Carr, A. (2009) 'The effectiveness of family therapy and systemic interventions for child-focused problems.' *Journal of Family Therapy 31*, 1, 3–45.

Carr, L., Iacoboni, M., Dubeau, M-C., Maziotta, J. and Lenzi, G.L. (2003) 'Neural mechanisms of empathy in humans: A relay from neural systems for imitation to limbic areas.' *Proceedings of the National Academy of Sciences 100*, 9, 5497–5502.

Cartwright, A. and Morgan, J. (2008) *The Teaching Assistant's Guide to Autistic Spectrum Disorders*. London: Continuum International Publishing Group.

Clark, C. and Dugdale, G. (2008) *Literacy Changes Lives*. London: National Literacy Trust.

Cline, F. (1992) *Hope for High Risk and Rage Filled Children*. Evergreen, CO: EC Publications.

Creeden, K. (2005) 'Trauma and Neurobiology: Considerations for the Treatment of Sexual Behavior Problems in Children and Adolescents.' In R. Longo and D. Prescott (eds) *Current Perspectives: Working with Sexually Aggressive Youth and Youth with Sexual Behavior Problems*. Holyoke, MA: NEARI Press.

Crittenden, P.M. (2005) 'Attachment and Early Intervention.' Keynote Address, German Association of Infant Mental Health (GAIMH), Hamburg, Germany.

Crittenden, P.M. (2006) 'A dynamic-maturational model of attachment.' *Australian and New Zealand Journal of Family Therapy 27*, 2, 105–115.

Crittenden, P. (2008) *Raising Parents: Attachment, Parenting and Child Safety*. London: Routledge.

Crittenden, P. (2010) 'The Importance of Attachment Theory for Children's Social Workers.' In J. Cooper (ed.) *Child Safeguarding, Children, Family support. Community Care*. Available at www. communitycare.co.uk/2010/11/29/the-importance-of-attachment-theory-for-childrens-social-workers, accessed on 13 January 2014.

Crittenden, P. (2014) *Overview: Courses, Assessments, Training, Research and Coding*. Available at www. familyrelationsinstitute.org/include/overview.htm, accessed on 26 October 2014.

Crittenden, P., Kozlowska, K. and Landini, A. (2010) 'Assessing attachment in school-age children.' *Clinical Child Psychology and Psychiatry 15*, 185.

Cook, A., Spinazzola, J., Ford, J., Lanktree, C. *et al.* (2005) 'Complex trauma in children and adolescents.' *Psychiatric Annals 35*, 5, 390–398.

Czarnecki, M.L., Turner, H.N., Collins, P.M., Doellman, D., Wrona, S. and Reynolds, J. (2011) 'Procedural pain management: A position statement with clinical practice recommendations.' *American Society for Pain Management Nursing 12*, 2, 95–111.

D'Andrea, W., Ford, J., Spinazzola, J. and van der Kolk, B.A. (2012) 'Understanding interpersonal trauma in children: Why we need a developmentally appropriate trauma diagnosis.' *American Journal of Orthopsychiatry 82*, 2, 187–200.

Dallos, R. (1997) *Interacting Stories, Narratives, Family Beliefs, and Therapy*. London: Karnac Books.

Dallos, R. (2005) 'Narratives of Young Offenders'. In A. Vetere and E. Dowling (eds) *Narrative Therapies with Children and Their Families: A Practitioner's Guide to Concepts and Approaches*. Hove, NY: Routledge.

Damasio, A. (2010) *Self Comes to Mind: Constructing the Conscious Brain*. London: Heinemann.

DeGangi, G.A. (2000) *Pediatric Disorders of Regulation in Affect and Behavior: A Therapist's Guide to Assessment and Treatment*. (Practical Resources for the Mental Health Professional.) London: Academic Press.

DeGangi, G.A. (2012) *The Dysregulated Adult: Integrated Treatment Approaches.* London: Academic Press.

Erikson, E. (1963) *Childhood and Society (Second edition).* New York, NY: Norton.

ESTYN (2006) *Behaviour in Wales: Good Practice in Managing Challenging Behaviour.* Available at www.estyn.gov.uk/english/docViewer1172126.5, accessed on 19 June 2014.

Fahlberg, V. (1994) *A Child's Journey through Placement.* London: BAAF Publications.

Family Futures (2014) *Day in the Life Form.* Available at www.familyfutures.co.uk/child-assessment, accessed on 4 March 2014.

Field, T. (2004) *Touch and Massage in Early Childhood.* Miami, FL: Johnson and Johnson Pediatric Institute L.L.C.

Finlay, L. and Gough, B. (2003) *Reflexivity: A Practical Guide for Researchers in Health and Social Sciences.* Oxford: Blackwell Publishing.

Fish, B. (2009) 'Harm's Touch: The Gifts and Costs of What We Witness.' American Art Therapy Association Conference, Dallas, Texas.

Ford, J.D., Grasso, D., Greene, C., Levine, J., Spinazzola, J. and van der Kolk, B. (2013) 'Clinical significance of a proposed developmental trauma disorder diagnosis: Results of an international survey of clinicians.' *Journal of Clinical Psychiatry 74,* 8, 841–849.

Franzblau, S.H. (2002) 'Deconstructing Attachment Theory: Naturalising the Politics of Motherhood.' In M.R. Dunlop and J.C. Chrisler (eds) *Charting a New Course for Feminist Psychology.* Santa Barbara, CA: Praeger Press.

Gaskill, R.L. and Perry, B.D. (2012) 'Child Sexual Abuse, Traumatic Experiences and Their Effect on the Developing Brain.' In P. Goodyear-Brown (ed.) *Handbook of Child Sexual Abuse: Identification, Assessment and Treatment.* New York, NY: Wiley.

Geddes, H. (2006) *Attachment in the Classroom.* London: Worth Publishing Ltd.

George, C. and Solomon, J. (1999) 'Attachment and Caregiving: The Caregiving Behavioural System.' In J. Cassidy and P. Shaver (eds) *Handbook of Attachment: Theory, Research and Clinical Applications.* New York, NY: Guilford Press.

George, E., Iveson, C. and Ratner, H. (2012) *Solution-Focused Brief Therapy: 100 Key Points and Techniques.* Hove, NY: Routledge.

George, C., Kaplan, N. and Main, M. (1985) *Adult Attachment Interview (Second edition).* (Unpublished manuscript.) Berkeley, CA: University of California.

Gerhardt, S. (2004) *Why Love Matters: How Affection Shapes a Baby's Brain.* Howe, NY: Routledge

Gil, E. (1991) *The Healing Power of Play. Working with Abused Children.* New York, NY: Guilford Publications.

Gitau, R., Menson, E., Pickles, V., Fisk, N.M., Glover, V. and MacLachlan, N. (2001) 'Umbilical cortisol levels as an indicator of the fetal stress response to assisted vaginal delivery.' *European Journal of Obstetrics, Gynecology and Reproductive Biology 98,* 1, 14–17.

Goddard, S. (1996) *A Teacher's Window into the Child's Mind.* Eugene, OR: Fern Ridge Press.

Golding, K.S. (2014) *Using Stories to Build Bridges with Traumatized Children.* London; Jessica Kingsley Publishers.

Golding, K.S. and Hughes, D.A. (2012) *Creating Loving Attachments.* London: Jessica Kingsley Publishers.

Goodman, R. (1997) 'The Strengths and Difficulties Questionnaire: A research note.' *Journal of Child Psychology and Psychiatry 38,* 581–586.

Green, A. (1986) 'The Dead Mother.' In *On Private Madness.* London: Karnac Books.

Green, J., Stanley, C., Smith, V. and Goldwyn, R. (2000) 'A new method of evaluating attachment representations in young school-age children: The Manchester Child Attachment Story Task.' *Attachment and Human Development 2,* 1, 48–70.

Greig, A., Munn, P. and Reynolds, S. (2010). 'Guest editorial.' *Educational and Child Psychology 27,* 3, 5–21.

Griffiths, J. (2013) *The Riddle of the Childscape.* London: Hamish Hamilton/Penguin.

Grunau, R.E., Holsti, L. and Peters, J.W. (2006) 'Long-term consequences of pain in human neonates.' *Seminars in Fetal Neonatal Medicine 11,* 4, 268–275.

Grunau, R.E., Whitfield, M.F., Petrie-Thomas, J., Synnes, A.R., Cepeda, I.L., Keidar, A., Rogers, M., Mackay, M., Hubber-Richard P. and Johannesen, D. (2009) 'Neonatal pain, parenting stress and interaction, in relation to cognitive and motor development at 8 and 18 months in preterm infants.' Pain 143, 1–2, 138–146.

Hammond, S. and Cooper, N. (2013) *Digital Life Story Work*. London: BAAF Publications.

Hargreaves, J. and Page, L. (2013) *Reflective Practice*. Cambridge: Polity Press.

Hart, C. (2012) 'The dead mother syndrome and the child in care: A framework for reflecting on why some children experience multiple placement breakdowns.' *Journal of Infant, Child and Adolescent Psychotherapy 11*, 4, 342–355.

Hawkins, P. and Shohet, R. (2012) *Supervision in the Helping Professions (Fourth edition)*. Berkshire: Open University Press.

Healing Resources (2014) *Trauma, Attachment, and Stress Disorders: Rethinking and Reworking Developmental Issues*. Available at www.healingresources.info/trauma_attachment_stress_disorders.htm, accessed on 25 October 2014.

Hebb, D. (1949) *The Organization of Behavior*. New York, NY: John Wiley and Sons.

Heller, S. (2002) *Too Loud, Too Bright, Too Fast Too Tight*. New York, NY: Quill.

Hendry, E. (1988) 'Play-based work with very young children.' *Journal of Social Work Practice 3*, 2, 1–9.

Hoffman, K.T., Marvin, R.S, Cooper, G. and Powell, B. (2006) 'Changing toddlers' and preschoolers' attachment classifications: The Circle of Security intervention.' *Journal of Consulting and Clinical Psychology 74*, 1017–1026.

Holmes, J. (2001) *The Search for the Secure Base: Attachment Theory and Psychotherapy*. London: Routledge.

House of Lords Select Committee on Adoption Legislation (2013) *Second Report of Session 2012–13 Adoption: Post-Legislative Scrutiny Report*. London: The Stationery Office Limited.

Howe, D. (2005) *Child Abuse and Neglect*. London: Palgrave MacMillan.

Howe, D. (2006) 'Developmental attachment psychotherapy with fostered and adopted children' *Child and Adolescent Mental Health 11*, 3, 128–134.

Howe, D. (2011) *Attachment across the Lifecourse*. London: Palgrave MacMillan.

Hruby R., Hasto, J. and Minarik, P. (2011) 'Attachment in integrative neuroscientific perspective.' *Neuro Endocrinology Letters 32*, 2, 111–120.

Hudson, J. (2006) 'Being Adopted: Psychological Services for Adopting Families.' In K. Golding, H. Dent, R. Nissim and L. Stott (eds) *Thinking Psychologically about Children Who Are Looked After and Adopted: Space for Reflection*. New York, NY: Wiley-Blackwell.

Hughes, D. (1997) *Facilitating Developmental Attachment: The Road to Emotional Recovery and Behavioural Change in Foster and Adopted Children*. Oxford: Aronson.

Hughes, D. (1998) *Building the Bonds of Attachment*. Northvale, NJ: Jason Aronson.

Hughes, D. (2004) 'An attachment-based treatment for maltreated children and young people.' *Attachment & Human Development 6*, 3, 263–278.

Hughes, D. (2006) *Building the Bonds of Attachment: Awakening Love in Deeply Troubled Children*. Oxford: Aronson.

Hughes, D. (2007) *Attachment-focused Family Therapy*. New York, NY and London: W.W. Norton and Company.

Hughes, D. (2009) *Attachment-focused Parenting: Effective Strategies to Care for Children*. New York, NY: Norton and Company.

Hughes, D. (2012) *Parenting a Child with Emotional and Behavioural Difficulties*. London: British Agencies for Adoption and Fostering.

Hughes, D. and Baylin, J. (2012) *Brain-Based Parenting: The Neuroscience of Caregiving for Healthy Attachment*. New York, NY and London: W.W. Norton and Company.

Iacoboni, M., Molnar-Szakacs, I., Gallese, V., Buccion, G., Mazziotta, J.C. and Rizzolatti, G. (2005) 'Grasping the intentions of others with one's own mirror neuron system.' *PLOS Biol 3*, 3, e79.

Iwaniec, D. and Sneddon, H. (2001) 'Attachment style in adults who failed to thrive as children: Outcomes of a 20 year follow-up study of factors influencing maintenance or change in attachment style.' *British Journal of Social Work 31*, 2, 179–195.

Ixer, G. (1988) 'Life story books can damage your health.' *Social Work Today 26*.

Jernberg, A.M. and Booth, P.B. (2001) *Theraplay: Helping Parents and Children Build Better Relationships through Attachment-Based Play* (Second edition). San Francisco, CA: Jossey-Bass.

Johnstone, L. and Dallos, R. (2014) *Formulation is Psychology and Psychotherapy: Making Sense of People's Problems*. London: Routledge.

Karen, R. (1998). *Becoming Attached: First Relationships and How They Shape Our Capacity to Love*. Oxford and New York, NY: Oxford University Press.

Keck, G. and Kupecky, R. (2002) *Parenting the Hurt Child*. Colorado Springs, CO: Pinon Press.

Kranowitz, C.S. (1998) *The Out-of-Sync Child.* New York, NY: The Berkley Publishing Group.

Landreth, G. (2012) *Play Therapy: The Art of the Relationship* (Third edition). New York, NY: Routledge.

Lanius, R.A., Bluhm, R. and Frewen, P.A. (2013) 'A Window into the Brain of Complex PTSD.' In D. Siegel and M. Solomon (eds) *Healing Moments in Psychotherapy.* New York, NY: W.W. Norton and Company.

Lanius, R.A. and Vermetten, E. (2010) *The Impact of Early Life Trauma on Health and Disease: The Hidden Epidemic.* Cambridge: Cambridge University Press.

Levy, T.M. and Orlans, M. (1998). *Attachment, Trauma and Healing* (First edition). Washington, DC: Child Welfare League of America Inc.

Levy, T.M. and Orlans, M. (2014) *Attachment, Trauma and Healing* (Second edition). London: Jessica Kingsley Publishers.

Lord, J. and Borthwick, S. (2008) *Siblings Together or Apart?* London: BAAF Publications.

Ludington-Hoe, S.M., Morgan, K. and Abouelfettoh, A. (2008) 'A clinical guideline for implementation of Kangaroo Care with premature infants of 30 or more weeks' postmenstrual age.' *Advances in Neo-natal Care 8,* 3, Supplement, S3–S23.

Lyons-Ruth, K., Bronfman, E. and Parsons, E. (1999) 'Atypical attachment in infancy and early childhood among children at developmental risk. IV. Maternal frightened, frightening, or atypical behavior and disorganized infant attachment patterns.' *Monographs of the Society for Research in Child Development 64,* 3, 67–96.

Maccari, S., Krugers, H.J., Morley-Fletcher, S., Szyf, M. and Brunton, P.J. (2014) 'The consequences of early-life adversity: Neurobiological, behavioral, and epigenetic adaptations.' *Journal of Neuroendocrinology 26,* 10, 707–723.

MacLean, P. and Kral, V. (1973) *A Triune Concept of the Brain and Behaviour.* Toronto: Published for the Ontario Mental Health Foundation by University of Toronto Press.

Main, M. and Goldwyn, R. (1998) *Adult Attachment Scoring and Classification System.* (Unpublished manuscript.) Berkeley, CA: University of California.

Main, M., and Solomon, J. (1986) 'Discovery of a New, Insecure-disorganized/disoriented Attachment Pattern.' In T.B. Brazelton and M. Yogman (eds) *Affective Development in Infancy.* Norwood: Ablex.

Main, M., and Solomon, J. (1990) 'Procedures for Identifying Infants as Disorganized/disoriented during the Ainsworth Strange Situation.' In M.T. Greenberg, D. Cicchetti and E.M. Cummings (eds) *Attachment in the Preschool Years: Theory, Research and Intervention.* Chicago, IL: University of Chicago Press.

Main, M. and Weston, D.R. (1981) 'The quality of the toddler's relationship to mother and to father: Related to conflict behaviour and the readiness to establish new relationships.' *Child Development 52,* 932–940.

Marschak, M. (1960) 'A method for evaluation of child-parent interaction under controlled conditions.' *Journal of Genetic Psychology 97,* 3–22.

McDonell, A.A. (2010) *Managing Aggressive Behaviour in Care Settings.* Chichester: John Wiley and Sons Ltd.

McMahon, L. (1992) *The Handbook of Play Therapy.* East Sussex: Brunner-Routledge.

Menzies, I. (1961) *The Functioning of Social Systems as a Defence Against Anxiety: A Report on a Study of the Nursing Service of a General Hospital.* Centre for Applied Social Research, Tavistock Institute, London.

Ministry of Justice (2012) 'Table 1, "Costs per place and costs per prisoner by individual prison."' *National Offender Management Service Annual Report and Accounts 2011–2012: Management Information Addendum.* London: Ministry of Justice.

Mitchell, A. and Boss, B.J. (2002) 'Adverse effects of pain on the nervous system of newborns and young children: A review of the literature.' *Journal of Neuroscience Nursing 34,* 5, 226–236.

Moore, J. (2012) *Once Upon a Time: Stories and Drama to Use in Direct Work with Adopted and Fostered Children.* London: BAAF Publications.

Moroz, K.J. (2005) *The Effects of Psychological Trauma on Children and Adolescents.* Report Prepared for the Vermont Agency of Human Resources. Available at http://mentalhealth.vermont.gov/sites/dmh/files/report/cafu/DMH-CAFU_Psychological_Trauma_Moroz.pdf, accessed on 8 January 2015.

Morse, R. and Wiley, M.S. (1997) *Ghosts from the Nursery: Tracing the Roots of Violence.* New York, NY: Atlantic Monthly Press.

Mosley, J. and Grogan, R. (2009) *The Big Book of Calmers.* London: Positive Press.

Murray, R. (2012) *Children and Young People in Custody 2011–12.* London: HM Inspectorate of Prisons and Youth Justice Board.

NACRO (2012) *Reducing Offending by Looked After Children.* London: NACRO.

National Child Traumatic Stress Network (NCTSN) (2014) *Secondary Traumatic Stress.* Available at www.nctsn.org/resourcesw/topics/secondary-trauma, accessed on 9 January 2015.

NIMH (2014) *The Teen Brain: Still Under Construction.* Available at www.nimh.nih.gov/health/publications/the-teen-brain-still-under-construction, accessed on 20 September 2014.

Nind, M. and Hewett, D. (1994) *Access to Communication: Developing the Basics of Communication with People with Severe Learning Difficulties through Intensive Interaction.* London: David Fulton.

Nishitani, N. and Hari, E. (2000) 'Temporal dynamics of cortical representation for action.' *Proceedings of the National Academy of Sciences USA 97,* 2, 913–918.

Obradovic, J., Bush, N.R., Stamperdahl, J., Adler, N.E. and Boyce, W.T. (2010) 'Biological sensitivity to context: the interactive effects of stress reactivity and family adversity on socioemotional behavior and school readiness.' *Child Development 81,* 1, 270–289.

Ogden, P., Minton, K. and Pain, C. (2006) *Trauma and the Body.* New York, NY and London: W.W. Norton and Company.

Orlans, M. and Levy, T.M. (2006) *Healing Parents: Helping Wounded Children Learn to Trust and Love.* Washington, DC: Child Welfare League Press.

Panksepp, J. (1998) *Affective Neuroscience.* Oxford and New York, NY: Oxford University Press.

Panksepp, J. (2010) 'Science of the brain as a gateway to understanding play: An interview with Jaak Panksepp.' *American Journal of Play 2,* 3, 245–277.

Panksepp, J. and Biven, L. (2002) *The Archeology of Mind.* New York, NY and London: W.W. Norton and Company.

Pearce, C. (2010). 'An integration of theory, science and reflective clinical practice in the care and management of attachment-disordered children: A Triple-A approach.' *Educational and Child Psychology 27,* 3, 73–86.

Perry, B.D. (2006) *The Boy Who Was Raised as a Dog.* New York, NY: Basic Books.

Perry, B.D. (2009) 'Examining child maltreatment through a neurodevelopmental lens: Clinical applications of the neurosequential model of therapeutics.' *Journal of Loss and Trauma 14,* 240–255.

Porges, S.W. (1998) 'Love: An emergent property of the mammalian autonomic nervous system.' *Psychoneuroendocrinology 23,* 8, 837–861.

Porges, S.W. (2001) 'The Polyvagal theory: Phylogenetic substrates of a social nervous system.' *International Journal of Psychophysiology 42,* 2, 123–146.

Porges, S.W. (2003) 'Social engagement and attachment. A phylogenetic perspective.' *Annals of New York Academy of Sciences 1008,* 31–47.

Porges, S.W. (2011) *The Polyvagal Theory: Neurophysiological Foundations of Emotions, Attachment, Communication, and Self-Regulation.* New York, NY: W.W. Norton and Company.

Prior, V. and Glaser, D. (2006) *Understanding Attachment and Attachment Disorders: Theory, Practice and Evidence.* London: Jessica Kingsley Publishers.

Reebye, P. and Stalker, A. (2008) *Understanding Regulation Disorders of Sensory Processing in Children.* London: Jessica Kingsley Publishers.

Rees, J. (2009) *Life Story Books for Adopted Children: A Family Friendly Approach.* London: Jessica Kingsley Publishers.

Rizzolatti, G., Fogassi, L. and Gallese, V. (2001) 'Neurophysiological mechanisms underlying the understanding and imitation of action.' *Nature Reviews Neuroscience 2,* 661–670.

Richardson, H. (1997) 'Kangaroo care: Why does it work?' *Midwifery Today 44,* 50–57.

Rogers, C. (1951) *Client-Centered Therapy.* London: Constable and Company Limited.

Roth, I. (2010) *The Autism Spectrum in the 21st Century: Exploring Psychology, Biology and Practice.* London: Jessica Kingsley Publishers.

Rose, R. and Philpot, T. (2005) *The Child's Own Story, Life Story Work with Traumatized Children.* London: Jessica Kingsley Publishers.

Rutter, M., Kreppner, J., Croft, C., Murin, M., *et al.* (2007) 'Early adolescent outcomes of institutionally deprived and non-deprived adoptees. III. Quasi-autism.' *Journal of Child Psychology and Psychiatry 48,* 1200–1207.

Ryan, T. and Walker, R. (1985) *Making Life Story Books,* London: BAAF.

Sapouna, M., Bisset, C. and Conlong, A-M. for Scottish Government (2011) *What Works to Reduce Reoffending: A Summary of the Evidence.* Available at www.Scotland.gov.uk/Resource/0038/00385880, accessed on 6 January 2015.

Schaefer, C.E. (2001) 'Prescriptive play therapy.' *International Journal of Play Therapy 19,* 1, 57–73.

Schechter D.S. (2012) 'The developmental neuroscience of emotional neglect, its consequences, and the psychosocial interventions that can reverse them.' *American Journal of Psychiatry 169,* 452–454.

Schon, D.A. (1983) *The Reflective Practitioner: How Professionals Think in Action.* New York, NY: Basic Books.

Schore, A.N. (1994) *Affect Regulation and the Origin of Self.* Hillsdale, NJ: Lawrence Earlbaum Associates.

Schore, A.N. (2001a) 'Effects of a secure attachment on right brain development, affect regulation, and infant mental health.' *Infant Mental Health Journal 22,* 7–76.

Schore, A.N. (2001b) 'The effects of early relational trauma on right brain development, affect regulation, and infant mental health.' *Infant Mental Health Journal 22,* 201–269.

Schore, A.N. (2002) 'Dysregulation of the right brain: A fundamental mechanism of traumatic attachment and pathogenesis of posttraumatic stress disorder.' *Australian and New Zealand Journal of Psychiatry 36,* 9–30.

Schore, A.N. (2003) *Affect Regulation and the Repair of the Self.* New York, NY: W.W. Norton and Company.

Schore, A.N. (2011) 'Foreword.' In P.M. Bromberg (ed.) *The Shadow of the Tsunami: and the Growth of the Relational Mind.* New York, NY and Hove: Routledge.

Schore, A.N. (2012) *The Science of the Art of Psychotherapy.* New York, NY and London: W.W. Norton and Company.

Schore, A.N. (2014) 'The right brain is dominant in psychotherapy.' *Psychotherapy (Chic) 51,* 3, 388–397.

Selwyn, J., Wijedasa, D. and Meakings, S. (2014). *Beyond the Adoption Order: Challenges, Interventions and Adoption Disruption.* Department of Education Research Brief.

Shapiro, F. (2014) 'Redefining Trauma and its Hidden Connections: Identifying and Reprocessing the Experiential Contributors to a Wide Variety of Disorders.' In D.J. Siegel and M. Solomon (eds) *Healing Moments in Psychotherapy.* New York, NY and London: W.W. Norton and Company.

Shemmings, D. and Shemmings, Y. (2011) *Understanding Disorganized Attachment.* London: Jessica Kingsley Publishers.

Siegel, D. (1999) *The Developing Mind.* New York, NY: Guilford Press.

Siegel, D. (2006) *An Interpersonal Neurobiology Approach to Psychotherapy: Awareness, Mirror Neurons, and Neural Plasticity in the Development of Well-being.* Available at www.lifespan.org/documents/siegel-IPApproach, accessed on 9 January 2015.

Siegel, D. (2007) *The Mindful Brain.* New York, NY and London: W.W. Norton and Company.

Siegel, D. (2010) *Mindsight.* New York, NY and Oxford: Oneworld Publications.

Spangler, G. and Grossmann, K. (1999) 'Individual and physiological correlates of attachment disorganization in infancy.' In J. Solomon and C. George (eds) *Attachment Disorganization.* New York, NY: Guilford Press.

Silver, M. (2013) *Attachment in Common Sense and Doodle: A Practical Guide.* London: Jessica Kingsley Publishers.

Smith, G.M. (1985) 'The collaborative drawing technique.' *Journal of Personality Assessment 49,* 6, 582–585.

Smyke, A.T., Dumitrescu, A. and Zeanah, C.H. (2002) 'Attachment disturbances in young children. 1: The continuum of caretaking causality.' *Journal of the American Academy of Child and Adolescent Psychiatry 41,* 972–982.

Stern, D. (1985) *The Interpersonal World of the Infant: A View from Psychoanalysis and Developmental Psychology.* New York, NY: Basic Books.

Stratton, P. (2010) *The Evidence Base of Systemic Family and Couple Therapy.* Warrington: Association for Family Therapy and Systemic Practice.

Streek-Fischer, A. and van der Kolk, B.A. (2000). 'Down will come baby, cradle and all: Diagnostic and therapeutic interventions of chronic trauma on child development.' *Australia and New Zealand Journal of Psychiatry 2000, 34,* 903–918.

Sunderland, M (2007) *What Every Parent Needs to Know: The Remarkable Effects of Love, Nurture and Play on Your Child's Development.* London: Dorling Kindersley.

Taylor, K., Menarchek-Fetkovich, M. and Day, C. (2000) 'The Play History Questionnaire.' In K. Gitlin-Weiner, A, Sandgrund and C. Schaefer (eds) *Play Diagnostic and Assessment* (Second Edition). New York, NY: John Wiley and Sons.

Teicher, M.H., Andersen, S.L., Polcari, A., Anderson, C.M. and Navalta, C.P. (2002) 'Developmental neurobiology of childhood stress and trauma.' *Psychiatric Clinics of North America 25,* 2, 397–426.

Teicher, M.H., Andersen S.L., Polcari, A., Anderson C.M., Navalta, C.P. and Kim, D.M. (2003) 'The neurobiological consequences of early stress and childhood maltreatment.' *Neuroscience and Biobehavioral Reviews 27,* 33–44.

Thomas, A. and Chess, S. (1977) *Temperament and Development.* New York, NY: Brunner/Mazel.

Trevarthen, C. (2001) 'Intrinsic motives for companionship in understanding: Their origin, development and significance for infant mental health.' *Infant Mental Health Journal 22,* 1–2, 95–131.

van der Kolk, B.A. (2003) 'The neurobiology of childhood trauma and abuse.' *Child Adolescent Psychiatric Clinic of North America 12,* 293–317.

van der Kolk, B.A. (2005) 'Developmental trauma disorder: Towards a rational diagnosis for children with complex trauma histories.' *Psychiatric Annals 35,* 401–408.

van der Kolk, B.A. (2014) *The Body Keeps the Score: Brain, Mind, and Body in the Healing of Trauma.* New York, NY: Penguin Group (USA).

Van Gulden, H. (2010a) *Introduction to Object Permanence and Constancy.* Adoption and Fostering, BAAF: YouTube. Available at https://www.youtube.com/watch?v=bd1-APMTiFY, accessed on 9 April 2014.

Van Gulden, H. (2010b) *Permanence 5: What Are the Symptoms of a Lack of Permanence?* Adoption and Fostering, BAAF: YouTube. Available at https://www.youtube.com/watch?v=uIVItjoJsu0, accessed on 3 February 2015.

Vaughan, J. (2003) 'The Drama of Adoption.' In C. Archer and A. Burnell (eds) *Trauma, Attachment and Family Permanence.* London: Jessica Kingsley Publishers.

Verrier, N. (1993) *The Primal Wound.* Baltimore, MD: Gateway Press.

Waycott, L., McInnes, K. and Carbis, C. (2012) *Adult-Child Interactions Assessment Checklist.* Cardiff: Stepping Stones (Child Therapy Consultants).

Weir, K.N., Lee, S., Canosa, P., Rodrigues, N., McWilliams, M. and Parker, L. (2013) 'Whole family Theraplay: Integrating family systems theory and Theraplay to treat adoptive families.' *Adoption Quarterly 16,* 3–4, 175–200.

Wesselmann, D. (2013) 'Healing trauma and creating secure attachments with EMDR.' In D.S. Siegel and M. Solomon (eds) *Healing Moments in Psychotherapy: Mindful Awareness, Neural Integration and Therapeutic Presence.* New York, NY: W.W. Norton and Company.

West, J. (1992) *Child Centred Play Therapy* (Second edition). London: Hodder Headline Group.

Wilson, J. (2005) 'Engaging Children and Young People.' In A. Vetere and E. Dowling (eds) *Narrative Therapies with Children and Their Families: A Practitioner's Guide to Concepts and Approaches.* Hove: Routledge.

Winnicott, D.W. (1958) 'Primary Maternal Preoccupation.' In *The Maturational Processes and the Facilitating Environment.* New York, NY: International University Press.

Young Minds (2014) 'Mental health statistics.' Available at www.youngminds.org.uk/training_services/policy/mental_health_statistics, accessed on 9 January 2015.

USEFUL RESOURCES

ADAPT Scotland

www.adaptscotland.org

ADAPT Scotland helps parents and children increase their understanding of the reasons why they struggle alongside offering strategies that create the safe base where change is possible. They work with professionals to ensure that there is wider community understanding of the needs of traumatised children, and promote the development of a coherent plan for helping children and families and the support to put this plan into practise.

Adoption UK

www.adoptionuk.org

Adoption UK are the leading charity providing support, awareness and understanding for those parenting or supporting children who cannot live with their birth parents.

Attachment Network Wales

www.attachmentnetworkwales.com

The Attachment Network Wales is a network of organisations, individuals, academics, practitioners, policy-makers and professionals who are working to promote understanding of the importance of attachment in bringing about better outcomes for children, young people, adults and families; through publications, training, research, lobbying and raising knowledge and awareness at a policy as well as a practice level.

Family Futures

www.familyfutures.co.uk

Family Futures offers an adoption service as well as adoption support, advice and child therapy services to children who have experienced trauma or attachment difficulties. They also offer post-placement support to birth families, adoptive families, foster carers or special guardians.

The Family Place

www.thefamilyplace.co.uk

The Family Place provides specialist and flexible therapeutic interventions for families, aiming to strengthen relationships between children and young people and their main carers by deepening understanding in a safe and therapeutic environment. They specialise in providing tailored interventions for foster and adoptive families and their support networks, alongside a range of other family issues.

Stepping Stones (Child Therapy Consultants) Ltd
www.steppingstonestherapy.co.uk
Stepping Stones offers therapeutic resources, training courses and therapy services to meets the needs of therapists and educators working directly with children, young people and adults in therapeutic and educational settings.

CONTRIBUTOR BIOGRAPHIES

Caroline Archer has four adopted children, now adults. Her experience of adoptive parenting aroused a determination to understand the issues affecting adoptees, including issues around sensory integration, attachment, neuro-development, self-actualisation, education and relationships, and to explore effective ways of enabling children to thrive. She is a keen supporter of regional and national rugby teams in Wales and loves following road and track cycling.

Emma Birch is in her final year of the Doctorate in Educational Psychology at Cardiff University. Prior to starting the course she worked for Cardiff Council running a project to promote independent travel and living for young people with a variety of special needs. She has also worked in a range of educational settings, teaching pupils ranging from three to 63 years old! She is particularly interested in the areas of attachment, fostering and adoption. Her doctoral thesis is about the stressors and coping mechanisms encountered by the sons and daughters of foster carers.

Clare Carbis has a BSc Psychology and an MSc Play Therapy and is a full member of the British Association of Play Therapists (BAPT). She has worked for Stepping Stones (Child Therapy Consultants Ltd) since August 2008, initially as a therapeutic play specialist and since 2011 as a qualified play therapist. Clare works therapeutically with children who have experienced trauma, loss and bereavement, those with attachment difficulties and those who have experienced neglect and abuse. Clare incorporates integrative techniques into her therapeutic work using attachment-based therapeutic techniques, Theraplay and Sensory Attachment Intervention in that she is also trained.

Ann Cartwright teaches at Crug Glas special school in Swansea. She is the co-author of *The Teaching Assistant's Guide to Autistic Spectrum Disorders* and is highly committed to meeting the educational needs of every child, whatever their abilities.

Charlotte Drury is the Chair of Attachment Network Wales. Throughout her career Charlotte has had a passionate commitment to children's rights and improving outcomes for children and families and sees awareness and understanding of attachment throughout the life course as fundamental to this. Prior to undertaking a PhD scholarship at Cardiff University she worked with Children and Young People's Partnerships and has also worked in social work, safeguarding and equalities. She has a background in applied research and her doctoral research is focused on complexity theory, social work and child neglect. She also bakes very good brownies.

Victoria Drury is an experienced independent social worker who has worked with children and families for well over a decade. Before qualifying she worked in residential care with children with learning difficulties and challenging behaviour, which is where she became passionate about the importance of providing high-quality, therapeutic support services for children and families. When not pushing the boundaries of social work, Victoria loves to kite-buggy along the Welsh beaches with her partner, her son and Spike, the dog.

Hannah Fryer is an adoptive parent with a particular interest in the inter-connections between trauma, attachment, development and dissociation. She has many years of experience in supporting adopters and their families, within PPIAS/ Adoption UK and as a therapeutic parent mentor. She feels most at home wandering the coastal paths and shores of Pembrokeshire and in the high mountains of France and Switzerland, identifying and photographing alpine wildflowers.

Christine Gordon gained her Certificate of Qualification in Social Work in 1981 and is co-founder of Family Futures Consortium in London. She now works as an expert witness in complex childcare situations. She recently founded Adapt (Scotland), an organisation offering bespoke parenting and therapeutic support programmes to adoptive and foster parents caring for traumatised children. She is involved in the training and support of parent mentors in Scotland and has written several books and articles on parent mentoring for adoptive parents of traumatised children. In her spare time, Christine is a keen cyclist and hill walker; she likes nothing better than exploring the hills of her native Scotland.

Tamara Gordon is an award-winning producer and director. She studied Politics, Philosophy and Anthropology at Manchester University and went on to complete an MA in Film and Anthropology. Over 18 years Tamara has produced numerous films and documentaries, mostly focused on human rights, and adoption and reconciliation. She has won numerous international film awards for directing. She is also trained in conflict mediation, which has been an important skill when working in conflict zones across the world. When not travelling Tamara lives in the bustling Welsh border town of Hay-on-Wye.

Jude Hills has recently completed an MSc in Play Therapy at the University of South Wales. She has had many years of experience working directly with children in post-adoption support and as a foster carer, and she has provided training for foster carers and social workers. She has four adopted and two birth children. Jude is particularly interested in attachment and therapeutic life story work.

David Howe is Emeritus Professor in the School of Social Work at the University of East Anglia, Norwich. He has research and writing interests in emotional development, empathy, developmental attachment theory and child abuse and neglect. His most recent books include *Child Abuse and Neglect: Attachment, Development and Intervention* (Palgrave/Macmillan 2005), *The Emotionally Intelligent Social Worker* (Palgrave/ Macmillan 2008), *A Brief Introduction to Social Work Theory* (Palgrave/Macmillan 2009), *Attachment Across the Lifecourse: A Brief Introduction* (Palgrave/Macmillan 2011) and *Empathy: What It Is and Why it Matters* (Palgrave/Macmillan 2012).

Helen Jury is an art psychotherapist who has worked with children in schools, NHS CAMHS and young people's services where she developed a strong interest in attachment and family issues and innovative practice. She is the course leader for the Health and Care Professions Council (HCPC) clinical MA Art Psychotherapy training at the University of South Wales and a guest lecturer at the Metafora Art Psychotherapy Intensive Course in Barcelona. As an artist, Helen has researched creativity in young children in partnership with educational and cultural institutions through the *5x5x5=creativity* research programme. She is also Associate Editor of *Inscape: The International Journal of Art Therapy.*

Jane MacNamara is the mother of five birth children. Over the 16 years she has been a foster parent, she and her family have shared their home with many children. Her interest in trauma and attachment has unfolded over the years and is something very personal to her, due to the early experiences of her firstborn son in an era when it was widely believed that children forgot early trauma. These experiences led her to train as a counsellor, play therapist and writer working with children and families needing therapeutic support. She likes freedom to roam, wide open skies, fires on the beach and an endless supply of good books.

Marie Martin is a lesbian adoptive mum with an interest in primary education. She is a sculptor, whose mindfulness practice, yoga, friends and 'doing something about it' keep her sane. She occasionally writes for Adoption UK and has just acquired a puppy!

Jonny Matthew is a social worker and criminologist who has worked principally in the field of youth justice. He has worked for many years as a specialist with children with sexualised histories. Before joining the Youth Justice Board he worked as the deputy manager of a secure children's home where he was responsible for interventions. He is currently leading on a project developing case management approaches for complex young people with prolific offending histories. His research interests are youth crime, attachment, adoption, abuse, safeguarding, therapeutic approaches and particularly how skewed developmental trajectories impact on children's behaviour. Jonny also writes a twice-weekly blog promoting recovery for troubled young people (www.JonnyMatthew.com).

Karen McInnes is a qualified speech and language therapist and early years teacher. She is a senior lecturer in Play and Human Development at the University of Wales, joint award leader for the MSc Play Therapy and MSc Play and Therapeutic Play and a member of the British Association of Play Therapists (BAPT). Her work incorporates integrative techniques, she is trained in Theraplay and is currently training in play therapy. Karen has extensive experience working with children in health and education settings and is currently working therapeutically with children who have experienced neglect, physical and emotional abuse and with children who have special educational needs. She has recently undertaken research with Stepping Stones (Child Therapy Consultants) to support and evidence their practice.

Vivien Norris is a consultant clinical psychologist. Vivien is additionally qualified as a certified Theraplay therapist and a Dyadic Developmental Psychotherapy (DDP) practitioner. Vivien has worked as an NHS psychologist and in private practice for many years and has developed considerable experience with foster and adoptive families. She is also Director of The Family Place, has written for a number of publications and is experienced in providing supervision and training.

Helen O'Shea is a clinical, counselling and educational psychologist who works in Aneurin Bevan University Health Board and is seconded to Action for Children, a national children's charity. She has worked with children and families throughout her career in education, health and the third sector, trying to make psychological ideas available to staff teams such as childcare staff and health visitors. Helen is particularly interested in early intervention and as such was part of the strategy group that developed the Family Intervention Team in Caerphilly (in that she now works) and was the first clinical psychologist in Wales employed to work in Flying Start, the Welsh Government Flagship Initiative for children under four and their families.

Elaine Simpson currently works as a children's service manager for Gwent family support (Action for Children). She has a background in mental health nursing and family therapy and has worked for many years in the CAMHS arena, initially in London and on returning to Wales where she managed the inpatient adolescent unit in Cardiff. Early on in her career she developed a real interest in attachment and has supported and developed attachment-based practice within the services she manages.

Tricia Skuse is a highly specialist child and adolescent clinical psychologist, working for the Wales Forensic Adolescent Consultation and Treatment (FACT) service. She previously worked at Hillside Secure Children's Home as the clinical lead for interventions. She teaches on the South Wales clinical psychology doctoral programme and has been involved in various research groups, including the Dartington Social Research Institute. Tricia's research interests include early attachment and trauma and the relationship of this to later functioning and behaviour during adolescence.

Lisa Waycott is Clinical Director of Stepping Stones (Child Therapy Consultants) Ltd, an independent agency providing therapeutic services for children and young people, training and consultancy. In addition to play therapy training, Lisa has a Master's degree in Social Work and is a senior lecturer at the University of South Wales. She has been instrumental in the delivery of the first accredited play therapy training course in Wales, as recognised by the British Association of Play Therapists (BAPT). She is trained in Theraplay and has worked therapeutically with children and young people in a variety of settings and with a wide range of needs, including severely traumatised and vulnerable children and young people with complex histories.

SUBJECT INDEX

AUTHOR INDEX